From

New Mills

To New Life

Joshua Spencer

From

New Mills

To New Life

"Believe it to achieve it. Believe it, do it!" ~Joshua Spencer

Joshua Spencer

Copyright © 2009 & 2020 by Joshua Spencer

Library of Congress Control Number 2009910479

ISBN: Softcover: 979-866-900-0202

Contents

DEDICATION

From New Mills to New Life is dedicated to all those whose existence made me in the person I am today. This includes my children Michael, Kaliese, and Kadisha, foster parents, Mr. Jim (James) Thompson and Mrs. Elethia Thompson, all my brothers and sisters, friends, and former wives.

ACKNOWLEDGEMENT

The writing of any piece, especially one's autobiography which, in my case, begins from the time of my birth, without a doubt, needs the assistance of many to come to fruition. First, let me acknowledge Mr. Michael Spence, a graduate of the Mico University and the University of the West Indies (U.W.I.), Mona Campus, Jamaica, who is a good friend, a former teacher, soldier, and a resident of New Mills. He is currently a businessman, and the owner of Bookmax Limited in Kingston, Jamaica.

Mr. Michael Spence and I both spent a significant part of our earlier years in this small district in the parish of Westmoreland, Jamaica. His mother, Mrs. Spence, was once my elementary school teacher and must be credited for preparing me to attend high school as will be gleaned later. Her son, Michael Spence created the title to this autobiography, on my behalf. To him, I owe much for a great title.

Second, I must thank the numerous relatives and friends who helped me to reconstruct my memory, in particular as it related to the period zero to the first ten years of my life.

As I had, in all my previously published books, I must thank some very special people. Mr. and Mrs. Jim Thompson who took me under their fold when I had no help to attend high school and college. Without them, none of this would have been possible. They are the direct reason that I can scribe this work, including the others I did in the past. The Honourable P.J. Patterson, former prime minister of Jamaica, for his encouragement in the 1980s as I read a few of my poems at a function of which he was in attendance.

Finally, I wish to thank Messrs. Glendon Lawrence, Grace Barbara Lawrence, Rosalee Forbes, Carlton Grant, Oliver Nelson, Taiwo Osuntoyinbo, Dr. Hixwell Douglas (my blind genius friend), Dudley Jennings, the Late Desmond Jackson, Renato Punu, and the Late Dr. Norman Buchanan, a good friend and fellow Jamaican, who had had a great amount of intellectual and other influences on my life.

The abovementioned individuals had some direct or indirect influence on the creation of this book. I owe them all immensely.

INTRODUCTION

I began to have a constant and uncontrollable urge to consider writing my autobiography just about the year 2005. See, I was born into a family, and grew up under circumstances that very few individuals who knew me then, expected me to escape the sufferings, trappings, and trimmings of poverty. I was part of a larger group whose most salient constants and hallmarks were one encumbered, inundated, and clustered in dire deprivation, a lack of motivation to succeed educationally or otherwise. I was part of a group that was destined to a dead-end road with no hope in view.

One may ask, but why did it dawn on you to consider writing this autobiography only in the year 2005 and not in prior years? Was there something special that happened in that year that led you to want to divulge your past to the whole globe? Was it merely an idea to get famous and possibly, wealth? Was it, that time and age had stripped you of all shame and pride? Frankly, it could have been all of the foregoing reasons. Importantly, though, it was in the year 2005, as you will glean in the reading of the pages of *From New Mills to New Life*, that I started to experience some semblance of respite from all the sufferings that I had endured upon emigrating to Toronto, Canada, on December 20, 1993 and even in prior years in Jamaica. Mine was a life of great hardship from an early age in Jamaica to my present life in Canada; the early separation of my mother and father, the murder of my father subsequently, the insanity of a younger brother, the imprisonment of a pregnant sister in England, a spate of marriages that blew up into flames right in my face, the mistreatment of my mother by stepfathers, the passing of close relations, including my mother, aunt, grandmother and uncle, all around the same timeframe, and my struggles in Canada to retain a job that was in line with my qualifications. It was in September 2005, when I finally acquired a teaching post as a Long Term Occasional (L.T.O.) teacher. This was the time that I considered to have been the engine of change. The time that had stirred into motion, a breath of well needed fresh air in my sphere, in my prior, struggling life.

So, since 2005, I had begun to organize my thoughts and mindset around writing this autobiography. I still could not get the guts to do it. I wrote not even a single letter down towards this goal until today (August 1, 2009). I thought of how people would view me, my colleagues, my acquaintances, the few friends I have. I even envisioned me being interviewed via the Oprah Winfrey Show, Larry King Live, AC

360 With Anderson Cooper of CNN, and numerous other talk shows. Quite ambitious thoughts too, I must add! The constantly roaming eyes as I walked the corridors of my school and its offices – were thoughts that glued to my cerebrum like the buttons on my shirt. I had great difficulties and struggles to overcome them. I got cold feet. How could I let the world know that this apparently grown and accomplished middle aged man had had a past of terror?!

Instead, on October 30, 2006, I had a book published, titled, *Let's Talk Africa and More*. The book was disastrous! I made a few cents in royalties from its sales. For one thing, there were many typographical errors in the book. I had advised the publisher about these problems. They promised to correct these problems in subsequent prints. However, every time that I purchased a copy, the errors would still show up. Consequently, I stopped promoting the book. It still makes a very interesting read, I am told, but the general errors and syntax errors make the work quite distracting to most readers. I decided then and there that my next work would be self-published. This route would give me more liberty with its editing and outlay.

On August 23, 2007, I published *Fluctuating Life*, a book of poetry which reflected on certain aspects of my life via the use of poems, even though in a concealing way. I employed a lot of symbols and metaphors in the creation of the work, even disguising my identity by referring to myself as a member of the feminine gender at times, or as a plant. I hurriedly put together all the poems that I wrote and on which I could lay hands. This urgency had come about as I, on February 17, 2007, had become ill unexpectedly and absent from work for approximately one month. As soon as I got out of hospital, I started to compile the work. I wanted to ensure that if I should die, there would have been something for my children, ex-wives, brothers, sisters, and friends to cherish in my memory which depicts my life's experiences in some way. It was the closest thing yet, to my memoir; a significant portion of the poems in *Fluctuating Life* was based on my experiences, my struggles, my financial challenges. The following year, February 12, 2008, I published *Contemporary Issues Science Africa and More*. This was a book of my original work with short essays pertaining to modern issues, some of which were of a moral nature and were highly debatable topics. I still, however, could not make up my mind to spilling my intestines and their contents to everyone, to the world.

Now here I am writing *From New Mills to New Life* – my autobiography. It will be organized around my life in periods, starting at zero year old to my current age, fifty years in October 2009. There will be some brief details on the history of my native country, Jamaica. This is to provide a backdrop and deeper understanding of the period I will allude to in this autobiography. It will also help you to make sense, and put into proper context, my earlier Jamaican experiences. Specifically, there will be information with respect to the creation, development, or lack thereof, of what is currently Jamaica.

In most cases, I will endeavour not to use the real names of individuals involved, apart from those mentioned in the acknowledgement and dedication and a few others. These are individuals who will not be affected adversely by their names being referenced in this autobiography. All situations mentioned will be non-fiction (fact) and based on reality as I recalled them from my memory or by the help of relatives and friends. Any relationships that are mentioned are all real, even if fictitious names are used to protect these individuals at times. All quotes and dialogues in *From New Mills to New Life* will bear the best approximation as possible to the actual, to the extent that my memory or those of my relatives and friends who assisted me, will allow. Some conversations and dialogues have been translated from patois, Jamaica's creole, to standard English for universal comprehension.

Later in this introduction, those whose true names have been used in this autobiography will be mentioned.

Notwithstanding all I have said in the preceding paragraphs, I guess the questions still linger, "Joshua, did you really have to do this?" "Did you, really now?"

The fact is, this work is cathartic in nature. It's like taking laxative for a constipated stomach. A constipation that had prevented you from enjoying the private facilities of the ladies' or men's rooms for a long time. Sprawling and unloading my pent up emotions will provide me with the needed therapy and assist me in bearing a salient portion of my emotional and residual trappings of my cognitive reservoir, deeply rooted feelings of sadness and hurt that had not totally and completely been erased from my being. A constantly stabbing thrust that gnaws away at my wellbeing. One that was brought about by a rugged, painful, and atrocious past. It was not exactly an easy task to put my life's experiences to paper. It elicited tears with gruelling pain, for the most part. However, I truly believe this emotional healing had been put off for far too long. It was either now or never, live or die! The latent, emotional air valve was either ready to explode to pieces or cause internal mental and/or physical damage. I could not afford for that to have happened. I was like a silent river ready to overflow its banks. The spilling of it all in this autobiography of mine, will, hopefully, bring about this desired relief from grief.

As you read *From New Mills to New Life*, you will find an honest description of my life's unfolding events as I recalled them. If there were any exaggerations or underreporting, it would not be a deliberate design on my part. I had taken care to corroborate all my thoughts and memories with those who should know, prior to committing them to this book.

I regard this book as my memoir/autobiography, worthy to be shared. This is, of course, not because I have lived a very long, complex, and interesting or accomplished life, where I met and encountered innumerable dignitaries and defeated unrealistic challenges. It certainly is no *Dreams From My Father* by former President Barrack Obama. It is simply because it represents my life's journey and those closely embedded in it for the last five decades. And even though, during this half a century of my life, I had not turned water into wine (Jesus) or commanded the sun to stand still, as was the case with my namesake, Joshua of biblical traditions (NB: The sun has stood still since.) I did paddle across some muddy streams, inundated enough to have effected deadly harm to my will to succeed. Having had to withstand all these blistering experiences, and having succeeded and being mentally stable, in my humble view, deserved to be shared and recognized. The true names of some individuals: uncles, aunts, siblings, friends, will be real and the events that so mentioned. These are events that will be unfolded as my recollection dictates, or that of reliable relatives and/or friends who advised me.

It must also be emphasized that any resemblance to those fictitious names or alias names mentioned in this autobiography of someone of whom you may be aware, *must* be treated as mere coincidence. This autobiography will not use the correct names of individuals involved *except* for those who will be mentioned later in this introduction.

In the end, I hope that apart from the psychological healing which I truly deserved and aspired for in its creation, that I shall have been able to relate to others of similar experiences. Even as my experiences might not have been unique, probably even considered relatively trivial, compared to the experiences of others, not everyone had taken the opportunity to share her or his with the world. Accordingly, the possibility that some poor, so-called, helpless soul on the verge of relenting, might be moved by it, is enough motivation for me. It gives me inner peace for such possibility in its sharing.

Let the words of these pages bring on a new meaning, as it will, according to your various and unique experiences and expectations. Tell a friend if you shall have benefitted from reading this book, who knows you might, in an indirect way, be helping to build a worthwhile future and a new outlook for a self-perceived hopeless soul.

Here are the true names that are mentioned in this work:

Mr. Jim Thompson, Mrs. Elethia Thompson, Wayne Colquhoun, Michael Spence, Mrs. Spence, Kadisha Spencer, Kaliese Spencer Carter, Michael Spencer, Reflor Spencer, Evelyn (Cornish), Almena (McDonald), Lucille (Griffiths), Gwendolyn (Spencer), George Spencer, Mary Spencer, Reuben Spencer, Benjamin Spencer, Fay, Dudley Jennings, Glendon Lawrence, Grace Lawrence, Beverly Ramgeet, Arthur Gilling (Leo), Carlton Grant, Taiwo Osuntoyinbo, Renato Punu, Maxine Ritchie, Mark Reid, Barbara Dandy, Everton Knott, Desmond Jackson, Oliver Nelson, Merfelin Spencer, Mrs. Norma Baichoo, Mrs. Joye Allman, Massia Morant, Mrs. Carmen Wynter-Ellis, Charles Spencer, Errol Snipe, Ilett Robinson, Christopher Suban, John Robinson, Adina Robinson, nee Topping, Donald, Mr. Lovell, Mavis Robinson, Jasmine, Don Evans, Mr. Blake, Joseph Campbell, Beatrice Campbell, Robert McTiernan, Alison Curtis, Kenneth Smith, Frank Smith, Mr. Jackson, Dr. Simon Clarke, Aubrey Campbell, Mrs. Andrea Douglas, Ms.

Russell, Hugh Solomon, Hixwell Douglas, Otmaro Service, Neville Vickers, Coleen Watson, Milton Buchanan, George Harvey, Joan Small, Everton Moore, David Garwood, Norman Buchanan, Mrs. Nancy Spencer, Renrick McFarlane, Cebert McFarlane, Dr. Cecile Walden, Mr. Shippey, Mr. Herbert George Nieta, Mr. Dixon, Ms. Michelin, Ms. Dennis, Rose Wallace, Olga Virgo, David Robinson, Lambert Robinson, Michael Weddemire, Mr. Blake, Levy Spencer, Wayne Taylor, Ike, Mr. Evans, Melaine Walker, Mr. Noel Monteith, Luther Buchanan, Michael and Brian Weddemire, Gee, Ms. Quest, Dannavan Morrison, Mr. Jackson, Don Foote, Paul Popwell, Ms. Stephens, Mrs. Mighty, Mr. Kassam, Mr. Batt, Joylyn Shakes, Edna Brown, Elizabeth Hall (Betty), Cely, Garrett Morant.

CHAPTER ONE

My Country and I – Birth, Political, and Historical Backdrop

Saturday of October 31, 1959 was no different from the many other Saturdays that had preceded it. For that matter, it was no different from the six other preceding days for that week's last day. The sun's scorching heat was already at 6:00 A.M., caressing the easterly walls of the many small homes that thickly juxtaposed one another in this suburban so-called ghetto, forming many arcs and circles in various arrangements in this small town, Albion of Montego Bay, Jamaica. Possibly, *Bob Marley and the Wailers, Beresford Hammond, Toots and the Maytals* or rhythm of similar artistes, pelted around the neighbourhood as warmly as the sun pounced against the walls and windows of these homes on this early Saturday morning. *The Beetles* might have even been part of that musical mix. The different music originating and dispersing outwardly, like the tentacles of an octopus, only that in the arrangement, the number and radii (radiuses) were much more multiplied. The sounds intermittently interspersed only by the running water from the taps, as children and adults alike engaged in their daily routines. The former soaking their faces and tearing away mattered substances and overnight grime from their less-than-spotless faces. The latter washing pots and plates, forks, and spoons mostly, getting ready to get the first meal of the day on track.

Sooner than later, all the children's faces would be as clean and sparkly as their bared feet or by now, like the sparkling utensils left in the trays to be dried by the sun's rays – the children chirping around like birds, playing tag, awaiting the special call for breakfast. The scent of ackee and saltfish, fried bammy, fried eggs, cocoa, tea, and coffee would soon join the mix of splashing reggae, water, and screaming children.

"Tiny, Tiny, where you going? Go and rest yourself dear. I don't want you to give birth in the kitchen," Aunt Gwendolyn chided at my mother.

My mother's registered name was Ilett Robinson, but like most Jamaicans she had a pet name which was Tiny. Mine was later to be 'Ricky'.

"Tiny, when did you get out of bed?" My dad joined in. "The reason I got my sister Gwendolyn to stay with us, is to help us in the house. You need to take it easy. Don't want anything to happen to my first son or daughter for that matter!"

"The doctor said I should keep active," my mother protested.

She, however, soon moved slowly towards the living room, accidently banged into a few of the items that crowded her path as she did so. She lay on the sofa for a brief while, prior to screaming that her water had broken.

Aunt Gwendolyn and my dad, Charles Spencer, hurriedly got my mother dressed and helped her into the car and quickly left for the hospital.

It would have been several hours later that very night of October that Joshua Spencer and his twin, "still birth" brother would have been born. That which caused the "still birth" remained a mystery or whether my parents knew they were expecting twins. As a matter of fact, this information about me being a twin had been kept secret for many years. It was only a few years ago, during my adult life, that I discovered this information from my birth certificate.

But what was ahead for me? How would my childhood be? Would I soon to join those screaming children, washing my mattered face, shaking my little full moon butt, very often as bared as the second I was born?

Jamaica had had a rich and full history. An understanding of its historical origins and that of its citizens, will give insight into the reasons that my experiences, to be unfolded in this autobiography might be shared by a large percent of Jamaica's young people and most Jamaicans in general. It probably is not as peculiar to me, as I would have hoped.

Like most of the Caribbean islands and North America, Jamaica was originally occupied by Native Indians, ours being known then as Arawaks (Taínos). This was all to be changed when on May 14, 1494, a fleet of Spaniards headed by the now renowned Italian-born, Christopher Columbus and sponsored by the Spanish Monarch of Ferdinand and Isabella. They swarmed upon Jamaica, the land we all love, like bees in search of nectar, or even worse, flies on faeces. Christopher Columbus buzzing around, sniffing like a canine, for all the spoils they could rip from our proverbial hibiscus flower.

"My fellow comrades," Columbus salivated, roared, and screamed from the bottom of his lungs, upon landing on what is now Jamaica. "We have come upon the fairest isle that eyes have beheld."

The Spaniards had great hopes of fortune to plunder, to return to Spain to empower the Spanish Empire. To drown their sorrows in more rum, other types of alcohol, and of course, adultery!

Christopher Columbus returned to Spain to advise Ferdinand and Isabella of his discovery of a land that he claimed was rich in gold and other minerals. They were to be disappointed. However, the Spaniards still went ahead to occupy Jamaica in 1509 under the supervision of Juan de Esquivel, a so-called Spanish adventurer. During this period, and until the coming of the British, headed by Oliver Cromwell in 1655, the Spaniards exploited the Native Indians and scraped all the little gold and other precious minerals that could have been found. The diseases brought into the country by the Spaniards, of which the Taínos had no immunity, also caused their extermination as much as the physical slave-like exploitation meted out to them by the Spaniards. They died quite swiftly and quickly under these inhumane conditions.

The English Naval Force, with Oliver Cromwell in charge, ceased the country from the Spanish in 1655 (a thief from a thief makes the gods laugh, is a popular Jamaican saying), even though it was not until 1670 that the British officially acquired (laugh, laugh) the island under the Treaty of Madrid. This meant that the English would not have had to be constantly on the lookout for Spanish attacks. I would also guess the less likelihood of them experiencing panic attacks and heart attacks as well.

It must also be pointed out here and now, that during the British invasion, some of the residents of African descent were prudent enough to escape into the hills to fight against their slavery status. They, in essence, became walking trees and entire forests, slashing and exterminating a few of the unsuspecting, former masters of European stock as they pounced upon the nervous souls.

These fighters for freedom were later to be known as the Jamaican Maroons. They now occupy the areas known as Accompong and Maroon Town in Jamaica, the land we all love. Here, the Maroons have basically their own State and laws, even as they still adhere to, and exhibit respect to the national laws of the country.

Jamaica's population at the arrival of the British in 1655, was just about three thousand (3,000) persons. This number quickly increased after the arrival of the British conquerors. This was as a direct consequence to Cromwell's efforts and ploy to have white British prisoners set free to engage in running this new colony of Britain. The population was also augmented due to the recruitment of indentured servants from Asia, particularly India and China. You will learn more on this later.

As soon as the Europeans had realized that there were no precious metals to plunder, they had begun on a new route and strategy in the cultivation of sugar cane to meet the market in Europe and for Britain, in particular. As a result of this, a new class was founded in these ex-prisoners, now white planters who owned the sugar plantations. Criminals and British 'jail birds', originating from the so-called Mother Britain, pretty soon became not merely owners of the captured lands but also the owners of African peoples (their slaves) on behalf of Britain.

The growing demand for workers for the sugar plantations intensified and led to the augmentation of the slave trade and slavery. During the late seventeenth century, for example, the slavery population of African descendants and fully Africans in Jamaica, my homeland, were approximately ten thousand. However, by the end of the seventeenth century to early eighteenth century, there were about fifty thousand African slaves in Jamaica, working the sugar plantations chopping canes, or as domestic slaves for their masters; cooking, cleaning, washing, and even offering coerced sexual favours to their masters to whom they were mere properties and laboured for free in all the above examples. What a shame! What a shame! How did they sleep at nights?

It is important that my readers understand that beginning in the fifteenth century, up until 1834, all Africans in Jamaica were connected to the plantation system as basically one of two types of slaves: (a) a field slave or (b) a domestic slave. The latter group, in general, was treated much more humanely than the former. Perhaps as the planters were being careful as the domestic slaves could easily do something untoward to their masters. The domestic slaves could easily and willingly share their saliva for one in their masters' meals, or even faeces for that matter, if they could have come up with the right ingredients. If domestic slaves were upset with their masters, they could also 'pepper' the masters' meals with poison. To a certain extent, the domestic slaves commanded some kind of direct power and respect, in a way, even if superficially and out of fear, on the part of the planters. Domestic slaves, even though in most cases, stripped of their religions, cultures, and names, among other factors and practices like the field slaves, they were spared the burden of receiving names such as Hogg, Pigmouth, Gutter, and would be assigned their masters' names such as Spencer, Stewart, Gordon, and so on.

It would also serve you well to acknowledge that in 1834, all Jamaica's slaves as well as a few other Caribbean islands started to embark upon that which was known as the Apprenticeship System. This was a four-year period that prepared the slaves for their freedom which was to come four years later in 1838 where they would be fully free.

The slave trade, the source of slaves arriving in the islands from Africa through the Middle Passage, chained together like four legged animals had actually and formerly ended in 1808. Jamaica finally was to gain its political independence from Britain on August 6, 1962. Its present political system comprises a Governor General, the Queen's Representative and the Head of State, the Prime Minister, the House of Representative and the Senate.

I am sure that at no surprise to you, my readers, after 1838, many ex-slaves, now free, refused to work on the sugar plantations for the small stipend that was being paid to those who remained. The planter class, the plantocracy, was therefore forced to bring in what they termed indentured servants who comprised mainly Asians but in particular, Indian and Chinese nationals. Most of the Indians would have come from the lower rank of their Caste System, the Shudras or Untouchables. This explains why we do have a fair share of Indians, Chinese, and other individuals of Asian extractions in places such as Jamaica and Trinidad, among other Caribbean jurisdictions.

Finally, on the political and historical backdrop of Jamaica, let's briefly explore the political structures from the time of colonialism to independent Jamaica. A civil governor was appointed to represent the country in 1661. The governor was appointed by the Crown. The governor acted at the advice of the nominated council in the Legislature. The Legislature consisted of the governor, and an elected House of Assembly, comprising mostly the local planters. This local body was not well represented, however. In 1662, for example, the second appointed governor to Jamaica, Lord Windsor, brought with him a proclamation from the King giving Jamaica's non-slave population the rights of English citizens, including the right to make their own laws.

Baby Joshua was born a little sickly, so he and his mother remained in the hospital for a few days before returning home. I understand that upon my return, and particularly about the age that I started to crawl (creep), that I enjoyed eating faeces but it was not any old kind of 'do do'. It had to be the droppings of the chickens walking around the yard or those of the domesticated pigeons that flapped around our surroundings and even flew from time to time inside our home. I understand that I liked these birds very well. Perhaps this was due to their very conspicuous and pretty feathers. However, now that I think about it, I might have liked those birds for completely different reasons than the grown-ups had established. My mother and father thought that I was just a bird lover. They even bought me a little book of birds that lived the long life of about three days!

The truth be told, I might have just learnt to have been extremely friendly and playful with these birds so that I would have an insurmountable amount of bird droppings at my beckon's call. These pigeons would bring me my meal of faeces right there on my parents' sofa. How much better could that get? I was told that I would clap and laugh, even jump at the arrival of these birds. I would ultimately figure that if I gave them my cookies and other so-called human goodies, they would come more often, and importantly, in their humongous numbers, and hopefully, would trade their delicious faeces for my human goodies, unrelentingly. If I should say it myself, I was indeed a pretty clever baby and toddler. Nasty, dirty, and weird, perhaps, but extremely smart, don't you think?

I was to join the others at the running tap water party as the months went by, but probably not as confidently and professionally as the others. I would break the cups and saucers in the trays outside until my mother learned the hard lesson. That she could not expect to leave them outside with me all the time and get a different result merely by admonishing me not to touch them. The idea that she needed to move them from my reach had completely escaped my mother's mind.

The years flew by quickly and before I realized it, my mother and I were now living alone in a part of a female friend's apartment somewhere on Dome Street or its vicinity in Montego Bay, Jamaica. I had no recollection of how this separation came about or how the moving out procedures took place. Did my dad pack my mother and I in his car then he sped off with us to this friend's apartment? Did he simply throw our clothes out? Did he just politely ask us to leave, probably with a kiss, a hug, or embrace of some kind? Did my love of the bird dropping delicacies contribute in a small way? I don't know and I, even at an older age when these questions started to have permeated my cerebral cortex, still bit my tongue, clinched my fists and swallowed the questions, shoved them to what I thought to be the recess of my mind.

My Aunt Gwendolyn had by then moved back to New Mills in Westmoreland, Jamaica. If indeed there was an explosive breakup, I did not notice. I might have been too much engaged in planning new tricks to con the birds out of their droppings, or I might have been sleeping or I just conveniently repressed the experience to my subconscious, and period, voilá, forgot the whole matter.

When I was around five years old, my dad and a Caucasian, male friend jointly opened a bar and restaurant on Hart Street, Montego Bay. I recalled him saying that he was always tired all the time, as he worked as a bookkeeper at an ice factory as well. He would leave work everyday to work in his business on Hart Street. He treated me as a king when I was there with him. I became a class dancer at five years old. Michael Jackson would have had a great competition in me. Everyone would clap and laugh and give me lots of money and candies (sweeties) for my stellar performances. I always enjoyed every moment of it. I remember the sadness that it usually brought when it was time to leave. During those moments, I was very sad. It was also the case when my dad ceased from coming to pick me up to visit.

My mother must have quickly given up on my father. In a few months, we moved to a place called Huntley in the parish of St. Elizabeth, Jamaica. My mother had met a gentleman who I remember only as Donald. At first, Donald was so kind to both of us. He would come home early, and we would all sit at the dining table to eat and talk. Then he gradually came home later and later. He would eventually make the midnight hour his 'homecoming hour' just about everyday. I know for sure that was about the time, as he would be always swearing and hitting my mom's face and all over her body whenever he arrived. Sometimes in the middle of the night, my mother would have to run with me on her hip to sleep at neighbours' homes. I became quite frightened and scared. However, because sometimes I saw him drive an ambulance home, I thought to myself, if my mother or I got hurt, there would have been no problem. He would simply have put on his ambulance's siren and rush us to the hospital to be cured before we died.

Now that I am writing this, and being an adult, I couldn't be sure if Donald was a paramedic or not. Who knows, he might have been borrowing the ambulance from a friend. In Jamaica, there is no problem! Everything is cool. Everything is irie! Everything goes!

I know for sure he had a Hillman Hunter motor car or some similar vehicle. However, I tried hard to remember the colour without luck. The constant, enduring image that floods my optical nerve and retina is that of a tall, dark, strapping, even handsome, but drunken man, staggering from his car always, and who was perpetually in a mood to practise boxing with my mother. Nowadays, as a grown man, I see him more like a jockey, striking his horse, not wanting to lose a very close race.

My mother returned with me to Montego Bay, but her friend had moved. She and I went to stay at the house of another friend until she could get an apartment of her own. This was her original plan. She must have thought about that decision all night because the following morning, she told me she would be taking me to visit my paternal grandparents in New Mills, that very afternoon.

CHAPTER TWO

New Mills and Berkshire – My New Homes

My mother had told me that she was taking me to visit my paternal grandparents in New Mills. I was now approaching five and half years old. Even though I was not very excited about the idea, I did not protest. I said in my little head that perhaps my mother simply needed a little break, perhaps to speak with daddy when I was not there. I even thought that I might have had a wonderful surprise gift on my return home – my mother and father cohabiting once again. Of course, I did not know the word, 'cohabit' but I was thinking along those lines.

We took the *Morning Star* country bus. The bus was big and red and the people all seemed dirty, extremely dark skin and uncouth in mannerism. At least, that was how they appeared to me. Again, not with this advanced vocabulary, but you get the idea.

I started counting the trees as the bus moved along, but they became too many for me. I attempted to count what appeared to be little huts along the road, but they too overwhelmed me. As I sat in my mother's lap minding my own business, the little, fat lady next to us, started saying how cute I looked, where I was from, and where I was going? As if my mother read my mind, she answered all the questions on my behalf.

The winding road to New Mills made me quite dizzy. It was almost evening. I started to think about how my cousins were. Did they speak funny like the country people in the bus, or even smell of fish like the one who was sitting next to my mother and me? Did they all wear aprons? Were they dirty all the time? Did they always ask so many questions?

The thoughts might have put me in a daze because suddenly an abrupt and hard shake, accompanied by a quiet call of, "Ricky, wake up," had brought me back to consciousness, and up on my feet, facing head-on, a forest-like area and rugged track that was to take my mother and myself to what was to be my new home.

The bus's brakes squealed to a halt and so were my heart and soul. I took a big clasp and grasp of my mother's left hand as she guided her handbag protectively onto the right shoulder. She led the way through the door and down the steps of the bus, endeavouring to avoid my soiling my clothes in a pile of marl left on the side of the road. I looked back at the dirty people in the *Morning Star* bus and wondered which would have been the lesser of the evils, my sitting beside a smelly bunch of market people of whom I had grown accustomed for approximately an hour, or relatives I had not yet met. Aunt Gwendolyn had spent time at my home in Montego Bay. She was actually there to witness my birth, but now I had no recollection of her. Like my experience with Donald, I was getting extremely nervous as the journey shortened along a tedious, out-of-breath, rocky and steep path, to that little structure on the peak of this sparsely populated district called New Mills.

They must have been expecting us, or so it seemed to me. There was a huge fire in an outside thatched kitchen and an immediate smell of coffee which briefly took my thoughts back to Albion, my original home. A young looking, very dark and beautiful woman rushed towards me, shouting, "Ricky, Ricky. Oh my God, little Ricky. You have grown so much. You are adorable!"

Before I could respond, they were all over me, squeezing, hugging. A tall, beautiful, grey hair woman approached from the kitchen. She said she was my grandma and her name was Mary Spencer, but to me she was Mammy.

"Hi Mammy," I said, testing the feel of the name.

It was not too difficult at all. They all seemed quite nice. My cousins and my grandpa all seemed a bit standoffish at first, but they too joined the party later.

As my grandpa, Reuben Spencer (Pa) chewed at his sugar cane, peeled by his long, dirty machete, he told me about my dad. He even attempted to hand me a piece of the cane, but I shook my head when I observed how dirty his hands, clothes, and machete were. He continued talking as if he had not noticed the rejection, I had just offered him. He stated how my father was a nice boy growing up. That he would take him to the field with him sometimes but, like Uncle Ben (Benjamin Spencer), his brother, now a school principal, they did not like the field too much. He said both boys were extremely bright. That they got straight A's in school and studied and passed their Senior Cambridge at the first sitting of the exam. Something that was unheard of by many students as the exams were quite difficult to pass at a first sitting. Pa continued to speak of my other uncle, Uncle George (George Spencer). He said that Uncle George did well in the field, but he was not too keen with the books. He said that he wanted him to learn a trade, but he left to live in Montego Bay before he could have helped him to realize that dream. For all I knew, Uncle George was doing well in Montego Bay as a truckdriver. I recalled him visiting my dad at the bar and restaurant while I was there.

It was strangely a great evening, so far. For one, my mother was still with us and there were so many people, including two children. I felt readily at home. As we talked though, I suddenly noticed that the place was getting quite dark, and where I thought I saw trees before, I was now seeing ghosts and images. I looked around more closely and realized that there were no outside lights but worse, there were no lights in the house either. A strange feeling of fear suddenly overcame my prior comfort and joy.

"Grenda, could you light the lamps, please?" Mammy yelled from the still smoky kitchen.

In a second, she jumped onto the verandah with match in hand to obey Mammy's command. The lamps at first failed to reveal the boarded and holey floors until the lampshades were cleaned. As Aunt Grenda (I now realized that was Aunt Gwendolyn's pet name), turned up the wick of each lamp, I could clearly see the two-apartment structure, plus its verandah. There was a little spring bed in what they called the hall which leaned against the boarded cedar walls. I also noticed that one of the window-panes was broken. My eyes went up to the ceiling that was made of zinc, but the inside was covered with a brownish material. My grandpa told me it was made from the trash of the cane. He also told me the name of it, but I quickly forgot. Opposite the bed, was a small table covered with a tablecloth made of plastic, bearing little fruits and vegetables all over its area. I went closer to examine the fruits to see if I could identify them all. There was another fruit there, but the table plastic had a big hole there that prevented me from properly identifying it. I wondered for awhile, had the tablecloth not torn, would I still have been able to identify that fruit or vegetable? I wondered how many people usually slept in that bed and whether those people would have been sleeping elsewhere that night. I noticed the bed was big, but I still questioned whether we would be able to fit. At one point, I assumed that if push came to shove, I could sleep on my mother's stomach as she slept on her back, on whichever of the beds they assigned to us.

"Ricky, come handsome. Sit on Mammy's lap. I made chocolate for you, 'cause coffee is not good for children's brain. I know you are going to be as smart as your dad with that brain."

I wondered if my grandma did not believe that my mother was smart. Why could I not get my mother's brain and still be a good student? I wondered briefly, what was the brain really? How did it work? How could the brain remember so many words and so many things, like Donald hitting my mother and we having to run to our neighbours' homes, with my mother crying and having me tucked to her hip like a belt? I also wondered how my brain did not let me remember what Aunt Grenda looked like until I arrived at the New Mills home. Like today, there were more questions than answers.

We gathered on the verandah for supper. I picked around the meal at Mammy's insistence to try foods which again, she thought was good for me and especially for my brain. I began to question why Mammy was so obsessed with the brain. I secretly wondered if her dad was a brain surgeon as I had heard my dad talk about brain surgeons in the past.

The hours passed quickly, and I realized that I was quite full and sleepy. I also wanted to urinate. It was at that time that it dawned on me that I had not seen the bathroom. Mammy pointed way down yonder; to show me where the toilet was. She said if I was scared, I could just pee at the root of the banana tree behind the house. She said the urine gives it manure so the plant will bear very large, nutritious fruits. I declined her invitation and asked my mother to accompany me to the toilet, way down yonder.

I realized when I reached there that I also wanted to defaecate but the only thing I saw there that resembled any form of paper to clean my bottom, was a Gleaner newspaper. My mother told me, to my surprise, that that was what they used to clean themselves after the act. I was in shock. I asked all kinds of questions, but my mother was getting quite tired of me, or simply just tired, period. I cleaned my bottom with the rough newspaper, my mother assisting a little, and returned to fetch water to wash my hands.

Mammy offered to have my mother and myself sleep in her big, giant, humongous bed. Aunt Grenda and one of the two kids would sleep on the floor, the other would sleep with Pa. I wondered how long this arrangement would last or how long I would have to remain in that strange house. As I pondered on all those things, I must have been flung into a deep realm of sweet sleep, as it was only when the roosters started to crow nonstop that I realized that the night had passed and the morning's sun was high in the sky. My mother had left. She left a little, smiley face on a piece of crumpled paper and drew a heart. She had told everyone that she did not want to wake me up as I was too deep in sleep.

That very morning, I realized that my cousins were girls. One was much older than me. She was called Fay. The other was about two and half years old. Her name was Jasmine.

Fay immediately started to show that she was in charge.

"I placed water in the basin on the bench for you to wash your face. The Colgate is there but don't waste it 'cause it's expensive," she beamed.

I pretended not to have heard her and went about my business, walking towards Jasmine, my younger cousin whose face in fact seemed to have needed a little more washing than mine did. There were bridles which ran from each corner of her mouth and stopped at exactly the same location, just below her very large and protruding ears. The matter surrounding her eyes were large enough to make cornmeal porridge, like the ones my mother used to make for me. I went closer towards her. She walked away. She probably sensed that I was describing her dirty face in my mind, or it could have been that she was too shy, or it just could have been that she did not like me too much.

"Ricky, you need to wash your face, now!" Fay repeated, but now much more like a Major in the army.

"Go tell Yasmine to wash her face," I uttered back, unable to pronounce the 'J' in 'Jasmine' properly.

Shortly after I insinuated that Jasmine's face needed more washing than mine did, I noticed that she went to the kitchen and returned with what I thought at first was chocolate. I soon realized that it was water. Mammy must have given it to her to wash her face.

I started to wonder in my little head, why did Mammy not give Jasmine water in the basin to wash her face? Why did she not help her to wash her face? She seemed so tiny, struggling with the mug, the size of her head, which wasn't that small either. Was it that boys wash their faces in basins and girls from big, white mugs? Was it because I was cute and she not so cute? Mammy interrupted my thoughts with her call.

"Ricky, come here handsome. Come taste Mammy's breakfast."

"But he did not wash his face yet!" Fay screamed.

"Come on. Leave the boy alone. He is new and just getting used to the place," Mammy explained.

I jumped onto my Mammy's lap. She fed me an egg sandwich and gave me hot chocolate which was actually cold by the time I got it. I watched her pour the once hot chocolate from one mug to the next, without a spill. I began to wonder how long she had been pouring hot chocolate from mug to mug, or whether she did it with coffee and tea and other hot liquids. I thought of asking her but changed my mind.

She rubbed my stomach and tickled me. I laughed and giggled as all kids do when tickled. I felt so loved, right then and there.

A few years had passed and there was no sign of my mother. I had virtually forgotten about her until one day while Jasmine and I played dolly house at the back of our place, she got me upset. I grabbed her the same way Donald grabbed my mother and slapped her in the face. Fay heard Jasmine's screams and came to her rescue. She pulled us apart and warned us never to fight again. She also said something about what she would do if I did such thing to Jasmine ever again.

I honestly did not hear what punishment my older cousin had in store for me. I had by then started to think of my mother. I was asking myself all sorts of questions. Why did Donald slap her all the time? Was it something that guys do to girls? I wondered whether my dad had also slapped my mother but because I probably had my mother's brain, I forgot it happened. I questioned whether my mother and dad were back together, but they were not ready to tell me. I also wondered if my mother not returning to see me was a result of her thinking that I would slap her too.

I spent the rest of the day mostly with Fay. She was beginning to teach me to read and write and review letters of the alphabet. My dad had already taught me a lot of that stuff, but Fay did not know.

At about six and a half years old, I was registered at the Bethel Town All-Age School – a school that contained grades 1 through 9. It was a little over a mile away from my New Mills home. I was placed in grade one. As Mammy walked away the first day of school and Fay went to a higher grade class, I cried uncontrollably. I was very afraid. At New Mills, I would usually stay home in the confines of my little home, well protected by Fay, Pa, and to some extent, Jasmine, and definitely by my Mammy who showed me so much love and care. However, now I was on my own. There were no cousins, no mother, no father, no Mammy. I thought of the distance away and the length of time I would have to be away from my Mammy. I cried some more.

My teacher, Ms. Michelin, was a great individual and I think she also had her own son in our class, if my memory serves me correctly. I found that cool. She taught us the same things Fay and dad had already taught me. I started to think why it was necessary to walk over a mile on a hot tarry road to burn the sole of my feet, to learn that which Fay and my dad had already taught me at home. I thought Fay could have continued to teach me at home after school, each weekday and during the weekends.

The days passed quickly, and I got acquainted to my new life. I made some friends. Each lunchtime I would take my three pence (three cents) to buy 'archie', a kind of fried dumpling and a snow cone. I always looked forward to recess. We played marble and rolled in the ground, enough to make Mammy a little upset at times, but not too mad. We would stop on our way from school to pick the oranges from Mr. Blake's orchard. I would never go over there though. I would just stand on the embankment while my new, 'Caucasian' friend, Michael Weddemire, and sometimes Brian Weddemire, the older brother, monkeyed up the trees as fast as lightning bolt. Dozens of oranges would be thrown down to the ground in seconds. If the truth be told, I was no better than the Weddemires in this regard. I did not climb the orange trees like my friends used to, as I did not know how to climb. I hid that fact from my friends up to this day. We would then peg the oranges and suck the juice as we played.

One evening, Mr. Blake caught Michael and warned that if he did not stop picking the oranges, he was going to tell his parents. However, Michael stopped only for a few days.

It was not merely the act of picking the oranges, but the risk of getting caught that made it exciting for us, at least for them.

A little about Michael and Brian Weddemire. Their parents were wealthy. They had a stone mill business in the adjacent district to New Mills known as Struie. They also had a huge shop. Although Michael and Brian seemed to be fully white, they were mixed, their mother being Chinese and their father, German (white). They usually took a lot of money to school. We liked walking with them from school, as they usually got rides from their parents' friends. Whenever that happened, they would throw us all the money they had left in their pockets. We would use the money the next day (sometimes the same day) to buy marbles, red herring, and snow cones.

Sometimes Michael upon hearing the roar of a vehicle as we walked from school, would jump over the embankments to hide, as he did not want to leave us by ourselves.

I had just completed grade 2 and it was the summer holidays when my mother returned. She told us that she was now living in Berkshire in the parish of Westmoreland. She was in fact born in that district. She had left Berkshire at a young age to live in Montego Bay where she met my father. Now with sparkling eyes, she told us that she had met a new boyfriend by the name of Mr. Lovell. They were living on the property of my maternal grandparents in this district and they wanted me to come home to live with them. I could tell by the look on Mammy's face that she was not too happy about something. She, upon hearing what my mother said, walked away towards the kitchen. My mother went to say something softly to her. I did not hear exactly what she had said to Mammy as I stood at my original spot.

Mammy offered my mother something to eat but she said she had to go and did not want to miss the bus. My clothes were prepared and placed in a bag. Mammy came over and hugged me tightly and told me to visit soon and often. I promised, then I walked away after saying bye to Aunt Gwendolyn, Jasmine, and Fay. Pa was in his field, so I did not get to say goodbye to him. I walked away gingerly toward the rugged, downhill slope, only to turn slightly to take a glance at my Mammy to see her using her dirty apron to wipe the tears that flowed from her eyes.

We arrived at Berkshire about dusk. We stopped at a shop that sold everything, sardines, mackerels, flour, beers, cigarettes and much more. There was a gentleman around the counter serving the many customers. He was playing dominoes and was drinking beers with guys who appeared to have been his friends. As I was about to try and make sense of what was going on, my mother interrupted my thought.

"Ricky, this is your stepdad, Mr. Lovell. He and I recently opened this shop," she said, pointing at the short, stocky-looking Mr. Lovell.

Mr. Lovell was nice. He spotted my head and said something like I was a handsome, young man and that I would have lots of girls in the future.

I immediately noticed that there were lit bulbs hanging in the shop and the streets were lit. My mother invited me around the counter to the back, to wash my hands. She offered me something to eat. There was a little bed in a very compacted bedroom at the back. I was wondering if Mr. Lovell, my mother, and myself were going to be sleeping on that little bed at the back of the shop. As if my mother read my thoughts, she blurted out,

"This is not where we live. The house is up the road. We rented this shop to make some money to help send you to school."

Later that night, all three of us walked to our home. It took us about thirty minutes. We had to walk through a narrow passage that led from the main road and which was set a little apart from the main road itself. It, however, was not far from the main street. The track was dark, and they had to use a torch for us to see.

We arrived at the house which, unlike the shop, had no electricity. The building reminded me of my grandparents' home in New Mills. The only difference was that it seemed smaller because it had no verandah.

Shortly after, I was shown my bed in the hall similarly placed as Pa's in New Mills. I was then invited to go to visit my grandma's tomb. I found it a bit strange, even scary to have been visiting a tomb at night. I had heard that ghosts were quite busy at night times and would rest during the day. They were nocturnal. As I did not want to disappoint Mr. Lovell and my mother so early after moving in with them, I went to visit.

The tomb was beautiful. It read:

"Adina Topping

May Your Soul Rest in Peace."

It also mentioned a date from so to so, but I couldn't recall it at the time of writing. I felt a weird kind of comfort came over me, similar to when my Mammy in New Mills hugged me.

My mother told me that my grandma was Indian with long hair that flowed to her bottom and that she died in child's birth. I wondered whether her bottom was flat or hilly like Mammy's. I laughed quietly at the thought. But really had no idea what 'died in child's birth' meant. I decided not to ask, at least not that night.

Berkshire was okay. My mother also got a part-time job in a place called Pisgah in the parish of St. Elizabeth. She worked as a domestic helper with a family whose surname was Warwar. I always wondered if these people liked war or what. However, when I got to know them and visited my mother at work, they were always so kind and their children would play with me and their big dog, Dragon. The first time I saw Dragon, I thought the dog was a cow. The dog was that big. Strangely though, I had never heard that dog bark. He was truly a big pet.

Not too far from the Warwar's was a big farm owned by one, 'Mass' Ken. Mass Ken cultivated Irish potatoes. Sometimes, he would load several pounds of potatoes in crocus bag with a bundle of firewood. He had really great guava and pimento firewood that Mr. Lovell and especially my mother liked. Mass Ken would pack the crocus bag with Irish potatoes or firewood or both. He would help the bag to my head, and I would walk the close to three miles home with it to Berkshire. Sometimes my bare feet would scorch on the melting tar or got pricked on those parts of the road that were only covered with marl and stones. Some of the very stones of the stone mill of that of my friend's dad, Mr. Weddemire. He might have sold the stones from his stone mills to the government's Public Works Department, or they could have been stones broken mostly by small hammers by the many poor, country women of these depressed districts.

My stepdad, Mr. Lovell, was from a district called Stonehenge in the parish of St. James. He did most of his farming on his parents' property there. Stonehenge was about eight miles from Berkshire. He had a bicycle and would often tow me on it to get food in Stonehenge, to return to Berkshire. On the way back, I had to walk with the load on my head.

I remember that one day while I was returning from Stonehenge with the usual crocus bag of yam, pumpkin, and other ground provisions on my head, I decided to take a shortcut. Mr. Lovell had already ridden his bicycle ahead with his bag of food as well. I had completely forgotten that it had rained heavily and that the Simon River usually overflowed during heavy rain. I walked for over forty minutes to reach this shortcut. As soon as I reached the Simon River, I would have only about thirty minutes or so, to reach my home in Berkshire. However, as I reached the river, I realized that it was overflowing and that it was quite turbulent. I started to think what I was going to do. It would be too time-consuming to turn back, plus my parents would get upset that I took so long to get home. I decided that I was going to try to cross the river. I looked for what I thought was the shallowest part of the turbulence to cross. I stepped on a big rock and slipped, the crocus bag of food slipping from my head. I grabbed onto the bag with all my life. I knew that if I lost that bag of food, so would be my life with caning I would have received from my mother. At one stage, the water had its way with me. It dragged and banged me against stones, but I decided I was not letting go of that crocus bag of food. I can't explain how it happened, but I eventually got tossed with my crocus bag of food over the other side of the river. Soaked like a rat, my heart racing, I hurried home, happy that I did not lose the crocus bag of food or had to turn back or drowned.

Mr. Lovell saw me on my arrival and narrow escape from death and remarked that I was a fool to have walked at the shortcut after a heavy rain. I kept my silence, not wanting to upset my mother whose eyes were still sparkling for having found love once again, interestingly, in a man called Mr. Lovell.

I was about nine years old when my sister Georgia was born. At about the time when my mother was due, she got her half-sister, her father's daughter, Imogene, to come and stay with us. I did not like the arrangement because I now had to share my little spring bed with my young aunt, Imo, as we soon started to call her. When Georgia was only weeks old, at Aunt Imo's request, I left to go to the shop to collect some items that she could cook supper. Upon my return, there was no Imo, only a screaming baby soaked in urine and faeces. Aunt Imo had run away with a male friend, leaving my little sister, Georgia all alone crying and covered in filth. Upon my discovering what had happened, I was so confused. I was a mere nine years old! I had no one with whom to leave Georgia to go to tell my mother. Those days there were no cellphones. We didn't even have electricity in the house much more the luxury of a house phone. I was devastated. I started to cry as much as, or even more than, my few weeks old sister, Georgia. I changed her nappy (diaper) for the first time and bathed her. I then put on her clothes and brought her to the shop, to let my mother know what had happened. They were so outraged. So much so, that at one point, I thought they were mad at me.

For the first time since I arrived in Berkshire, the entire family was home by six in the evening.

CHAPTER THREE

The Disappointments

The sparkles in my mother's eyes got dimmer and dimmer as the days went by. I noticed the change not merely in her eyes but in her general deportment and mannerisms in her relationships with me and others. She had lost the bounce in her steps, the spring in her bosom, and her shoulders slouched. Her head now hung loosely and bubbly like a bubble head to her shoulders, connected ironically, by an apparently taut and stiff neck. Her beautiful smiles had slowly disappeared from her face like a small pot of water left out in the blazing, open sun for days. Her very light complexion started to take on a deep, dark, and scaly tone. The screaming at me, not to mention the flogging, and cursing, gradually climbed like a crescendo. I could guarantee a slap as hard as the greatest of those she had received from Donald several years ago, or the atrocious shove she received from Mr. Lovell only days before. This would occur for the slightest of transgression on my part, or for no transgression whatsoever. I noticed too that she had become a heavy smoker as well. Mr. Lovell would spend less and less time in the shop like Donald had done to the home in Huntley and had also started to return home very late at nights, often tipsy, though not drunk. My mother learnt not to ask questions after she was pushed to the floor with little Georgia in her hand one night, the shove I mentioned above.

Things had certainly changed drastically. My attendance at the Dundee Primary School where I had registered shortly after arriving in Berkshire, was being affected because I found myself spending more and more time in the shop. I remember months ago being told that they had opened the shop to send me to school. Now the shop had the opposite effect – a weird and contrary impact! It was a big impediment to my going to school. It was indeed a huge stumbling block to my acquiring an education.

I loved school very much. I had met some great friends and the work was always manageable. Wayne Colquhoun, my new-found friend was kind and his birthday was just three days apart from mine, having been born on November 3. We got along at school very well. There were also my cousins: Cecil Salesman, Winston Salesman, Radcliffe Daley, pet name, Dave, and many others.

Dave is my second cousin, being the son of Mrs. Stephenson, a teacher, who is my first cousin. Her mother, Aunt Linda, was my mother's sister. At the time, the positioning of cousins as if they were in a competitive race did not make a darned sense to me. Now the concepts are more comprehendible, but I still believe a better way could have been found to define such relationships among relatives. I was also getting interested in girls, and as far as I was concerned, girls were also getting interested in me. I wanted to be at school for those reasons and more.

I spent so much time in the shop, I now became an expert at Mathematics. If a customer needed three tins of sardines, in seconds, I could tell them that it was fifty-one cents, three times seventeen, without using pen and paper or a calculator. The same for Red Stripe Beers. I found it quite interesting at the time that most items were being sold at seventeen cents each. As fascinating as that was, I was quite upset that I was only going to school every other day and not every school day. I had gathered some information that my father was now an accountant at Pemco Hotel at East Street, Montego Bay. At the time of writing, I could not recall how I got that information, but I did.

I secretly wrote my dad a letter to the Pemco Hotel address, outlining my condition, advising that my mother had me selling in her shop and would not send me to school regularly. At first, after writing the letter to my dad, I thought my dad did not receive the letter or that he might have gotten the letter but did not care about education anymore, or worse, he no longer cared about me or that he might have died. I reflected on the stories he had read me as a toddler and young boy, and the complicated and complex things he attempted to explain to me then. I remembered that at one stage he explained what happened to my cookies in my body from the time they touched my tongue until the moment they hit my intestines. He said there were little guys called enzymes that broke up my cookies, beginning in the mouth. That these little guys were great guys, that the ones in my mouth actually lived in my spit (saliva). That there were others in my stomach and intestines, and that all the enzymes work like a team. Each one had another specific job to do in the chain of actions. He said that there were little nets in my small intestines that were able to absorb these broken down cookies into my body and take them through little roads in my body that lead to building blocks (cells) that make us up. He compared it to the making of soft drinks (pop) that he had taken me to see upfront at the Desnoes & Geddes factory, many, many years ago.

I got really interested in such stuff. I considered that I should be careful not to spit unnecessarily because I did not want to destroy these great enzyme guys living there. Later when I got older, I went to the library to read up on these things and found out that the enzyme in my saliva was called ptyalin. I found out that different things happened to foods such as the beef or the vegetables that I eat and that their end-products during digestion were quite different. That carbohydrates and starches become glucose before they are absorbed into the villi of the small intestines. Proteins such as our chicken legs become amino acids, and fats become fatty acids and glycerol. I found the whole thing quite engaging as well as interesting. Consequently, I acquired and developed a great liking for Science, particularly Biology and Chemistry in my later years.

It was therefore quite unusual that the man who was so fond of education seemed to have turned his back on the very thing in which he wanted me to have an interest as a younger child. I found it strange that he did not respond to my letter. A letter that was a boisterous cry for help. A cry that would let me realize my dream and his.

About three months passed before I got a typed letter from the Dundee Post Office or it could have been at the Pisgah Postal Agency. Now that I have revisited this matter, I now believe it was at the Pisgah Postal Agency. I am not absolutely sure which post office or postal agency. Anyway, I received a typed letter. The returning section (the top left-hand corner) of the envelope said, 'Charles Spencer' and it had the hotel's information and address. He addressed me as 'Master Joshua Spencer'. I found it quite interesting and amusing. He started out by saying he was "sorry for the tardiness in response". It was the first time learning the word, 'tardiness' but from context, I understood what dad meant. He went on to say that he was sorry that I was not going to school regularly and that he would contact my mother about it, with a view to have her change her ways. He closed by saying he loved me, and I felt very happy when I read those words. Below the typed 'Signature', he drew what seemed to have been a huge 'C' and in the middle, he flashed the word, 'Spencer'. To this day, I write my signature from modelling my dad's signature. I draw a big loopy-looking 'J' then I write a flashy-looking 'Spencer' in the middle of the 'J'.

My dad was indeed a man of his word, for the very next day, I got two letters which I originally thought were at the Dundee Post office. However, I could have collected them at the Pisgah Postal Agency in St. Elizabeth, a few miles outside of Berkshire which is actually located in Westmoreland. One of the letters was addressed to 'Ilett Robinson'. That, as you will recall, was my mother's 'real name' (registered name), even though everyone called her Ms. Tiny. One of the letters had in the 'return address' section, the name, 'Charles Spencer' typed. The other had 'Mavis Robinson' scribbled in a grade two kind of writing. The address said something about London, England. I immediately realized that it was sent from my aunt who lived there. I recalled my mother telling me that when she was little, her sister May May (That was my aunt's pet name) left for England. However, she was not registered or her birth certificate (age paper) could not be found or some such nonsense. As a result, Aunt May May (Mavis Robinson) had to use Mama's birth certificate to emigrate to England. So, 'legally', Mama was actually Mavis Robinson and Ilett Robinson was actually Auntie May May. I found it both confusing and intriguing. I felt a little important then, too. I could tell my friends that my mother lived in England. I considered about the thought for awhile and realized that that would not have been a great idea. My Mama and Aunt May May could have gotten in trouble if this became public. I later wondered why they used their real names in the mails.

One last point on this matter. I recently realized that of the six of us that my mother gave birth to, only me has her name on my birth certificate. All my siblings, unfortunately, one had died a few years ago, have birth certificates bearing the name, Mavis Robinson. Now that I am thinking of it, I would not have been able to sponsor my siblings to Canada, even if I had the means to do so which I did not have anyway. The record would show the relationship between my siblings and I as first cousins, not siblings. Intriguing state of affairs!

I handed the letters to my mother. She seemed very excited to have received them. I noticed she opened the letter from England first. She unsealed the envelope. The letter from England was quite interesting in design. She had to take great care in opening the letter. I watched her fold her tongue in a curved kind of carpet-like way and then splashed saliva all around the edges of the envelope. She seemed to enjoy the taste of the envelope or something on it. I thought about those poor enzymes. I wondered whether they would survive the onslaught of Mama's tongue and the rugged edge of the envelope. To make matters worse, she took a pen and rolled it inside between the edges. The envelope eventually relented, exposing a broad note which had a funny symbol on it with numbers juxtaposed next to it. My mother's face lit up in joy. I wondered what was so funny about the note. I peeped over my mom's shoulder but did not see any funny pictures on it. I heard her murmur that she would have to go to the post office the next day to change it. I realized that Aunt May May had sent Mama money from England. The sign on the note was the symbol for pound, the currency of England. I then noticed that there was no writing paper in the letter. I soon realized why my Mama was so careful with the letter when she tried to open it. The envelope was also the writing paper. I thought that the British people were either very clever or very mean or possessed a bit of both traits.

It was time for daddy's letter to be read. I was somewhat nervous. I felt like leaving but I wanted to get my mother's immediate reactions as she read the letter. To my disappointment, she threw the letter down on the bed.

For most of the rest of the evening, I was a nervous wreck. I wondered what she would say when she found out I had actually written my dad about not going to school. Would she get mad, or would she just give me one of her lectures about how she had to feed me and that my dad was not giving me anything? I wondered if she would mention for the umpteenth time that Mr. Lovell was not my dad and that he only got money when he travelled on the farm work program in the USA once a year. I also imagined her getting angry and slapped me with her shoes. The thoughts were unbearable. I went outside to talk to the little boy who lived a little way down the road. Upon my return, I could tell Mama had already read the letter. Her face was pink. She was in a rage. How ungrateful I was to have complained to my dad about her not sending me to school. As far as she knew, I went to school almost every day, would catch up on the little I was missing as, according to her, I was very bright. She howled at me that I had never been hungry, even when sometimes she went to bed hungry. She started to throw my clothes on the floor.

"You ungrateful wretch! You can go to your father if that's what you want," she screamed.

I waited patiently for her to calm down, then I put the clothes back onto the hangers under the closet, which incidentally looked exactly like the one at New Mills.

A few weeks had passed. Mama called me in her room one day when we were alone with my baby sister, Georgia. Come to think of it, I think Mama, Georgia, and I were always home alone than was Mr. Lovell with us. She asked if I really wanted to go to my dad. I thought about her being alone and found it hard to respond.
"I'll tell your dad to come to get you," she said.

I was not sure whether I should laugh or cry. I ate supper, brushed my teeth, washed my feet, then went to sleep with a heavy heart.

My dad had decided that my mother should send me by bus and that he would meet me at Charles Square (now Sam Sharpe Square) in Montego Bay, Jamaica. He would be meeting me just at the roundabout where the buses used to park by the terminal those days. My mother packed my few pieces of clothes and placed them in a bag similar to the one she had brought to New Mills to retrieve me. I thought of the fun times I would have in Montego Bay. I imagined watching cartoons on television when it signed on at 5:00 P.M. in the afternoon and sometimes in the mornings when it signed on about 9:00 A.M. to about 11:30 A.M. and all day on weekends, after doing my homework. I thought about watching Ms. Lou (Louise Bennett) too. I imagined my dad and I going to the cinemas once awhile, eating peanuts and ice cream as we did so. My friends would come over to play sometimes or I would go to their homes. I imagined that my dad might have sold his car and now bought a more expensive one, probably a Volkswagen bug or an Anglia or Zephyr. I imagined him introducing me to his girlfriend or his wife. I said, no, my dad was not married. He had a girlfriend. He would have invited me to the wedding had he gotten married.

I went to my friend's house a little down the lane, not only to tell him that I would be going to Montego Bay the following day for good, but I wanted a break from all the thoughts that inundated my brain. I ran up to his fence. As I always did, I placed two fingers from each hand together and rested them on my pink tongue. I blew hard and the familiar whistle summoned my friend to come out of his house. Harry McDonald, I think his name was, but I just referred to him most of the time as my friend. He did not go to government school but to Seventh Day Adventist School. Sometimes when I was lonely and wanted a friend to talk to, I would go whistling by his fence. He would say that it was his Sabbath and he was not allowed to come out, or I had to wait until the sun would set. I remember my dad saying that the Earth was on an axis like other planets and that the Earth was moving around the sun. So, when the sun seemed to set here, it might have very well been up and about somewhere else, providing life and energy I thought. I never said it to Harry though. He was my friend. He was entitled to think the way he wanted. My dad and my mother also taught me that people were different. That people look differently, talk differently and believe in different things. It means that we must respect others' beliefs and practices, even when we don't necessarily practise or believe in the things they do.

My friend came to the fence and opened the gate. He handed me some marbles and we started to play marbles. He gave me six marbles, but he won them all back. We then played chase. Finally, we sat on the ground and chatted about all things that boys talked about. He said his dad was going to build him an eight-wheeler and would paint it red. An eight-wheeler was a truck with eight wheels. Strangely enough, we had never talked about our parents. I asked him his dad's name and the work he did. He said he was a truckdriver and that his name was Ferdinand McDonald. I awaited patiently for him to ask me similar questions, but there was only a big, great pause between us. I started to say something when his mother screamed out his name. He said goodbye and I left, somewhat dejectedly.

Mr. Lovell shook me awake that early morning. He asked me if I changed my mind about going to Montego Bay. I shook my head. He said he would miss me, but a boy needed his dad.

Mr. Lovell was indeed a good stepdad. At least, in comparison to Donald. He had never hit me or even screamed at me, other than when he thought it was stupid of me to have walked across the Simon River after that heavy rain. I also remember him asking me to read from the newspaper to him from time to time. At that time, I thought he was just proud that his stepson was such an excellent reader. However, as I got older and became an adult, the thought that he could not read came to my mind. That I don't know for sure. I had never seen him read anything whatsoever. In a way, I admired Mr. Lovell, and hoped he and mother could have gotten along much better than they did.

I couldn't recall the time that all four of us, baby sister Georgia, were all at the dining table together. They gave me mint tea and egg sandwich and they had the same – I think. We chatted and my mother said she loved me. That I was her first child and she wanted me to be happy. I listened attentively and did not say a word until Mr. Lovell grabbed my bag and beckoned that we should go. We embraced and left to get the bus. As we were on the little track that led to the main road, my mother shouted that I should remember that my father would be wearing a grey pair of pants and a white shirt. He would say, 'Ricky?' when we meet, and he knew that I was wearing my pair of khaki pants and blue shirt and blue crepe. I was not at all worried about that because I had secretly sent him my photo in the letter that I mailed to him.

The bus arrived and Mr. Lovell spoke to the driver. He told him that dad would pick me up at Charles Square, now Sam Sharpe Square, in Montego Bay. He also described what clothes my dad would be wearing and the password, 'Rick?' that would be said before I would go to him.

As the bus started to roll away, I felt an uneasy feeling. At that moment, I was not as excited anymore. It probably had to do with the uncertainties, the anxieties, the possibility that my dad might have forgotten, and I would have had to return to Berkshire. I felt as if I was becoming nauseous. I slowly managed to calm my thoughts. I began to focus on the people around me. There was a gentleman with a white cane, and he wore dark glasses. I wondered how he seemed to be travelling by himself. How would he know when to come off the bus? The bus roared along. Every now and again, someone would shout, 'one stop' or simply pulled the string in the bus and it would stop to let them off. Sometimes, someone standing on the pavement would wave her or his left hand or right hand at the bus as it approached, and the bus would stop to pick up the passenger. We drove through Cambridge, where the bus stopped for a long while. Even the driver left the bus. Many passengers left the bus too.

Finally, the driver returned. He pulled a long, wiry horn and the bus bellowed like a bull. The many people scampered back to the bus and hurried to resume their seating positions in the vehicle as the bus resumed its journey. I noticed that the blind man came off at Montpelier. My assumption was right. He was alone. He and the driver spoke as if they knew each other. He clapped and banged his cane along the sidewalk as he walked along. The bus was moving so fast. I did not get to see if he had in fact made that left turn into the track that I was betting myself that he would. I was a little upset with the driver for driving so fast that I did not know if I had won the bet with myself or not.

In literally seconds, we were going down the scary-looking Long Hill, near Reading, Montego Bay. There was a deep gully on one side of the road, the left side of the road on which the bus was driving. In Jamaica, drivers, drive on the left side of the road. There was no solid structure to prevent it from going over the gully either. If the driver made a little error, we would all be dead in that gully, I thought.

I did not get to worry for long. The driver sped along quickly to the intersection of Reading in Montego Bay. He made a right turn and now once again, I was in my town, years later to be named Jamaica's second city. I started to think of Albion and my father's business on Hart Street. I wondered if any of the boys who I left there a few years ago, were still there. I also wondered whether we would recognize each other. As I thought all those thoughts, the driver screamed:

"Charles Square. Charles Square, final stop."

The driver beckoned me to come forward. I checked the zip on my bag to have made sure the bag was properly secure. I placed the bag's strap on my shoulder and started walking nervously and with trepidation towards the driver and the front door. There was dad in his grey pair of pants and white shirt! We seemed to recognize each other instantly.

He shouted, 'Ricky!' and I said, "Dad."

I said to myself, his password was not quite right because he said it with an exclamation and not an interrogation. But I figured, what the heck, he said it! He called my name and to me, that was what was really important.

On disembarking from the bus, and within arm's length of dad, I felt like hugging him, but I was waiting for him to make the move first and then I would reciprocate. He did nothing. I quickly followed behind as we tried to cross the busy round-a-bout to get to the other side of the street. Once again, I began to wonder what colour his car was, the size and make, and whether my original thoughts were correct. As my thinking persisted, a cab drove along. He flogged it down to a stop. He pushed me in the back seat and went to sit at the front. I overheard him say to the driver, "12 ½ Upper King Street."

The address to which my father took me was known as Canterbury or Gully. It was the real ghetto area of Montego Bay, with a lot of violence and even hard drugs. I could not understand. My father was not explaining anything. As a matter of fact, he spoke very sparingly to me. I felt like we were strangers. I roamed in my now medium-sized head and questioned myself, "Where was that dad I knew at five and a half?"

Was I remembering incorrectly all the experiences I described above? Where is the dad who taught me all those stuff about Science and took me to Desnoes & Geddes to witness firsthand, the manufacture of pop (soft drinks)? The dad who took me to the cinema and was constantly talking with me and stimulating me educationally? What happened to the dad who would take me to his partnership bar and restaurant on Hart Street and clapped and shouted, 'That's my boy!' when I danced for money and candies (sweeties), for all his patrons at his bar? What happened to his home in Albion? What happened to his car? Did it get too old and dilapidated that he had to abandon it? If so, why did he not buy another? Why had my dad become so strange?

There were more questions than answers. Worse, I did not have the guts to ask them out loudly. At this point, I really felt closer to Mr. Lovell than I did with my dad. I felt a big gaping hole inside of me, a longing for affection, a longing for a feeling of belonging. I started to think about my mother and Mr. Lovell. I asked myself whether Mr. Lovell was still leaving my mother for long hours all by herself with my baby sister, Georgia. I questioned whether my mother had felt the same way I was feeling in the presence of my daddy at this moment. I was confused.

I was constantly being by myself. My dad had introduced me to the adults living upstairs his little one-bedroom apartment. He had told me that I could ask the lady, Gee, upstairs for anything I needed when he was not home. She was the lady who was cooking for my dad. She would also be cooking for me. Gee was nice. I was thinking that Gee was my father's girlfriend until I saw the beautiful wedding band on her finger and heard her speak of her husband. I couldn't recall seeing her husband at the home, however. Could they have been married and they wanted to keep it away from me? They just wanted to keep it a secret from me, no? I would never know for sure, even though I currently doubt that was the case.

I found it ironic that the main reason I wanted to leave Berkshire was to go to school. I know it was some time in May and schools would have been out in July for summer holidays. However, I thought my dad would have had me enrolled in a school. He did not. At one point, I started to question if I was captured by a dad impersonator. I knew that those thoughts were nonsensical because I saw dad with pictures of me when I was five and a half and younger. He also had the picture I mailed to him from Berkshire.

I started to get very depressed and bored. There were books for me to read, but nothing else. There wasn't anything in his bedroom, other than a radio and books. I also noticed that he had some strange looking books. The language was not in English. I wondered if my dad spoke other languages, but I did not ask him about these strange books when he came home. He said I should keep in when he was at work as the area was bad.

I started to read my father's mind, but not his books. I started to think he was caught between a wall and a hard place. I had begun to think that he wanted to please me, but things had changed drastically in his life. It was as if he felt ashamed that things did not work out as he envisioned, and he did not know how to explain himself to me.

I began to feel sorry for him. I began to realize that the reason he did not send money to Berkshire for me or came to visit was that he couldn't. It came as no surprise then, when my dad came home one night with alcohol on his breath and said:

"Ricky, I am so sorry. I don't think this place is good for you. I will have to take you to New Mills, until I sort out myself. Ricky, do you understand?"

My dad hugged me for the first time in two weeks since I had arrived in Montego Bay.

"I understand," I murmured in both disappointment and sorrow.

My dad inquired of me when I would like to go to New Mills. I told him that the coming weekend would have been fine if he had the time. He agreed to take me on the Saturday that weekend.

New Mills had not changed much. My uncle, Benjamin Spencer, the principal, had added a room to the house and they had built a new latrine, this time a little closer to the house than the older one. There was now toilet paper in the toilet and there were more drums to hold drinking water. A gutter was built around the zinc roof, forming a circle that led into one of the drums. I imagined that when one drum was filled, they would lift it to the next, until each drum was filled to capacity. Mammy looked a little bit older now and so was Pa. Fay had grown older and left for Kingston, Jamaica's capital but another cousin was born by the name Otmaro. His full name was Otmaro Woodrow Service. I thought the name was a little strange, frankly, ridiculous, but I said nothing.

Pa was still doing his farming. He had a few cattle over the back land and one or two tied around the home. There were sugar cane, ginger, corn, peas, yam, and other ground provisions all around the house. There were also lots of coconut and breadfruit trees as well as mango and pear (avocado), among others. Some that I did not notice before or I had forgotten about them.

Mammy got me registered for the second time now at the Bethel Town All-Age School. I think I was placed in grade 5 or 6. I can't really remember of which class I was precisely placed. At school, there were still many of the kids when I was there prior. So, making friends was quite easy. I resumed buying archie and snow cones and the playing of marbles and now, football (soccer) and cricket.

I quickly got to grade nine in this school. I was always placed in the top five of my class. A few times, I placed first or second in my class. I can recall that in grade nine one year, Errol

Snipe who came first, beat me by just a half of a point.

I discovered something about Mammy that I had not known before. My grandma was a market woman just like the ones I had met on the *Morning Star* country bus some years ago. I had seen her wear the apron, but I thought it was just to prevent dirt from getting onto her dress. Or it simply was the fashion statement for old people who lived in those areas. She would go around from house to house from Mondays through Wednesdays each week. This was to purchase goods to sell at the market in Montego Bay. She would leave on the *Morning Star* on Thursday morning and would return Saturday night.

When Mammy was at the market, I would wonder whether she was able to have had a bath. One thing though, I would have more room on her big, giant wooden bed. I would have a little more room to sleep. This was, of course, if Aunt Grenda did not decide to sleep in Mammy's space.

One day, I actually visited Mammy at the market. The place was so crowded and noisy. They screamed and shouted at potential customers to buy their goods. They were competitive but at the same time, they were all friends and worked as a team. I remember as I was about to leave the market, Mammy asked me to stay for a moment so she could go to use the bathroom. I got nervous because if someone came to purchase something, I would not know what to do. I would hate for her to miss a sale because of my incompetence. A quite dignified-looking lady approached to ask the price per pound of the yam. To my surprise, and before I could muster some courage to speak, the lady next to me came over and told the lady the price. After the lady was told the price, she was about to walk away, but the market lady reduced the price. As a consequence, the customer bought a whole heap of my Mammy's yellow yam. She gave me the money which I handed to my Mammy upon her return.

I told her what had happened. She explained that was how they lived and worked as a team. I started to imagine how beautiful a world it would be if we could just live like these poor and dirty market women. I smiled at the thought of describing my Mammy as a dirty market woman, but I knew if she had read my mind, she would have understood what I meant.

At New Mills, things were sometimes very hard. When it did not rain for a few days, we would have to take containers and travelled two to three miles away to fetch water to drink, bathe, and wash clothes. There was a pond behind the house but when the water was getting too low, Pa said we should leave the water in the pond for the cows and goats. I was shocked to realize that goats drink water. I was even more shocked when I saw grandpa milk one of the goats and drank the milk without boiling it. Sometimes during the weekends, I would accompany Pa to the field at he back land. He would show me stones that shaped like tanks, filled with water from which he would quench his thirst. He would show me where he and my daddy, Johnny, would sit and talk when he was a child. I had just discovered that my dad also had a pet name, Johnny.

Pa and I were getting quite close. He and Mammy would argue all the time. He sometimes argued with Jasmine and Aunt Grenda too, but he never argued with me. I thought that he liked me. I thought that Otmaro Woodrow Service (Ottie) was too young for Pa to argue with him. As the months and years went by, I realized that my grandpa would argue with anyone. I remember him telling the gas station owner, Mr. George Harvey, in Bethel Town Square, that he was a thief and that he didn't have any love for poor, black people. That the fore-parents of Mr. G. Harvey came from England and captured Jamaica and exploited black, Indian, and Chinese peoples. Imagine that! My grandpa in his stained, dirty clothes and water boots, smelling like an overnight dead rat, telling Mr. G. Harvey, the most powerful man in Bethel Town that he was a thief – standing right next to him and in his face.

Apart from Mr. Lewis, Mr. G. Harvey seemed to have owned the whole little town. He lived in what to me, from a poor child's eye, seemed to be a palace. He also had a club which was called the Underground Club. I remember going there after graduating from high school some time later. The place was fantastic and only so-called decent people went there at the time. They usually wore their Sunday's best to attend that club.

I quietly adored the man for his guts. I immediately wished I had that kind of guts. I would have told Mr. Lovell not to treat my mother poorly and inquired of him where he was when he stayed out late at nights. If I suspected he was lying, I would have had the nerves and propensity to shout, "Don't lie!"

I would also have asked my dad all the questions that were hovering in my medium-sized brain at the time. I would ask Gee if even though she was married, whether she was having an affair with my dad or if not, if she found my dad handsome and attractive. I really thought that it took a real brave person or a fool to have had the audacity that Pa showed that day at Mr. G. Harvey's property. I knew for sure, that Pa was certainly no fool.

Some several years later, my old cousin, Uncle Brother (His real name was Levy Spencer) who lived a little further away on the Spencer family plot, came to our house and sat on the verandah. It was April 1. He said I told him that my Mammy wanted to see him. I told him that I had done no such thing. He insisted that I told him that my Mammy wanted to see him. I figured that my third cousins, his nephews, whose parents lived in England, might have stopped by his little shack and told him that Mammy wanted to see him. He mistakenly thought it was me.

As he continued to persist that I was the one who came to his house to advise that Mammy needed to see him, I remembered how the little Pa stood up to the powerful Mr. G. Harvey. I started to give Uncle Brother a piece of my mind. He hurriedly got off our bench and scampered away to his home. From that day, he was careful how he talked to me. How important it is for parents and guardians to be mindful of how they serve as role models to the children put to their charge.

I remember it was a bright and sunny Friday in August. My neighbour, Vadney (Joseph Campbell) and I went bird shooting. I remember this nice, little doctor bird came from nowhere to perch on my right shoulder. I was so happy. I took the doctor bird home to show Pa as Mammy was at the market. While I was there fooling around with my doctor bird, it just quickly flew away.

That very day, at about six in the evening, I was sitting under a big breadfruit tree when I saw someone coming up the hill. She looked like my Mammy. I looked for awhile and said, it couldn't be. First of all, it was a Friday and second of all, the old lady I saw coming up the hill had nothing in her hands. Mammy always picked up a few items like hot, baked bread that we used to eat with butter when she returned from the market. So, I continued to relax under the breadfruit tree until suddenly I heard a big roar like someone was crying. To my surprise, it was Mammy and she was really bawling. I ran towards her to ask her what was wrong. But she did not respond and kept crying and walking. She hugged me really closely and tightly that I thought I was going to be stifled. She kept saying statements such as,

"Ricky, you're going to be fine. Ricky, you're going to be okay. We'll take good care of you."

I got very concerned and I screamed, "Mammy, tell me what you're talking about!"

Aunt Grenda questioned whether Uncle George was fine.

Mammy responded by nodding her head. She then asked if Johnny was fine, to which she screamed even louder. I started to realize that something might have happened to my dad. I asked and shook Mammy gently, "Mammy, is dad hurt?"

She burst out in even more tears then said, "They murdered Johnny at his work and his body was found in the Pemco Hotel swimming pool, this morning, floating. It was the Pemco Hotel manager who alerted the police."

I was in dire shock. I did not cry, nor speak. I went to resume my sitting position under the big breadfruit tree. I stared in space. And wondered, why?

Even though my dad was found dead at the Pemco Hotel, East Street, Montego Bay on August 18, it took a few days before he was buried. Mammy and Aunt Grenda had sent off telegrams to my aunts in Canada, USA, and my Uncle George in Montego Bay as well as to Uncle Ben, the school principal at King's School, near White House in Westmoreland, Jamaica. Uncle Ben and Uncle George came almost instantly to

New Mills. My aunts and other relatives abroad came later. They rented cars and stayed in hotels. Everybody kept hugging each other and me. Some cried and there were all sorts of discussions. Pa said that he knew that there was some foul play. At the time, I did not yet understand the term foul play. I thought that it had something to do with getting killed while playing or going after a hen or two. I wondered if Pa thought that my dad had time to play with chickens. Where did Pa think my dad would keep all those chickens in his little one bedroom at 12½ Upper King Street, I thought? I was quite surprised when I found out later that the term simply meant murder.

There were several nights of 'wakes' where people who lived in the adjoining districts and even far away, would visit. There were, the singing of hymns, clapping, drinking of rum and beers, serving of coffee, tea, bread, and the playing of dominoes, cards, and so on. This happened every single night until the funeral. I wondered how Mammy was able to afford so much liquor and food. I questioned myself, where was all this money when I had to drink home grown tea because there was no money to buy Milo and Ovaltine, or the times Mammy had to walk the full mile and a half to Bethel Town School to bring me turned cornmeal for my lunch as there was no money for me to buy my usual archie and snow cone.

Everywhere I walked, there were some kind of conversations related to my father's death.

"I heard that Johnny was having an affair with a married, coolie woman and her husband hired a killer to do the trick," I overheard a lanky, rum-breath, ruggedly bearded man say to another, a shorter looking, almost midget-like figure.

"Did you know Johnny was a lodge man?" queried another.

The other person questioned what that had to do with anything. He said that lodge people were sometimes required to make great sacrifices, like how God had to sacrifice Jesus. That Johnny might have required to kill his only son but refused, and that was the reason they killed him.

I started to think if there could be some truth in the latter conversation. I remembered seeing strange books in my father's tiny bedroom. I remembered him behaving as if he was avoiding me and did not talk to me much. I started to think if he was endeavouring at the time, not to develop a relationship with me so his sacrificing of me like a sheep to the slaughter, a helpless lamb, would not be as painful for him. I also remembered how he avoided hugging me at Charles Square upon my arrival. That he placed me in the back of the cab while he sat at the front. I suddenly and briefly experienced an immediate state of bitterness, hatred, and sorrow within me. I felt like saying, "Served you right, you bastard!"

I quickly came back to my senses and said that what those men were gossiping was all foolishness! I had already understood why my dad was acting weirdly; he had no money and was ashamed that he was unable to take care of himself and me. At that thought, I felt like returning to the two men and tell them to shut up and mind their own business. I remembered that both my dad and my mother said that we should never tell anyone, especially adults, to shut up.

I continued roaming about when I ran into my Aunt Evelyn, next to the breadfruit tree in front of the yard. She lived in Boston. She asked whether I was okay. I nodded. I was about to continue along my lonely path and thoughts, but she literally hijacked me.

"Ricky, I know how you feel. It's okay to show some emotion," she said.

I shook my shoulders.

"You must be missing your dad very much. I miss him too and I am an old woman," she said.

I did not say anything. I stared at the breadfruit tree under which I was sitting when I heard and saw Mammy crying, and where I got the most devasting news of my life. I started to focus my attention at the top of the breadfruit tree. I saw a pair of breadfruits connected to the same branch, sharing the same stem. One appeared ripe, the other was the same size but appeared green, and not yet fit to be eaten. Yet the sister breadfruit was ripe. Interesting, I thought. I thought a little longer about that for awhile. I wondered how the same stem could give birth to two different fruits at the same time, one being ripe and now useless for consumption, and the other not. I dropped my eyes from the tree's gaze and moved more closely to my aunt who was still standing and talking to me, even though I was not listening. My eyes travelled up from her feet to her head. I noticed that she was somewhat bent and seemed very old. Much older than her brother, my dad. I thought back to the two paired breadfruits in the tree and thought that life was indeed very strange, or was it?

I quietly slipped away from my aunts and uncles, and all the commotions at the New Mills home. I ran down the slippery slope, to the New Mills main road. It had been raining all day earlier in the morning and afternoon. Up by the house earlier, I heard a very old-looking lady who had on a nicely fitted black frock and matching stockings with spike-heeled shoes, remark that Johnny was blessed and that was the reason for the rain. Again, the 'S-up' phrase came to my mind to offer the lady, but I resisted the temptation. Like before, I remembered what my dad and my mother had told me. That I should show respect to everyone, particularly to elders. I still searched my medium-sized head for the reason someone in heaven's sake could regard the possibility that one's funeral was about to be rained out, a blessing.

Sitting on the damped sidewalk, down by the New Mills main road, I was very surprised to see so many vehicles parked along the road. The last time I saw so many vehicles was during a political campaign with Michael Manley and I heard that all the vehicles were paid for by the PNP party, or some said the taxpayers and private sectors. I was not sure who to believe. I wondered who was paying for those vehicles. I wondered why the people wore black to the funeral but drove in white cars and mini vans.

I started to scrutinize the mini-buses and the cars. I noticed that most of them had on Montego Bay licence plates. I had not known that my dad had so many friends. When I was at 12½ Upper King Street in Montego Bay, I saw no friends.

"It takes death to know who your friends are," I murmured.

I made a quiet chuckle before I realized once again that it was my dad who died here.

I had only seen a couple of cars pass while I was there. New Mills was a quite quiet and remote area at the time, with very far and in-between traffic in the area. I remembered that usually in these Jamaican, evening funerals, the hearse would arrive first, and the procession of vehicles and mourners would follow next. However, Montegonians seemed to have done things differently. I was hoping to see the hearse down by the road, but it was not there.

I got to my feet, off my damped rear and wiped off the bottom of my trouser. I made a step towards the track to return home when I thought I heard a calm roar. I stopped to rest my head and one of my ears to the surface of the road, to listen, and waited patiently. It was daddy – I meant the hearse. A vehicle was coming for sure. In a few seconds, a black, almost scary-looking vehicle appeared. Suddenly, the inescapable struck, that my father had actually passed away. The vehicle slowed and I wondered if it was my dad who was pulling it back, wanting to say hello to me. It attempted to go up the track, but its wheels started to skid on the muddy pathway.

One guy said something that children should not repeat and then they parked the hearse. They opened it to reveal the loveliest coffin I had ever seen. I wondered who paid for it. I said it must have been Uncle Ben as Uncle George seemed poor like a church mouse. I had heard the saying from my Mammy. After all, my dad and Uncle Ben were also quite close and they both hated going to the field with Pa. I also understood that Uncle Ben had houses all over Jamaica, rented out. They both thought they were intellectuals. I changed the thought. I started to think along the line that it was possible that everyone might have pooled together like what my friends and I used to do at school to buy archie and red herring. I wondered whether the intellectual, Uncle Ben, had outsmarted his siblings and gave little or nothing toward the casket.

I walked quietly and pensively behind the six guys or so, who were taking the casket up the hill. The fouled mouthed one uttered the swear word once again, after having twisted his ankle in the mud a second time. This time, between concealed rocks or stones. I imagined how that made my dad feel. My dad hated people with dirty, fouled mouths. I imagined him saying that the guy should go watch his mouth with Dettol. I watched to see if the coffin would have gotten heavier because of my father's anger and disgust. However, they seemed to have been moving well. He might have been cold and weakened by the freezer on which he was kept for so many days, or he might have been anxious to get up to the house, I thought. I slowed to take a rest and to face and ponder on the reality that my dad had actually and really passed.

I was just on time to see them passing a little boy, around five years old, over the coffin. As they passed him across the casket, the congregation roared in the words of this very sad song:

When the roll is called up yonder

Oh, when the roll is called up yonder

When the roll is called up yonder

When the roll is called up yonder, I'll be there....

Aunt Evelyn turned around and grabbed me.

"Ricky, where were you? We nearly lowered the coffin without you crossing it," she scolded me.

Without waiting for my response, she tossed me like a marble to the two men with the physique of wrestlers who wheeled me across the coffin like they did the little boy before, to the singing of a new song:

> Across the bridge
>
> There's no sorrow
>
> Across the bridge
>
> There's no pain
>
> Hey no, no pain
>
> The sun will shine
>
> Across the river
>
> And you'll never
>
> Be unhappy again.

My Aunt Evelyn then took me under her arm. A sudden flow of emotions enveloped my being, and for the first time since I was told that my father had died, I allowed the tears to flow, freely.

Through the blur of tears, I saw two images approach us. I pulled out my shirt from my trouser and used its ends to wipe away the tears from my eyes. The images turned out to be an

Indian-looking lady and the little boy who was passed across my father's coffin earlier.

"Ricky, meet your brother, Johnny," she exclaimed.

I stared at her and the boy, questioningly.

"Your father and I had little Johnny about five years ago. Please you two must not be strangers now," she said, as she walked away.

I assumed that she must have given my Mammy her address, so I did not call after her. I watched them walk gingerly down the hill towards the New Mills main road. That was the first and last time that I would ever see these two individuals.

From time to time, I think about my little brother but unfortunately, I had never seen him again. I thought the Indian lady behaved strangely. My thoughts went back to the remark of the two gossipers sometime ago, but I quickly let the thought die, just like my dad.

———————

The funeral had passed, and everything was getting back to normal as it was possible to be. My Uncle Ben had approached me to inquire if I would have liked to live with them. I was ecstatic! Finally, I was going to have the good life. My uncle's wife, Aunt Avona (not her real name, was the vice principal at the school. They had two children, Tony and Marcia (not their real names who were younger than me. My uncle also had a nice car. I could not believe I was so lucky. I had heard either my mother, dad, or my Mammy, or all three say, that everything happened for a purpose. I started to believe that was true. Here was this little 'dead-left' boy who was now going to get everything he desired in one shot. Not only would I get to go to school five days a week with my uncle as principal, I would also live at the school, a place I loved so much. In Jamaica, during those days, the principals were provided a house (cottage on the campus of the school of which they were in charge. My uncle had a car and money and ran a school. I was so excited.

The journey to the King's All-Age School, near to White House in Westmoreland, seemed further than the fifteen miles Uncle Ben told me that it was from New Mills. The car ran smoothly and hugged the curves nicely as we travelled along, sometimes climbing slopes, other times descending them or simply rolling along horizontal planes. Uncle Ben told me the names of the different districts as we entered them. He was such a nice man. I felt like I had found a new dad. Only that this one was more conversant and understanding.

We approached a town that seemed quite lively. I was about to ask Uncle Ben if it was White House, when the *You are entering White House* sign appeared. There was a nice, fresh breeze that permeated the interior of the car, which emanated from the surrounding sea. The houses seemed nice like middle class or upper middle-class people lived there. Uncle Ben slowed almost to a stop when we arrived in the square, long enough for me to see a man with a humongous fish in his hand. There were also people selling food on the sidewalks and near, and in, shops. Again, I was quite excited. I asked my uncle how far we were from King's School, my new home, to which he said we had about two minutes to reach home. We took a left turn off the main road. The secondary road was just as great as the major road. It was well paved. It was part of the constituency of Mr. P.J. Patterson who was a top-ranking member of the P.N.P. (People's National Party) and he later was to become Prime Minister of Jamaica.

I saw the school on the hill and a lovely church at its base. Uncle Ben said it was the Anglican Church and that he preached there every third Sunday. I started to think why every third Sunday. What was so special or awful about third Sundays that he had to preach on those days, and not the priest? I wondered if he had ever asked the priest, "Why not preach on random Sundays, even on first Sundays or even second Sundays?"

I started to question myself, "What was meant by third Sunday, anyway?"

I quietly murmured in my medium-sized head that I would ask my new dad all these questions and more, some time in the future, maybe even starting tomorrow.

That September, I started school as a grade nine King's All-Age student. this was my second year being in grade nine. I had just completed grade nine at Bethel Town All-Age School when my dad passed away. Had I not gone to my uncle's school, I would have been in grade nine at the Bethel Town All-Age School, just the same. I had skipped a couple of grades along the All-Age School System. Now I was stuck in grade nine with nowhere else to go. The highest grade in the All-Age School System was grade nine. From there, one would graduate into the realm of work or would go to learn a trade. There was also the Junior Secondary School System, but they too, at the time, terminated their studies in grade nine. It was some time later that they added two grades to the Junior Secondary System; grades ten and eleven, at which time it was referred to as the New Secondary School System. In those grades, children would just learn such things as plumbing, welding, auto mechanic, Home Economics, and so on. There were also the traditional high schools whose main focus was to train students for preparation to attend university and other tertiary institutions to become professionals, such as doctors and lawyers. To attend these schools, one had to pass the Common Entrance Examination (C.E.E.) or the Grade Nine Achievement Test (G.N.A.T.). During most of my time in the All-Age School System, I had no idea about the Common Entrance Examination (C.E.E.) or the Grade Nine Achievement Test (G.N.A.T.) which I was to take later. In chapter four, I will provide more detail as to how I became cognizant of these exams and how I eventually took one of the exams to attend a traditional high school. I must also point out, that as far as I can recall, those days a student could attend an All-Age school up to, and until, she or he was sixteen years old. That meant, I still had some time on my hand in that system before I would have been kicked to the curb, hopefully to a vacant job opportunity or by a trade school to learn a trade.

In essence then, there were two separate secondary educational systems. I guess one could say, there was a two-tier system. The

98

traditional high schools that took in students from the more affluent middle and upper classes, and the All-Age and Junior Secondary School System that catered significantly to students of my ilk. Students who originated from, and lived in, dire poverty. The quality of the curricula in the two systems was as distinct as night is to day. The All-Age/Junior Secondary System basically acting as a holding area until these students reached sixteen to take up their places in/as factories, small subsistent farms, domestic hands, and the likes. The traditional Secondary Educational System, on the other hand, moulded the young minds to become local leaders and thinkers. The facilities, teaching aids, and the quality teachers were mostly the enclave of the latter cohort.

This was my third week at King's All-Age School. The teacher had assigned Psalm 24 to us to study. We were basically to memorize the biblical chapter, so that we would have been able to recite it in class. It was now my turn to recite it when Uncle Ben – (Mr. Spencer, I called him at school) walked in the class. I rose nervously and I began:

The Earth is the Lord's

And the fullness thereof

The world and they

That dwell therein

For he hath founded it upon the seas

And established it upon the floods

Who shall ascend in the hills of the Lord?

Or who shall stand in his holy place?

He that hath a clean hand and a pure heart

And hath not lifted up his soul unto vanity

Nor sworn deceitfully

He shall receive the blessings of the Lord and righteousness from the God of his salvation.

Who is the King of Glory?

The Lord Strong and mighty

The Lord mighty in battle

Lift up your heads, all ye gates

And be ye lifted up ye everlasting gates

And the King of Glory shall come in

Who is the King of Glory?

The Lord of host, he is the King of Glory.

(NB: I wrote this chapter from memory and might have omitted parts of it. Psalm 24)

The teacher congratulated me for a job well done, and then turned to the student next to me.

"John, your turn," the teacher screamed.

"John, your turn," Mr. Spencer echoed, only more sternly and with an air of authority.

John, obviously shaking, stood and began, "The Earth is the Lord. Aaaaaam, and... the earth is the Lord and the fulness they have."

John was muttering or attempting to, under his breath, trembling like a leaf being blown in high wind.

Mr. Spencer moved towards us, to John, like an army Major, with his cane high in hand. He ordered me to step aside. If one did not know we were related, even lived in the same house, one could never tell in his interaction with me at that moment. After his order to me to step aside, he climbed onto the desk. I wondered what would have been his reaction if one of us, students should have stood on the desk. I said to myself, "Donkey said the world wasn't level." I tried to remember where I learnt that thought. Oh, I said, it was from my Mammy.

She had also said, "What was good for the geese, was good for the gander."

By now, Mr. Spencer had settled himself well on the desk.

To Mr. Spencer's command, John held out his right hand, and right up in the air. I said to myself, that must be quite tiring for John – to hold his hand up and out. As he did so, it reminded me of the third Sunday just passed at the Anglican Church, when Uncle Ben was handing out communion to the church people. I wondered which he enjoyed more – handing out communion or handing out licks? If I were to guess, I quietly thought, I would settle on the latter for his pick.

Mr. Spencer continued to inflict discipline in the palms of John's hands, but he was not crying. As if Uncle Ben felt a little bit dissatisfied, somewhat as a failure for not having elicited a 'deggy' inch of tears, he suddenly started to inflict the force of the cane anywhere and everywhere that it could find a surface area for landing. And note, that included John's stomach. For every stroke missed, Uncle Ben seemed to have added an extra one. John screamed and 'whaled' in agony. A sudden flash of accomplishment and joy washed over Mr. Spencer's formerly, sterned face as our teacher nodded approvingly. As the howling sounds permeated the entire school's walls, the lunch bell joined in unison, summoning that it was time for the atrocious ordeal to end. Mr. Spencer looked at his watch and ordered John to sit and wait for instructions from the teacher to leave the class. I wondered if John would be able to have lunch, or even used his arms or even sit on his butt for long, but I had to go quickly – to prepare and organize lunch for my Uncle Ben, Aunt Avona, and my cousins.

One evening at supper time, I overheard Uncle Ben and his wife, with the children. They remarked how the students were useless and lazy. As they spoke, the male child pinched the female in her face.

"If you two don't behave, I'll have you sit at the corner dining table with Ricky," Uncle Ben screamed.

I quietly hoped that the two would have continued their pranks. Heaven knew I would have done well with their company, irrespective of any brawls that might have emanated among us.

The house (school cottage) was huge, at least in my eyes. There were six bedrooms, a front and back verandah, two bathrooms, a living and dining room, a kitchen, and a little library of sort in the house. The back verandah was where I would be routinely washing dishes. The materials for cleaning the floors were neatly stuck under the house in a little butchery-like cellar. I was quickly shown where to locate all items during my first full and complete day at my new home, including the wash pan that I would use to have a bath. I quietly wondered why apart from cleaning the bathrooms, they were out of bounds for me. I, however, was not as brave as Pa. I kept my mouth shut. The domestic helper was now requested only to report to work on 'wash day' as Uncle Ben had to save money to take care of me, the dead-left boy. Even though the house had a generator owned by and supplied by the Jamaica Ministry of Education, the dishwasher would no longer be used as a means to save money and energy. I truly believed if Uncle Ben was being honest, he would have added to the foregoing reason as well, "So that I could enslave the dead-left boy."

Each Friday after school, we would go to the Black River market in St. Elizabeth, to replenish the home of its supplies in food and delicacies. I liked driving in a car and watching the trees and animals along the way. It sometimes reminded me of the earlier days with daddy, being driven in his car.

One Friday, on the trip to the Black River Market, Uncle Ben nearly hit a cow as he drove. Man, it seemed that in this area of St. Elizabeth the cows fed on the asphalt or stones that lined the narrow streets because there were always scores of them to be found walking around those roads. In a way, as I recalled it, I always saw more cows and donkeys going for a walk on the streets than did people.

One day, I said to Uncle Ben as he drove, that there must have been a club or something like that, that cows, donkeys, goats, and pigs went to relax around those areas after a long week on a Friday. Uncle Ben and his wife certainly did not find me funny at all. They thought I was stupid to say things like that. I also thought it was their belief that children should not be seen or heard, especially lower-class children whose roles were simply to serve as the contemporary slaves.

I promised myself never to be funny or being a comic in their presence ever again! As a matter of fact, I would always keep my mouth closed and spoke only if a question was asked of me.

At the Black River Market, the routine would always be the same. I guess, that's why it is so called. I would either go to fetch the big, old, out-of-shape basket from the trunk of the car or Aunt Avona would fetch it on my behalf, throw it my way. If, by chance, I did not catch it, I would have been told how clumsy I was or worse, how stupid.

My two little, first cousins would always be crying for one thing or the other as I would move steadily behind, the basket getting progressively heavier and heavier with every passing moment, as the volumes of the produce in it increased.

One day Aunt Avona and I were home alone with my younger cousins. The strangest, most uncomfortable conversations started between us.

"Ricky, how comes you're so brown?"

"I don't know. Perhaps, because my mother is brown and her mother was Indian," I babbled.

"But the Spencer's blood is strong. You don't seem to have anything for the Spencer's," she quipped.

"What do you mean?" I asked.

"You know what I mean. You read, you know – Not too slow," she remarked.

"Well, isn't Uncle Ben a Spencer? He reads, no?" I tried to control my anger.

I thought right then and there that I should have had Pa's temperament and bravery. I would just put the forward woman into her place. Let her know that she was classist, that she was rude and impertinent! But I had to be humble and respectful – for more reasons than one. I began to think that probably after all, I wasn't a Spencer. How else would I be putting up with this woman's freshness?

"Your Uncle Ben is different! He grew up with his grandmother and an aunt, Aunt Maud who were elementary school teachers," she persisted.

"Well, my dad was educated too," I protested. "He passed his Senior Cambridge just like Uncle Ben, at the first sitting, something that was unheard of those days," I reminded her.

"But your dad was also partially grown with his grandma and Aunt Maud," she corrected.

I was happy when the children were back at their screaming match. She had to go to see what was going down with them.

I really did not know that my dad had spent time with my great grandmother who I actually met. She died at age one hundred, eight years old. I wondered why Pa or Mammy, or my dad did not tell me that story or whether they had told me, and I forgot.

The school year had gone well and was coming to its close. The teachers, the school's cleaning lady, and the canteen cook, were preparing an end of the school year get-together for themselves. Uncle Ben and Aunt Avona had collected money from them and bought liquor, soft drinks, and so on, which were left over by our home. The night of the function, I could hear the music and merriment by the school. I thought if only I could go to join. I knew that was mere wishful thinking.

At about 11:00 P.M., a teacher I knew very well by the name of Ms. Quest, came over the house. She advised that they were running out of drinks and that I should give her a case of the soft drinks to take over there. I told her that I did not want to touch Uncle Ben's stuff. However, she assured me that everything was all right and that Uncle Ben knew she was coming to get the soft drinks.

Some days after the party, and in July, Uncle Ben said that a missing crate of soft drinks could not have been accounted for. I asked him whether he had checked the one I had given to Ms. Quest that night. In a flash of a second, both Uncle Ben and Aunt Avona got extremely irate. They accused me of behaving as if I was running their home. I told them that Ms. Quest advised that Uncle Ben was aware that she took the drinks. They got even angrier.

The next day, I did my chores, and everything seemed fine until about 5:00 P.M. Aunt Avona said she was watching to see if my uncle would let me get away with what I did. Uncle Ben immediately ran into his bedroom and got the cane. The same one that was tested on John, not too long ago. He reached for me and caught my shirt. I slipped out of the shirt, ran into my bedroom and through one of its windows. There were shirts on the outside clothe line, so I grabbed a shirt from it. I was barefooted and had no money. I decided I was not returning into that house to be caned, even if it meant I was going to die that night. I knew too well the damage of which that cane was capable. I ran down the school's road and climbed over the school's gate, to freedom.

CHAPTER FOUR

The Onset of Change in a Runaway Boy

There were a few boys, girls, and elderly people standing outside of the King's School onto to the road. One boy seemed to have been playing marbles with a girl. I thought that was cool. I had not played marbles with girls ever. I was soft-hearted. I thought I was a better player than most girls, even though I was terrible as a player with my male friends. I did not want to crush them and then had to apologize every single game when they lost. I suddenly remembered that my daddy, my Mammy, and my Mama had all told me that we should not judge a book by its cover. That everyone was equal, boys and girls. I also remembered that my Mammy in particular, believed that God made us all. That he was an excellent God and that he would not have made some people inferior or even superior to each other. She said that God gave each boy, each girl, each woman, each man a talent. Something that he or she was truly great at doing but sometimes due to circumstances mostly beyond their control, these people never discovered that they really had possessed these talents, these powers. I wondered why God would give you something and not sit around to ensure that you made use of it. I said if I reached New Mills safely, the next time I played marbles, my first partner would be a girl.

I moved swiftly, trying not to be noticed. I did not want to draw attention to myself. I did not want to have to answer any questions as to why I dressed so shabbily, barefooted and all. I wanted to avoid questions as to why I was on the street without Uncle Ben, the King's All-Age School principal. A few people had even rumored that I was the son of the principal with another woman.

At the intersection of the King School road and the White House road, I made a right, just like Uncle Ben had done with us in the car numerous times. I then continued straight. The streetlights were shining in all their glory by then as the evening's sun had started to set. I was concerned that it was going to be extremely difficult to pass through the White House Square undetected. A sudden sadness and fear wrapped, blanketed, and unnerved me instantly. I wondered what was the chance of me turning back, and Uncle Ben either forgave me, had pity on me, or said, after all, I was his best brother's kid, that I was a poor dead-left and was still a child. Everyone was entitled to one chance, I imagined him thinking. I looked back and then remembered how angry he got while he caned John. Every time the cane's strike did not make contact with some body part of John, Uncle Ben seemed to have gotten even angrier and seemed to have doubled the number of canings for every one that he missed.

The thought encouraged me to take the risk and to walk somewhat bravely towards, and into the White House Square. There was a stream of parked cars on either side of the road. There were loud music and chatter. A young man with an older-looking woman seemed to have been in embrace. I wondered whether they were parent and son or lovers. I walked closely to the cars and stepped with confidence through the Square. I had the urge both to run and look back but I resisted the impetus. As I said earlier, I wanted to do as little as possible to have avoided bringing attention to myself.

The sun was really disappearing from out of sight. It had suddenly started to set completely. I remembered my friend and his obsession with sunset. To be fair, he did not have an obsession with sunset, his parents did. He was only following orders. I wondered about him for awhile, and Mama, Mr. Lovell, and my sister, Georgia and the other siblings who had been born while I lived in New Mills. I was thinking whether Mama had heard that my dad had passed. It suddenly dawned on me that I did not write her. I felt ashamed. I comforted myself by saying that I was too busy with housework at Uncle Ben's home to have to have engaged in writing. I thought probably Mammy, Pa, Aunt Grenda, or Uncle Ben should have ensured that my mother was informed of my father's murder. I said, to myself, that was exactly the problem in the world and our country. Everyone was thinking that the other person would do it, would have informed my mother. I wondered what else in life or our country was not getting done because each sat patiently hoping that someone else would do it.

I often heard the P.N.P. and the J.L.P. (Jamaica Labour Party) supporters, even the ministers and members of parliament in power, blaming each other that the P.N.P. or the J.L.P. when in power, did not do this or that thing or the other. I now understood why it happened.

The road grew darker and darker and the number of vehicles passing, had been reduced to a trickle like the water in the pipes we had to travel more than a mile to, from New Mills during drought. I was not sure whether I should have been happy or sad about that situation with the vehicles. When the cars passed, I felt somewhat afraid that someone might have been in the car and recognized me. If that was the case, I was afraid they would stop to ask me a whole courthouse of questions. I also worried that there could have been the take-away men in the cars. As a young boy at New Mills, the boys told me about the take-away men. That they would stop their cars and would ask for directions or give you candies (sweeties), then they would grab you and take you away in their cars. Then I thought, why would the takeaway men take you away? What would they do with us? Is it that they were lonely and wanted a big family? Would they cook us and eat us like Pa would munch his roasted pigs? If not any of the above, why then? Were they so rich that they had to have some extra mouths to feed? On the other hand, despite all those questions, I felt like I had company when the cars were constantly passing me on the now lonely thoroughfare.

My thoughts suddenly subsided when I realized that it was really getting late and dark. I imagined that it was about 7:30 to 8:00 P.M., or later. The sun sometimes set so early and a whole flood of darkness would appear upon the land like thieves about to rob a bank. I started to think about ghosts and my dad. I wondered whether he was tiptoeing behind me all along. I wondered whether he had seen what his favourite brother had attempted to do, or what he had been doing to me since they took me into their home last summer.

I suddenly recalled that a few days after moving into the Kings School cottage, that while I was washing dishes on the back verandah late one Saturday night, I saw what appeared to have been two legs walking up the steps, wearing a similar pair of grey pants and an upper body, no head, wearing a white shirt similar to the one daddy wore to meet me at Charles Square in Montego Bay.

I had run inside to tell my Uncle Ben. He retorted that I was talking foolishness and that my Mammy had taught me foolishness about ghosts. Later that same night, I recalled hearing something rubbing against my bedroom's walls and saw a bright light being shone through my window. I ran out to tell Uncle Ben. Again, he thought it was stupid to have been thinking of ghosts. However, about five minutes later, he came back to my room and was asking me a whole bunch of questions. I figured that whatever had come rubbing on the walls of my bedroom and lighting up my room must have done the same thing with his, on the other side of the house.

The thoughts got me scared. It was now pitched dark. I arrived at the Ferris Square. The streets formed a fork. One could either keep left and end up in the capital town of Savanna-La-

Mar or keep right and go towards Whithorn to Darliston to New Mills. I stopped and tried to figure out which should be the route to travel. The direct route through Whithorn to Darliston to New Mills would have been shorter. Uncle Ben had travelled both routes in the past, depending on his mood. The Savanna-La-Mar route was longer but there were brighter lights, better roads, and there would have been people. Furthermore, the direct Whithorn to Darliston to New Mills route was quite hilly, bushy, and tiring. The thought of making a decision overwhelmed me.

Suddenly, I saw two persons who appeared to be workers at the Ferris Gas Station. I walked over to them. I did not want to have to explain that my father was recently murdered, so I told them that my dad wanted to beat me for no reasons. As a result, I was on my way to my grandma's place in New Mills. I told them that I was getting scared and afraid as it was getting so late and dark. To my surprise, the guys said I could stay there overnight. I was very happy. They spread clothes on the floor inside the building at the back and we all slept there until early dawn.

The next morning, I resumed my journey. I settled on travelling the direct route to Whithorn to Darliston to New Mills. When I thought about it now that I was rested, it dawned on me that either route would have ended with me going to Whithorn to Darliston to New Mills unless, I was going to walk to Chester Castle, walked up Galloway, through Bethel Town, passed the entrance to the district of Castle Mountain to New Mills. I walked and ran as much as I could. As I began to climb the steep hill to ascend into my Mammy's home and bosom, I heard the roar of a motor vehicle coming up the rugged hill. I started to run even more. I was growing breathless, but I had to keep running. I ran pass the breadfruit tree of which I sat when I heard of my father's murder, and quickly headed for under the house.

My Mammy had spotted me and had also heard the engine of Uncle Ben's car. I placed my index finger on my lip, indicating to my Mammy that she should not say anything. I knew I could count on my Mammy.

I went to the far corner under the bottom of the house. There was a black hen that was sitting on what seemed to be more than a dozen eggs. She got a little annoyed upon my uninvited arrival. I quickly slid to the other side, a little distance from the hen, just in time for the hen to keep quiet and my Uncle Ben to make giant steps into our yard calling, "Mammy!"

"Ben, what happened? What happened? Why are you here so early, Ben?" Mammy queried.

I knew my Mammy had some genuine concerns. She had seen me go under the house, but she did not know why I had to go under the house. Could I have been involved in a fight? Could her precious Ricky have stolen something from someone at King's School or White House, bringing shame to Uncle Ben and his family? Worse, could I have unconventionally struck a boy and he died? So, it was not that she was pretending to have been worried or concerned. She was indeed genuinely worried and concerned after seeing me. She must have been dying in her heart that she did not get the opportunity to find out what had really happened before my uncle arrived at our home.

Mammy's black cat joined the hen, the eggs and I under the house. At first, she seemed a little startled to see me by her usual resting place but unlike the black hen, she did not protest. I placed my index finger at my lips, the same signal I gave my Mammy and the cat seemed to have understood perfectly well. It came over and rubbed against me slightly. I felt so great for a brief while. Since I left New Mills, I didn't have much or any physical or emotional expression of love from any family member or anyone. No cats, no dogs. Not even the rats I heard in the ceiling of the King's School cottage had any respect, much more to show me love. Certainly, no slight rubbing against my body or embrace from anyone. The cat made me feel that I was still appreciated. That I still had family.

"That idiot you have as grandson, ran away last night," he uttered.

"What do you mean idiot? How could you be calling your own flesh and blood idiot? What has come over you?" grandma asked.

Uncle Ben did not respond, neither to the comments nor the questions.

"Ever since you married that woman, I noticed the big change in you! It is as if she has you in a trance," she continued.

"Mammy, I am sorry, but the stupid boy will get me in trouble. He walked out of the house and nobody knows where he is," my Uncle Ben said.

Mammy cleared her throat. I thought she was about to say something, but she didn't.

"I can't stay much longer," he continued, "Who knows if something has not already happened to him since he left?"

"When did he leave?" my grandma asked.

I got concerned that Mammy would let Uncle Ben know that I was under the house in hiding. I said to myself, let's face it, Uncle Ben is her son. I am only her grandson. According to all those questions Aunt Avona was asking me the other day, there was a big chance that we were not even related. She was not going to let her son go through so much agony and concerns while she knew I was under the house with her cat and hen, I thought. I waited nervously for Mammy to disclose my little, but safe haven.

"Ben, have you been treating that boy well?" she questioned.

Again, Uncle Ben did not respond.

"I have been dreaming of Johnny ever since you took his son over to your place. Believe me, he seems angry all the time. Something is not right, Ben."

Uncle Ben mumbled inaudibly.

"Listen me, Ben, are you treating your own blood and flesh right? Ricky is your nephew, your own flesh and blood," she remarked.

I heard steps receding from the house. I heard some murmuring in the distance. I assumed it was Uncle Ben leaving for the Bethel Town Police Station to report my being missing. I wondered what the reason he was going to tell them for me leaving the comfort of his posh government school cottage for the street, or wherever he thought I was. I thought that the cops might have become suspicious of him if I was not found. That I might have been considered dead like dad. I thought, they would have now had two unsolved cases of two closely related persons on their hands whose cases were still unsolved. The last after a full year had elapsed. They might have even considered my Uncle Ben a suspect in my going missing.

I wondered how that would have affected him being a principal and a third Sunday priest. He might have also been considered a suspect for his brother's death in that case as well. The thought made me feel sad. I was proud that I had an uncle who was a principal, even though I was ashamed of the way he treated me.

It suddenly dawned on me that my expressed concerns re my uncle might have been unnecessary. Daddy had told me that one could get out of trouble by bribing some cops, not all. For a moment, I had a sigh of relief to know that after all, my uncle being a principal, would probably not have lost his job if I were to remain quiet in hiding. Upon further analysis, it made me feel rotten. How many of our police officers were involved in bribery? I questioned. Could those cops not involved in bribery arrest their colleagues and throw them into jail for giving the Jamaica police force a bad name?

Mammy came to the side of the house where the black hen still sat. The black hen was quite a protective fowl. As long as I was under the house, the black hen would never go for a break from her eggs. If only some parents and families were as protective, loving, and caring as the black hen, I thought. What if they could just show a little tender care to someone like me without a father, even an active mother? Would there not be less pain in the world? Those were my thoughts.

Mammy finally got on her bony knees and peeped under the house. She laughed in the fact that she did not realize that I had moved away from the side I entered. All along, she thought I was lying under the house quite close to her, listening. I was listening alright, but I was not as close as she thought. She wondered why I moved away from what she thought was a safe hiding spot. I explained that the hen would not allow me to sit on that side of the house, however, the cat was quite understanding and accommodating.

Mammy said that the black hen, Peck, was like that when she was preparing to hatch her chickens. She said that she knew something was up with her because when she was feeding the other hens, she scarcely ever came to feed and normally, Peck loved corn very much. When she planted corn around the house, Peck would scratch out all five grains from each hole and leave only the three peas. But when she was preparing to hatch her chickens, she was a different hen.

I thought Mammy would have said she was a different person because that was exactly how Peck behaved, like she was a person, a very responsible and great person, not a hen.

I told my Mammy what had taken place at King's All-Age School, the school of which Uncle Ben was principal. I told her that I did not want to return and that she, or Aunt Grenda could go to fetch my clothes.

The next day, my Mammy and I walked to the Bethel Town Police Station to let them know that I was safe. They wanted to know why I left, but my Mammy interrupted by saying that I had just about year ago lost my dad tragically. I held onto my Mammy's hand, while she made her tiny steps towards the long journey in the direction of New Mills.

Before we had gone to the Bethel Town Police Station, Mammy had taken me to Mr. Don Evan's home. Mr. Evans was this old and wise man in the district. He knew every subject and could have a very intelligent discussion with anyone. I was told that he had a brother or some relative who was a big-time politician. The most interesting thing I discovered about Mass Don (that was his pet name) was that he did not use cooking oil. He used only margarine. I noticed that his margarine gave the food flavour and it tasted nicer. Even today when I started writing the above line, I could not resist the urge to have some dumpling, corned beef, and margarine, just as Mass Don used to do.

Mammy had brought me to meet Mass Don because recently he had some relatives who had come from the parish of Hanover to stay with him. I recall that their surname was Nugent, but I can't recall any of the children's first names. Two of the boys were about my age and size. Mammy wanted to find out if Mass Don could have them lend me some clothes until they were able to go to pick up mine at Uncle Ben's or until when Uncle Ben had returned them to New Mills. That is, of course, after we disclosed that I was at my Mammy's home. Mass Don was glad to oblige. He called the boys and outlined the situation. The boys basically shared their clothes with me. Some were somewhat big, patchy even, but I was glad for them. I got all types of clothes and they were foreign clothes. The boys had relatives in Canada, I was told.

Sometimes while I was outside playing with them, I would recall the joke of a man and his friend. The man had lent his poor friend party clothes so they could all go to have a good time. However, one night while these two friends were at the party, the one who lent his friend the pants was having a ball and the other was not. The lender danced with all the girls and the girls were all over him. He might have had a little too much to drink. He looked across the room and saw his friend sitting lonely, all by himself. He saw that his friend was not dancing, looked sad and detached. He suddenly shouted, unfortunately just about the time the music had stopped, "Leonard, dance and prance man, dance and prance; it doesn't matter if my pants I lend you get soiled or torn. Leonard as you know, I have many more where that one came from."

Every time I was wearing the boys' clothes and I saw them I would suddenly get into my shell. I remembered the story and I wondered if they were going to shout, especially when they were among other friends, that I shouldn't worry about staining their clothes because there was much more from which the clothes I wore came. I wished I could have truly said the same with respect to my clothes and its then source, albeit the King's All-Age School where my Uncle Ben was principal and his wife, the vice-principal.

I was re-admitted at the Bethel Town All-Age school. This was my third year in grade nine as well as my third attendance to this school. As I said earlier, I got stuck in the system. In those days children like me from the dearth and girth of poverty had little or no choice but to stay in the All-Age School System and the Junior Secondary System, holding areas for us, until we reached the good ripe age to be some handyman, mason, plumber, factory worker or domestic helper for middle class and upper class folks, among other undesirable work, at least so I thought. In a way, I thought Uncle Ben was a smart man; that he wanted me to be acclimatised to the rough life at the King's School Principal Cottage in an apprenticeship role, so that I would have been better able to master what, inevitably, would be my lot in life. At least that was what my mindset was until Mrs. Spence, my now grade nine teacher requested a private meeting with me at lunchtime or after school. I thought about my friends leaving me after school and settled for the lunchtime meeting with my teacher, not the after school.

All morning I could not focus on my schoolwork. I was concerned that I was in trouble or something. Otherwise, why would Mrs. Spence want to talk with me? I thought. As far as I knew, I was a good student in my schoolwork, so the meeting couldn't have anything to do with my performance in school. It was also unheard of for those teachers to discuss students' performance with them outside of the teaching hours. I found Mathematics, English, Spelling, Composition, Dictation, Social Studies, Civics, General Science, Health Science and Biology, quite easy and interesting. As a matter of fact, I had passed some of these subjects, including English at the Jamaica School Certificate (J.S.C. level even prior to leaving for King's All-Age School.

As Mrs. Spence taught and gave us work, I wondered about everything I had done in the recent past and whether any of them could have landed me in some kind of trouble with my teacher. I tried to read Mrs. Spence's every move, her body language. Did she seem angry? Did she avoid looking at me? When she looked my way, did she appear angry or not? I recalled me laughing at this boy because he had a runny nose while he ate his snow-cone and 'archie'. I remembered that at the school tank where we drank water by throwing a Berger paint tin hung from a rope, that I had cut in line a couple of times. I wondered whether the persons I had gotten in front of were so offended that they went to tell tales to Mrs. Spence or worse, Mrs. Spence might have seen me herself. There was also this girl, Rose Wallace, who I loved very much, and I always bothered her. She could also have been the culprit why I would have to meet with Mrs. Spence. It could also have been that she heard about us stopping at Mr. Blake's orange orchard after school, on our way home. Come to think of it, I thought, Mrs. Spence also lived in New Mills and could have seen me catching those oranges, standing on the bank while my friends picked and threw them to me. It could have also been because I teased the grade six boy whose big toe seemed so far from the nearest toe to it. There was a wide gap between the two toes. So one day, out of the blue, while I was doing my usual staring at the two toes and the huge gap in between them, the idea of calling him 'Catapult Foot' jumped into my medium-sized head and flew from my lips.

I could no longer take the 'guess and spell' situation I found myself in with respect to the impending meeting between my teacher and myself. I wondered what was taking the lunch bell so long to be rung. I peeped across the opposite side of my class and noticed that the principal was sitting there, head down. I wondered whether everyone had forgotten to ring the bell. It was not too long when I saw a boy come forward with the big bell and clumsily started to ring it, bingy ling giling, giling.

Mrs. Spence, like all the other teachers, instructed the class to leave orderly for lunch. She enquired whether I wanted to go and get a bite first. The way she said that caused me to laugh. Now that I think about it, it was really a bite, An 'Archie' a type of fried dumpling, and a snow-cone. I responded in the negative.

I was beckoned to her desk. I walked steadily, trying to be brave and not to show my nervousness. She pointed to the chair. I sat.

"Joshua, did you ever write the Common Entrance Examination?" she questioned.
I searched my medium-sized head before I responded. I did not want to say 'yes' and it was something that would make me look bad or said 'no' and that would make me look as if I had no ambition or that I had no idea about that which she asked me.

"Remember I passed four subjects including English," I said, referring to my passes in the Jamaica School Certificate Examinations.

"I know, I gave you the free lessons," she shot back.

"To go to a school that would develop the kind of talent you have, you need to go to Cornwall or Manning's or Munroe," Mrs. Spence said.

I felt so great. Here was Mrs. Spence, who was the best teacher I ever had, telling me that I had a lot of talent academically.

I asked her, "How did one go about sitting the Common Entrance Examination?"

To which she said that I was too old to sit the exam. My heart sank to the floor. I thought, how comes no teacher had told me about the Common Entrance Examination before. They had me skipping grades like a rope because I was finishing my schoolwork too quickly, but they had not seen me as fit for the Common Entrance, to even mention it to me, in a whisper. They could have written it on a piece of paper, if the term, 'Common Entrance Examination' should not have been mentioned here I thought.

My mind started to go wild. Was it that it did not dawn on any teacher that someone from New Mills, living in a three apartment board house without electricity, on Spencer Hill, could ever cope with schools such as Cornwall where rich people's children attended.

My thoughts were quickly interrupted.

"Joshua, it's not all doom. You still have an opportunity to do the Grade Nine Achievement Test," Mrs. Spence said.

I lost my pride or figured that Mrs. Spence by now knew I was ignorant of these exams.

"What's the Grade Nine Achievement Test?" I asked.

"It's an exam similar to the Common Entrance Examination but it is prepared for more mature students like you," she said.

I asked Mrs. Spence if the exam was difficult and if she thought I could pass it.

"I am absolutely confident that you will pass this exam," she shot back, ignoring the first part of the question.

"Thanks," I said.

My only concern is that sometimes when you pass the G.N.A.T., they send you to a technical school such as STETHS. However, if a student scores very high, they will send you to a grammar school, such as Cornwall," she encouraged.

STETHS stands for St. Elizabeth Technical High School. These schools had more status than the junior secondary schools and were also considered calibre schools, but still had a heavy inclination to the technical aspects of education such as Mechanical Engineering and Technical Drawing. Mrs. Spence was implying that she thought I was more suitable to attend the traditional grammar schools such as Cornwall College or Manning's. She said I should tell Mammy that I was going to sit the Grade Nine Achievement Test (G.N.A.T.). My teacher said that she was going to keep extra lessons after school for the students who she would be sending to write the exam. I can't recall whether Mrs. Spence had charged the other students for her extra lessons after school, but I know for certain that she did not charge me anything.

Upon arriving home at Spencer Hill, that high rise area of New Mills that all the Spencer families lived, I told my Mammy what had transpired between Mrs. Spence and myself.

"Ricky, don't be ridiculous. Where do you think money will come from to send you to these rich people, posh school? You will only waste your time 'cause if you pass, you will not be able to go," she chimed.

I certainly could not believe my ears. Here was my Mammy being tricked by the system herself. Having a feeling of helplessness. That it was impossible for people from her stock to attend Cornwall College. That's how they referred to some high schools in Jamaica, college. For example, there are Munroe College, Jamaica College and so on, but they are all top-ranking high schools. There are also Wolmer's Boys and Girls, and Manning's School, Kingston College, Calabar High School—All top-class high schools in Jamaica at the time.

"Mammy, how comes you are always telling me that God or Jesus, they will provide? That no-one should worry," I reminded her.

"Jesus and God are one. It's not 'they'. It's one God. Jesus and God are the same," she explained.

I argued that whether there was one God or a million that was not the issue. That the issue was that from her own standpoint and mouth, God would take care of everything and everyone, but now that I was trying to go to rich people school, God was going to turn his back on me.

"Ricky, stop blaspheme. You can't talk 'bout God like that. You don't reach at rich people, corrupt schools yet, and already you start to disbelieve in God!" Mammy shouted.

"I did not say I did not believe," I protested. "It's just that what you people say sometimes, don't make sense, most of what you all say, have no logic," I could not believe I was talking to my Mammy like that.

I had never, before, heard Mammy speak like this or never heard her lose her cool before. Neither had she heard me talk like that. It was always Pa who was losing his cool. Not my Mammy nor I, but today was different. I thought about the reason that Uncle Ben might have sat the Senior Cambridge and even my dad in their days, but not the other children of Mammy and Pa. I remembered Aunt Avona's remarks about these two living at their aunt's and grandmother's house in Ashton as children. I also questioned myself how Mammy and Pa were able to have children? They didn't even talk to each other or sleep in the same bed. I interrupted my thoughts.

"I will be writing the G.N.A.T. come high or low waters, and I will be attending Cornwall College that September," I said firmly.

I truly don't remember if there was a fee to sit the Grade Nine Achievement Test (G.N.A.T.) and if there was, how I got the money to do so. All I knew was that I sat the exam. I will assume that if there were fees involved, I must have written to my aunt Evelyn in Boston, U.S.A. to ask her for help. She, once in a while, would send me a little pocket money (allowance). The exam was held in the district of Darliston. The district of Darliston which I was later to teach and reside for five years, and where my two girls, Kadisha and Kaliese were consumed, was approximately seven miles from New Mills.

By the way, Kadisha was actually born at the Cornwall Regional Hospital in Montego Bay but Kaliese, the younger of three years, was both consumed and born in Darliston. She is truly a Darliston girl.

The arrangement for the examination was made. All the candidates who were to write the examination, including me, would all travel in a van to Darliston. We would pay individually for the return trip. I also cannot recall what the fee was to take us to the exam and back. If memory serves me correctly, the van was supposed to pick up those of us living in New Mills at about 7:30 A.M. at Mrs. Retinella McFarlane's home. Ms. Rittie (That was her pet name) was a teacher at the Barneyside Primary School at the time. Barneyside is an adjoining district to New Mills. She also had a son, Renrick McFarlane who was also going to sit the examination as well, that day. I believed the examination was scheduled for 9:00 A.M. at the examination centre in Darliston.

It happened that the morning of the examination, I must have been the first candidate to wake up. I woke about 5:30 A.M. I washed my face and got a bath from the wash pan that I always do and got ready. My Mammy and aunt Grenda had prepared my breakfast. When I was finished eating and drinking my hot chocolate, I wanted to leave immediately and Mammy and my aunt Grenda told me that it was still too early, and dark, so I should wait a few minutes more. I lay all the six HB Medium Soft pencils I had, sharpener, and geometry set on the windowsill in a case and lay on the verandah's bench, to rest for awhile. It seemed I had dozed off, but I was still early when I awoke. I jumped up quickly and grabbed the little package off the windowsill and ran down the hill to get to Ms. Rittie's house. On approaching the New Mills main road, I doubled checked to see if I had everything. I suddenly realized that I did not have the examination card, so I had to return home to get it. The examination card served as a kind of identification card for each candidate, as I recall it. I could not have entered the examination centre without it, or so I thought.

I reached at Ms. Rittie's home at about 7:35 A.M. and 'Mass' Stanley, Ms. Rittie's husband, told me they just left but that the driver said he would come back to get me. He said I should not worry. Tears started to roll down my eyes. Imagine, I thought, the last chance I had to go to rich people school and see what happened to me. I told 'Mass' Stanley that I was going to walk until the car reached me on its way back. I guess the correct term, I should use was 'run' because by the time I got at the lower section of Darliston, to my enquiry, I was told that the vehicle had just passed with the students. I could not believe that I ran so fast that the vehicle was merely a few minutes ahead of me. It should be noted that the journey to Darliston was mostly uphill. I now think about that and realised that so has been my life literally and figuratively. My numerous struggles were a sort of uphill run. I had built up a kind of inner toughness that I, myself, didn't even know I had. The going up and down the Spencer Hill in New Mills had not gone in vain. I was really fit and I was now being rewarded because of that uphill experience seven days a week and throughout most of my life; going to the shop, to fetch water, to look firewood, to go to school, or simply, to play with my friends and cousins and importantly, my changing addresses and schools, like how rich people changed their clothes.

I walked onto the school's compound where the examination centre was located, to see that some of the candidates were still disembarking from the vehicle. The driver whose name I think was Wreckter, the brother-in-law of Ms. Rittie, recognised me. He asked me who dropped me there. He could not believe that I had actually walked to Darliston and got there so quickly. He said he could understand my anxiety, but he would not have forfeited on his commitment to take me to the Examination Centre and he was just about to come to get me.

The examination was about to start an hour or so later. We were all seated at our desks after having located our candidate numbers, attached to each respective student's desk. My heart started to race. I wondered if this was so, because I had run so fast just an hour or so ago or was it because of anxiety over the examination that would decide my future. Would I have to go to learn a trade in a few months' time or would I be studying at Cornwall college? I thought. I took a deep breath and tried to count backwards, from twenty to one. I had some difficulty doing so. I said, oh God, if I couldn't count backward from twenty to one, how would I pass the Grade Nine Achievement Test? As I started to get fearful and harbour doubt, I recalled Mrs. Merlin Spence's voice.

"I am absolutely confident that you will pass this exam."

An unusual calm came over me. I got back my confidence. I started to remember how great I was at Geometry, calculating areas and volumes of shapes, work with Pythagora's Theorem, $a2 + b2 = c2$. I remembered that 'a' and 'b' represent the legs that meet to form the right angle, that the c2 represents the hypotenuse, the line that was opposite, and runs diagonally. I started to remember the sweet compositions I had written in school and for my J.S.C. English, and that I was among the few who had passed English at the Jamaica School Certificate level at such a tender age. I also recalled that there were pre-trained teachers at one of my schools who had failed the J.S.C. English several times before they passed it. I knew, for a fact, one of my grade six teachers, a pre-trained teacher then, who was among those teachers at the time. I was ready to write this exam and I finally was confident that I would be at Cornwall College rain or shine, that September.

The examiners asked us to listen carefully. One of them advised that we should shade in our candidate numbers, write and shade in our names, date of birth, and so on. They remarked that most of the examination was marked by a computer. I started to imagine how could that be, but I quickly refocused my thoughts to the rest of the directives from the examiners. They instructed us not to look at others' work, that we could not go outside once the examination was started, not even to the bathroom. There obviously could not be any talking. I started to feel the earlier uneasiness I experienced, began to reappear upon me, once again. I said to myself, are these people trying to scare us poor people's children so that we get scared and fail, and don't go to rich people's children school?

Finally, we got the go ahead to start working. I kept my head straight on my papers. I could not afford to glance at my friends and to get kicked out of the examination centre. I found the examination quite easy. I said that rich people work was not that hard, so how comes more poor people didn't do these tests and go to rich people's school and become rich people too? As I worked away at my test, I recalled how I did not know about these exams until Mrs. Merlin Spence told me. I wondered why Uncle Ben, being a principal, did not tell me about the Common Entrance and the G.N.A.T. I almost said it out aloud but caught up with myself and merely mumbled in my mind that that was how rich people prevent poor people's children from progressing. It made perfect sense, I thought. If all the little poor children from places like New Mills and Barneyside and Lambs River and all those places, heard of these examinations and take them and pass, what would happen? Who would become the domestic helper, the factory worker, mason; who would chop the grass on the pavement? I almost felt that I should not have been so mad with my teachers anymore. They had to maintain a system. If it was now, I would certainly have used the term, 'status quo'. I wondered if they had a course in teachers' colleges that trained them how to keep the poor, poor.

I had finished my examination but would not risk to find out if other candidates were also finished. I held my head straight in my book until I started to feel a pain in my neck. I did not trust people anymore. I still remembered that not even my Uncle Ben let me in on the secret of this examination business. I was not going to give them any reasons to disqualify me now that Mrs. Merlin Spence had let me in on the secret.

One of the examiners screamed in a rough voice, "You have fifteen minutes to go. Those of you who are finished, and you have double checked your work, may come up to my desk with it."

I rose from my desk and realised that I was not alone. Many of us were finished. I handed in the documents to one of the examiners. He looked at a sheet he had in his hand and then on mine. He asked me to sign something which I signed without even reading it. Later I wondered if I had agreed to them having the option to remain in all-age school, even if I had passed. I said to myself, oh silly me.

We proceeded to the outside of the building. I was endeavouring to find out how my friends thought the examination was, but no one seemed to want to say anything. I shocked myself when I said it was hard. Everyone agreed. I wondered if they were just saying that to be on the safe side in the event they did not pass as I was. Deep down in my heart, I knew I passed. If I did not pass, I would have been very disappointed, as I knew the work well. Probably, because I spent so many years in grade nine. Some of these students had just completed their first ninth grade stints, even though several of them would not have had a second chance to write it, no different from me.

We returned to school the following week or day. I can't remember for sure. Several teachers, many of whom taught us in the lower grades wanted to know how it was. I now changed my response from 'hard' to 'not too bad'. I, too, wanted to create a safety net in the event I failed. The thought of failing brought cold sweat all over me. I started to wonder if I had misread any of the questions, whether I had made any mistakes. I tried to put it to the back of my medium-sized head, but it kept coming back.

Some strange rumours started to spring up around the community about me. Every time I walked in Bethel Town square or anywhere for that matter, I could see that some kind of whispering was going on. I wondered why everyone, all on a sudden, whispered any time I approached. I began to get a little withdrawn and was not my jovial, provocative self as I used to be. One day as I walked in Bethel Town square, I realised that I was the centre of discussion. The two ladies apparently did not see me coming.

"You know that little, poor boy from Spencer Hill in New Mills?" the short lady asked.

"Ricky?" the other confirmed.

"I heard that the other day, they had an exam in Darliston and he had to run all the way there as he did not have any money to pay the taxi driver," she explained.

When I heard what was being said I quickly turned back. I was about to go to the post office, but I felt very ashamed and hurt. I knew I was poor but why were people telling all these lies about me? I thought. I started to judge everyone. I thought one of those students who sat the exam must have thought that I did not have any money and that was the reason I walked. I quickly recalled that I had the money with me in Darliston and had actually shown it to them as proof. It meant that someone was just trying to put me down. I had eventually found the source of the rumour and decided to let it be.

As the weeks drew closer for the publishing of the results of the G.N.A.T. in the newspapers and/or the submission of the lists to the respective schools from which we were prepared for the exam, everyone was getting nervous. I could not focus. At nights, I could not sleep, I tossed and turned all night in our bed. So badly that my cousins and grandma with whom we shared bed, were also losing sleep because of me. I was an ardent reader of the Hardy Boys' series that I enjoyed very much, but even those books could not get my mind off the exams or get my nerves settled. The night before the results were published, I was a disaster.

The result came to the Bethel Town All-Age School, and of the twelve or so, of us who wrote the the Grade Nine Achievement Test, only Joshua Spencer had passed. I was quite sad that my friend, Renrick McFarlane's name was not among the results. He was my close friend and his mother was a teacher at the Barneyside Primary School as I alluded to earlier. Ms Rittie was a very kind lady. She had later gone to the Ministry of Education's office in Kingston and Renrick was deemed to have passed and subsequently sent to the Knockalva Agricultural School where after graduating, he had acquired a job as a pre-trained agricultural teacher. Ms. Rittie was later to have played a very important role in my life as you will see later in this chapter. I had passed to attend my second option, Manning's High School. I was extremely elated! This school is the second oldest high school in Jamaica. It was founded in 1738. Second only to Wolmer's. However, the jubilation and excitement would not last for too long. I started to ask myself how I would attend Manning's School. Those days, there were no buses travelling daily back and forth from New Mills to Savanna-La-Mar where Manning's is located. It meant that I would have to board in Savanna-La-Mar as was the practice at the time. Where would the money come from to pay the expensive boarding fee? Where would the money come from to buy the numerous books that were sent on a list of things required to attend Manning's? The khaki and the epaulettes? The shoes? The Physical Education outfit?

The Michael Manley Government of the 1970's had just made secondary education free to all, but it did not provide free books or dealt with the problem of travelling, etc. If I had gotten my first option, and had gone to Cornwall College, an all-boys school, I would live on the campus of the school at a cheaper rate I thought. However, Manning's School was a non-boarding, co-educational institution. The way was going to be tough.

As the weeks of the summer holidays got closer to coming to a close, so were my wits with coming up with a strategy to make my dream come true. My Mammy had contacted my aunts and uncles and asked if they could help, but they all responded in the negative. I was utterly frustrated. September had come and I was still at home in New Mills. There was no money to get me to attend Manning's School.

My mother and Mr. Lovell had moved to Stonehenge to live with my siblings. My parents by now had a few more children in addition to

Georgia. I think by then, there were Georgia, Anzil, Raffick and Polly or she could have been pregnant with the latter. My last brother, Oliver was definitely not yet born. They were staying at the family house. Mama and my stepdad both opened a little shop over there. The truth be told, as I type the immediate bit of information above, I truly cannot recall who had told me that my parents had moved to Stonehenge to live. I can't recall whether we received a letter or not, or whether we were simply told by someone. As a last resort, I decided I was going to travel to Stonehenge to seek help from my mother and Mr. Lovell. I remember that Mr. Lovell was an American farmworker. I thought he might have had a few cents tucked away, and might have been able to help me, to at least, purchase some of the books or to pay a month's or two, of my boarding fee.

I took a bus to the Montpelier Railway Station and took the train to the Stonehenge Railway Station. The house was not too far from the Station. I outlined my dilemma to my parents. Mr. Lovell indicated that he had a little savings and would try to see what he could do. I was totally taken off guard by my mother's response.

"Lovell, you better not do it. When the boy grows up, who said he is going to remember you?" she remarked.

Upon hearing the remark, I was dumbstruck. How could one's own mother not want to help her son? I searched inside my now, more-than-medium-sized head for answers. Could it have been that my mother did not understand what she had actually just said? I started to beat up on myself. Why did I bother to go to my mother for help to go to rich people school? She did not even want me to attend poor people school, that I secretly had to write to my dad, to take me back in Montego Bay sometime before. I started to wonder if this lady was really my mother. I knew she was, as I looked so much like her, but I couldn't help the thought. I questioned why some people had children without any sense of responsibility. I was deeply disappointed, hurt and hurting.

Mr. Lovell eventually agreed that my mother was correct, after he thought long and hard about it. Today, I have no hard feelings against Mr. Lovell who was still alive at the time of writing. He wasn't even my dad and he initially thought that he should help. Neither did I harbour any hate or negativity re Mama, but since that date, that conversation that occurred among Mr. Lovell, Mama and I, had never totally left my mind. I wondered if it had left theirs!

I returned to New Mills from what I considered the most disappointing experience I had ever had up to that stage of my life. I was cloaked and choked in depression and hopelessness. I walked in a daze. I hid away in Spencer Hill, that hilly section of New Mills seemingly made for the Spencer's, a geographical area and family tribe that had no hope like was true with the absence of electricity, water, television and other basic amenities.

Just around mid October, my Mammy was insisting that I return to Bethel Town All-Age School instead of just staying home to which I responded that I would rather die first. The Sunday, following this discussion, Mammy asked me to accompany her to church. I was reluctant to go at first, but then decided to go. I thought, who knows, I might have been able to meet someone who could help me.

At church, there was a local Caucasian by the name of Mr. Sturridge. Mr. Sturridge was someone I knew very well from my attendance at church before. He had also built my Mammy's house and carried out repairs from time to time. I felt comfortable with him so I outlined my situation to him. Upon my outlining my problem, he said he would definitely try to help me. He told me that he was the leader of a People's National Party (PNP) group in the Constituency of the then North Eastern Westmoreland of the ruling Peoples National Party. He promised to call an emergency meeting and he would seek the attendance of the then Member of Parliament, Mr Jim (James) Thompson.

To my surprise, the meeting was called on the following Tuesday with Mr. Jim Thompson present. He was presented with the detail of my case by Mr. Sturridge. He asked to be excused immediately after he got the information to go to his car. He returned with his cheque book and wrote a cheque for six hundred dollars (J$600.00) and handed it to Ms. Retinella McFarlane. Ms. Rittie, her pet name, as you gleaned earlier, had the responsibility to purchase khaki, shoes, and books. Mr. Thompson had contacted a boarding home located at 10 Beckford Street in Savanna-La-Mar, owned by one Mrs. Edna Brown. I had not even met the gentleman yet, and this was what he was reported to have said, upon his being told about me and my struggle to go to Manning's School.

The boy must go to school. I am not even sure where I will be getting the next cent after today, but I am sure, if God spares my life, Joshua will be in school no later than this Friday. Ladies, and gentlemen, listen to the young man's name, we could be talking about the next prime minister of Jamaica.

Mr. Thompson, who was our MP, visited me at the New Mills location. He, Ms. Rittie, and I left for Savanna-La-Mar. Everything was taken care of inclusive of boarding, books, etc. I met his wife, Mrs. T. (Mrs. Elethia Thompson). From that point, they had taken me under their wings and had continued to support me through college as will be gleaned in chapter five. I spent time with them at their Fort Williams home in Westmoreland, Jamaica, their Save-A-Dollar Supermarket in the Negril square, Jamaica, and at their Bar-B-Barn Hotel on Norman Manley Boulevard in Negril. They began to tell everyone that I was their child, so I elatedly accepted their love and yes, their money that took care of my education and me. I have never been afraid to tell anyone that Mr. and Mrs. Thompson were my foster parents, because they were, even if my biological relatives are uncomfortable about this claim.

I moved into the 10 Beckford Street address, the Thursday of the same week to start attending Manning's School the following day, Friday. The owner of the boarding house, Mrs. Edna Brown had immediately exhibited some fondness for me. She remarked how handsome and cute I was and that she was sorry that her only daughter and child was much older than me and was already a student of the University of the West Indies (U.W.I.), reading for the Bachelors of Science degree in the Natural Sciences. Upon her mentioning the Sciences, I said I liked the Natural Sciences too. I told her how my father had actually stimulated me, in developing a love for Science and outlined the cookie story to her. She laughed and touched me on the head and enquired what had become of him. That is, my father. I told her what had happened, and she said she was really sad to learn of that. She, however, outlined that Mr. Thompson was a very nice man and would take over that role. I felt that she was really a genuine and kind person. And she was.

We moved along the passage of her huge house. The long passage that ran from immediately beyond the living room was flanked by numerous rooms on either side of its length. The passage led to a back door. Outside of the back door was another house, probably a four-bedroom house all fit with kitchen and bathroom. She told me that that house was her original home. She smilingly said she fell upon some money and decided to go into the boarding business. She told me she had boarded some of the finest people who attended Manning's School, teachers, doctors, lawyers, professors, judges, politicians, pharmacists, and so on. Currently, she said there were some Manning's School teachers who boarded at the home. I had mixed feelings about that fact. I wondered, wow! I would be living at the same place as some of my teachers. She pointed out that the teachers were all from abroad. Two of them were from England and one, I remember his name, Mr. Kassam, was from India and he taught Physics. Mr. Kassam was later to teach me Physics, but I thought he was not a very good teacher though he new the material well. The last, two opposite rooms at the end of this very long and rectangular structure were the kitchen and the dining room. I found it interesting that she had designed her house to have the kitchen opposite (opposing) her dining room and being divided by this long passage. I laughed at the idea. She eventually took me to my bedroom. It was the first room from her personal bedroom, on the left side, going toward the end of the building. I felt safe and secure with her bedroom being so close to mine. Then I said, If I get up at nights or anything like that, I might wake her up. I said I would have to be extremely quiet at nights, especially if I needed to go to the bathroom.

The day had come to a close, and the Manning's teachers and students had returned home. Some of them were looking quite old. The students that is. Some of them wore beards and even looked older than the teachers. Among some of the students I can recall, were David Garwood, later to become a doctor, Everton Moore, one Michael Walker, also known as Three-Finger, Maxine Smalling, and Joylyn Shakes, among others. I found it quite interesting that Mrs. Brown would board both boys and girls in the same house. I said how could she ensure that strange things wouldn't happen between these boys and girls as she slept.

I was shocked when, about six o'clock of the evening, I heard the ringing of a hand-held bell. My thoughts quickly flew back to Bethel Town All-Age School, Dundee Primary, and King's School. I recalled how nervous I was when Mrs. Spence indicated that she needed to speak to me at lunch time. How I thought all kinds of weird stuff. That I was in trouble because of cutting in line at the water tank or because Catapult Foot had complained that I gave him his fancy new name that would probably stay with him for life. How Rose Wallace might have told that I was always pestering her. I wondered what had happened or would be happening to those students who did not get into the rich people schools. Would they continue to live a life in the girth and dearth of poverty? Then I remembered Dundee Primary. The day I got the letter from my dad and later, another from my dad, and Aunt May May and how they swapped names, Mama and Aunt May May, that is, like how my friends and I used to swap marbles for cashew, especially when I visited Stonehenge and got a whole bunch of cashew. I remembered my friend, Wayne Colquhoun at the Dundee Primary School. How we played and chatted together. And my cousins Winston Salesman, Cecil Salesman, Paul Salesman, Radcliffe Daley, pet-name, Dave, and his mother, Mrs. Stephenson, my first cousin, who was also a teacher. Everything just popped right up in my head like a well blown Christmas balloon. I saw Uncle Ben walking in my grade nine classroom at King's School, asking me to step aside, like I was a stranger, as he threw licks on the bottom, back, legs, just about everywhere of poor John's slender and frail body. How Uncle Ben tried to beat me for nothing and I ran away barefooted, braved it and slept at a gas station, on the floor with strangers, then sped home to my Mammy who shielded and protected me from the vampire, Uncle Ben.

Mrs. Edna Brown came to my room and explained that that bell meant that it was supper time and that we all should gather at the huge tables in the dining room. I felt awkward at first.

"Mrs. Brown told me that you will be starting school at Manning's tomorrow," the man with British accent said.

"Yes, sir," I replied.

"Do you know of which class that might be?" he asked.

"I think, I think it's 3G," I said.

"Oh 3G, Oh, you're Joshua Spencer, I have your name on my list," he proclaimed.

I was thinking what kind of list this gentleman had my name on when he interrupted my thought.

"Joshua, I'll be your teacher of Mathematics," he said.

"Please to meet you. I hope I don't disappoint you," I said.

Mrs. Brown came and introduced me to the other students and Mr. Kassam and a fireman by the name of Mr. Dixon. My Mathematics teacher was called Mr. Batt, but I can't use the name that most students called him behind his back. Many of these students, like my fellow Jamaicans, could be cold at times, I thought then, even though in general, we were a warm and loving set of people, I reassured myself.

"How convenient, a fireman right here when we burn the place down," I could not believe I actually said that out loudly.

Ms. Brown smiled and so was everyone else. Joylyn said she would take me around the school the following day. I wondered if she liked me, but she was one form ahead of me.

I was up bright and early Friday morning for the first day of school at Manning's. I beamed with pride when I put on my nice khaki suit and my epaulettes. I placed the books in my bag and sat on the bed, awaiting the bell to ring or something to happen, informing us that it was time for breakfast. There were banging and all types of sounds everywhere. The noise and banging reminded me of some kind of steel band music. Finally, the bell rang and I went for breakfast. I noticed the teachers did not come for breakfast with us though. As I looked at Mrs. Brown somewhat quizzically, she indicated that they would come later.

Joylyn and I sat at the same table. She asked me if I was nervous about school and I said, "No." I was expecting her to ask me why I was just starting school and school was in nearly two months, but she did not. I said to myself how considerate of her. I assumed she must be a very intelligent person. Some students would let the inquisitive nature of human beings get the upper hold of them but not Joylyn Shakes. I thought she must have figured out that to ask too many uncomfortable questions, would probably make me uncomfortable or she probably new the whole story. I started to wonder if Mrs. Brown had told them my experience. I wished that she didn't and they probably didn't know from how they related to me.

Joylyn took me around the school and showed me the important areas. This place was massive. There were about two to three physics labs, the same numbers of chemistry labs, about two biology labs, a huge library and book-store or some book related facility, as I can recall. There were also various other buildings some of which were classrooms. There was a long rack on which were hung hundreds of bicycles. Savanna-La-Mar is a flat plane. Everybody but me and Joylyn seemed to ride a bicycle. I soon discovered that Mr. Batt even rode a bicycle to school as well. Our boarding home and Manning's School were on the same street and it was pretty close to school, and convenient as well.

I recalled that I had to go to the office, so I did. In there, I had to do all manner of stuff. There were some books that were paid for, that I did not yet receive. I also had to get exercise books and dictionaries, I think. I had to meet the principal, Mr. Herbert George Neita, for one reason or the other, but I couldn't recall what it was, at the time of writing.

As much as I can remember, my first class at Manning's was the third period Spanish class already in progress. The class was already well on its way in the old building at the front of the Manning's compound when I walked in. I tiptoed quietly and sat near to the door of which I entered, not wanting to disturb the class. The Spanish teacher who also turned out to have been my Chemistry teacher as well, was one Mr. Shippey. I don't think he realised that I had just come in the class or he wanted to pick on me for the fun of it. To this day, I didn't find out.

"¿Como te llamas?" he said.

"I don't know," I said.

The class roared in laughter. "¿Como te llamas?" means 'what is your name?' I wanted to tell Mr. Shippey not to have embarrassed me, because I was new and was coming from poor people school, and that I did not learn Spanish there. However, I did not have the guts. I thought about how I should have been like Pa and put Mr. Shippey in his place.
"¿No sabes?" he said

I wanted to crawl under the table and chair on which I was seated, and in front of it. Probably, I truly don't belong here. This is really for rich people's children, I thought.

Mr. Shippey continued to aggravate me until he realised that I was really a dummy or that he was satisfied that he had embarrassed me long enough or he felt sorry for me afterwards, and wished he hadn't done it.

I started to think, why would a teacher try to embarrass a student who is obviously unaware of what was being said or what was going on in the class? What gain does one get from that act? I asked myself. To give him the benefit of the doubt, I thought he was probably an absent-minded teacher. He probably thought I was a Common Entrance Examination student who was enrolled at Manning's since first form or I came through some advanced elementary system, and should have known what was going on. As a teacher now, I endeavour not to put anyone of my students in the position I was placed in, the first day of my first class of the third period at the otherwise great Manning's School.

That evening after school, I made sure I studied Spanish a lot. Joylyn came to the door of my room to ask me how I was doing but she realised I was in no mood to converse. Within a few months in the school, I had acquired the nickname, 'Spanish Prof'.

It had also turned out that in my class at Manning's was my long time friend from the Dundee Primary, Wayne Colquhoun who I knew some time ago. I was so happy. I had really found someone who I could trust and who trusted me. Wayne, boarded at a private family home on Ricketts Avenue which was merely a stone's throw from where I lived. We visited each other from time to time and studied together. Our friendship was to be a very enduring one. Even today as I write these lines, we are still in contact with each other.

The 1970's were tough in Jamaica. There were times when the fifty dollar boarding fee did not arrive on time. The Thompson's had a drugstore known as Thompson's Drugstore on Great George's Street in Savanna—La-Mar. During the end of the month when Mrs. Brown did not receive the boarding fee on time, I would go out by the drugstore, hoping that when Mrs. Thompson saw me she would remember that it was the end of the month and that the boarding was due. It was usually difficult to remind her. So, I would be there chit chatting briefly when she had the time. I would try to introduce some related subjects but never went directly to the point of mentioning that Mrs. Brown was getting upset that she was not paid the boarding. She would even ask me if I had pocket money. If I did not have, she would even give me pocket money (allowance) but usually no mention of the boarding. Sometimes, I just stopped short of reminding her, but choked at the last moment before I could acquire the courage to do so.

As a result of these sometimes, late payments of my boarding, I started to feel obligated to Mrs. Brown to do a little chores around the house, to keep her happy, as well as for her to keep my little secret from the others. It did not take long for me to have become the official domestic helper in the house. Every evening after supper, I would find myself washing the huge pile of dishes. On weekends when the other students were gone downtown for a walk or to the library, I would be the only student home at Mrs. Brown's, polishing the floors and shining each and every room. Some of the other students thought I was sucking up to Mrs. Brown to show me love or I was downright stupid.

One evening as I washed dishes one of the female students pranced into the kitchen, grabbed a knife from the dish rack and stabbed me in the back. I felt the stab and turned around to ask her what that was about, when she stabbed at my face several times. I used the frying pan I was washing to protect my face. I ended up receiving a stab below my right eye. She ran to the police station to report what she had done; I ran to the hospital to get my wounds treated. There was some pressure to press charges but I refused to do so. The incident had apparently happened due to some sort of jealously. To date, I still have the scar under my right eye, but many people mistake it for a dimple.

Notwithstanding all the above, Mrs. Brown and her home were always great. I had started to do these chores which overtime, I could no longer stop from doing. It became a natural. She would tell everyone how great a person I was and how the other students were lazy. Joshua was the best, she thought. How could I have withdrawn my labour after all that praise? Sometimes when my foster-parents remembered the boarding, it was almost the third month overdue. I started to notice that the amount and quality of meal that I got sometimes, started to be reduced. As a consequence, I worked even harder domestically, endeavouring to remain on the good side of Mrs. Brown. My experience at the King's All-Age School had groomed me for the situation I found myself in at 10 Beckford Street. I now started to thank Uncle Ben for having given me the exposure and experience in what I joked to myself as working in his Domestic Affairs Ministry at King's School.

From time to time, Mr. T, that was how we called Mr. Thompson, would write two or more months' cheque to avoid the problem but of all the boarders, it seemed my payments were still proving the most challenging for Mrs. Brown. She would sometime tell me that she had not received the money on time and that she needed the money to pay bills, buy food, and so on.

Now that I think about everything, I wondered whether there were other reasons other than not remembering, why Mrs. Brown was always telling me that the boarding was not yet received or was late. As I said earlier on, the seventies were truly tough times. Although my foster-parents had businesses, one could never know what the true financial health of these businesses were. Again, any conclusion here would be a mere assumption. I had no evidence of any financial challenges of any kind on their part during the seventies but the question of challenges did cross my mind.

Despite these challenges, I am always grateful to the Thompson's. They had never frowned one day, or showed me any sign that they regretted helping me. I visited them from time to time. As you shall see later, they had continued to assist me financially even through teachers' college.

Manning's School was great. I got involved in a few of their extracurricular activities. I did a few pieces of writing that got published in the yearly school magazines. I became a member of the Cadet Corp. I also took part in sports and ran for my house which I think was called Segre.

After my three years at the institution, it was now time for my graduation. We had an elaborate graduation service of which the only family members who attended were Mr. and Mrs. Jim Thompson. None of my biological relatives turned up for my graduation and this was to be the case with respect to all important functions and milestones throughout my life. All biological relatives, including my mother were always absent.

The Graduation Ball was held at the Manning's School Auditorium. The place was well decorated and romantically lit. We had a popular sound system, the We the People Band. It was indeed an unforgettable evening and night. That night I had actually got the opportunity to kiss a girl I had always liked throughout my three years at Manning's but never had the guts to talk to her. However, after a couple of alcoholic beverages, after all I was now no longer a high school student, I gathered the confidence to ask her for a dance. Upon our conversing as we danced, closely together at times, at other times far apart, I discovered she felt the same about me all along, as much as I had for her. However, I had never once noticed her noticing me during my three years at the school. Accordingly, I thought I was not being projected on her radar. Unfortunately, this very sweet, female student would be emigrating abroad, just days after her graduation. I had never seen or heard of her since.

I graduated from Manning's in 1978 and applied to the Sam Sharpe Teachers' College in the early part of 1979 to be trained as a high school science teacher. At first, at Sam Sharpe Teachers' College, my majors were actually Spanish and English then I changed to Science and Physical Education. The same year that I applied to teachers' college, it happened that I was in the capital city of Kingston, spending time with my cousin, Fay. While I was there, it dawned on me that I should go to write the police entrance test, at the Police Head Quarters. My cousin lived in Zadie Avenue. She asked her boyfriend who worked in the vicinity of the Police Head Quarters to drop me there and asked her boyfriend to pick me up later that day.

Frankly, those early days of my life, I had really little respect for a police officer in terms of intellectual potency. I knew that all one needed to join the force was a grade nine education, be trained for a mere six months and be given a gun, and maybe later a car to drive. I compared that to teachers' college where the matriculation requirement to embark on studies in the Secondary Education Faculty at the time, the candidate would have had to pass a minimum of three to four General Certificate of Education (G.C.E.), including English, and the Primary Education faculty, minimum matriculation requirements, 5 Jamaica School Certificate Examination (J.S.C.) which must have included English, Mathematics and a Science subject or combinations of G.C.E and J.S.C passes in the respective subjects outlined above. The training was for three years, two of which focused on pedagogy, methodology, content, child and/or adolescent development, etc. The third year was the internship period where the Joint Board of Teacher Education based at the U.W.I. (University of the West Indies) Mona, would supervise and assess one's teaching practice. Therefore, I was extremely surprised when I arrived at the Police Head Quarters to see over three hundred people in long lines, many of whom wore three-piece suits, waiting to do the police test. I had dressed as casually as one could get.

I started to get nervous and wondered whether I had in fact falsely underrated the qualifications and training of Jamaican police officers. However, I tried to calm my nerve by saying to myself that I had absolutely nothing to lose. It turned out that the test was not difficult. There were an essay and a grade 8 Mathematics test, in my estimation, that we had to do. However, what I found interesting was that by the time the tests were marked, we had only about seventeen people left behind from the original number of say, three hundred people who had sat the test and who had actually passed it. I said to myself one cannot and should not judge a book by its cover. I had gone on to do the interview and was successful.

Upon my returning home to New Mills, I told Mammy that I was successful in my application to join the Jamaica Constabulary Force (J.C.F.).

"So, Ricky, all the trouble you went through to go to rich people school, that all you could do is to become a police officer?" she questioned.

"I am not sure that I will be going yet. I just wrote the test as I was in Kingston," I explained.

"Are you saying that you doubt yourself about being accepted to teachers' college?" she queried.

"Mammy, not really. Just in case it does not work out," I said.

"Ricky, so help me God, if you become a police officer, I don't know you. I am not your grandma!" she screamed.

"Why do you hate police?" I asked.

"I don't hate police, but they have to swear to kill their parents and family. That's not of God," she explained.

I walked away and hoped that I would not have to swear to kill and/or arrest my mother, if needs be. I considered what if Mr. Lovell were to cheat on my mother and she got angry and fatally hit him. I was transferred to the Stonehenge area and had to arrest her. It bothered my mind for awhile, but I walked off to sit under the big, and now, my favourite breadfruit tree. Yes, the one I was sitting when I got the news of my father's murder.

I sat under the big breadfruit tree. My mind ran back to my life from Albion, Montego Bay, to my brief stay near Dome Street, to New Mills to Berkshire, back to New Mills to Uncle Ben's King's School. I remembered my running to Darliston, the trepidation that inundated me that exam day, that my last chance to go to rich people school was about to elude me when I missed Wrecktor's vehicle. I thought of how I was the only person who passed the exam and how, if it had not been for Mrs. Merlin Spence, I would have probably joined my Rastafarian cousins in New Mills, smoking marijuana, planting weed, and just taking things cool after getting red hot from the stuff. Here I was now, sitting under the big breadfruit tree of Spencer Hill, New Mills. The same breadfruit tree that I had received one of the most negative news in years gone by. However, it was not the same barefooted Ricky as before. I now knew what was being taught at the rich people schools and what the exams were like that one needed, rich or poor, to benefit from these so-called schools for the affluent. I thought that it was not as sophisticated as I had imagined, after all. I wondered if all poor people realised that with a little effort and luck, they too could be called part of the so-called middle class or even, upper middle class. I wondered in a few weeks whether I was going to embark on that journey to become an educator, perhaps later a principal like my Uncle Ben. I wondered if I was making the right decisions. I thought too about being a police officer, wearing my red stripes not only in my hands and to my lips, but on the sides of my pair of blue pants. I imagined the power that I would have had bestowed upon me by the law and the Constitution of the land, just after training for six months. I could pull over anyone and everyone including those who made the law. It gave me a sense of satisfaction. I thought of how I would have reacted if I cornered a thief or a gunman or gun-woman for that matter. Would I treat both genders equally in these circumstances or would I say, oh this gun person is a woman? I can't do it.

There were Mammy's objections to my joining the police force as well. I could understand her reasoning. It would be quite distasteful to have to arrest your own family, even shoot them. I thought about it a second time, and realised that my mother, my entire biological family, in essence, for most of my years, have been shooting me, had shot me head on. My mother, in particular, had shot, what could have been, a fatal bullet straight through my cerebrum and cerebellum, when she persuaded my stepdad from providing financial support to send me to rich people school. I was supposed to have died years ago, lie useless in jail, forgotten, I analysed quietly.

I tried to settle my thoughts like sediments in an extremely, dirty but a thirsty man's drinking water. A sudden emotion consumed my overwhelmed soul. The tears started to flow freely, but yet ruggedly down my distressed face, just like the Simon River that almost took away my life with my crocus bag of yam, dasheen, baddoo, pumpkin, and other ground provisions, several years ago. I bit my lip and my tongue, and ground my teeth. I felt like someone touched me gently and lightly on the right shoulder. I turned around and saw no one, not even a breadfruit leaf. Just like on August 18, 1978, the anniversary date of my father's death, while I sat under the big breadfruit tree at New Mills, the same poem started to flow throw my mind once again. This time I quietly pulled my pen from my pocket, and a piece of scratch paper and started to write:

Daddy

Daddy, the very word sounds strange

Slipping from my quivering lips, estranged

Endeavouring to escape a child's lonesomeness

Desiring your stern masculine voice

To make me happy, make me rejoice

Daddy, just uttering the word makes me daze

Reminder of a missed phase.

Daddy, you were long gone before your murderers attacked

Forthrightly, the moment you walked out the door

And turned your back

No hugs, no kisses, no rocks

Daddy, I longingly wished that even then, you were back.

Daddy, naturally, I have friends and foes

When they speak of their dad

It makes me feel very, very sad

Even more with a foe

Although, I wouldn't tell him so

I wanted you to father, to care

To take me to the cinemas and everywhere

Your slaughterers were cold blooded

Now I'm fatherless, exposed, unblanketed

Oh daddy, I only wish you were here.

But daddy, where are you now?

Are you, as before, watching in the distance

And not taking a stance?

Oh daddy, oh daddy, I really miss you so

I wish you'd come by my side right now

And flush away my uncertainties, my doubts

Oh daddy, I will always wish you were here.

I whispered the words slowly in my mind, that was what I thought. However, my lips were moving and my vocal chords vibrated to the rhythm of my so tired heart. I started to recite the words with fervour, with feel. A gentle breeze caressed the trees around me, unlike on August 18, 1978, the first time the poem came alive to form a part of my being. A couple of leaves, from the big breadfruit tree lost the battle with the wind and fell on my head. I looked up and smiled between my still heavily flowing tears.

I wondered what it would have been like if instead of the leaves that just caressed my head, it was both of my biological parents' arms. I could only have imagined the joy, a joy that I had never experienced, and certainly never would. Was there a direct path that each human being must trod? Was there a lifeline that was intricately linked with every human being from the time the male sperm (spermatozoa) fused with the female egg (ovum)?

The questions were many but, as always, the answers were few, and not forthcoming. I felt a deep sorrow in my being. I thought about God and Satan. Why a God and a Satan? I understood in a flash the symbolism of God and Satan. Yes, I thought. This is the reality. There must be white and black. There must be bad and good or good and bad. There must be an opposing force for everything. Capitalism versus Socialism, Socialism versus Capitalism, rich versus the poor, inferior schools versus quality schools, great parents and families and the incompetent and irresponsible parents and families. I realized I couldn't waste my entire life merely focusing on my struggles or yours. That I must take responsibility for my future, and to a certain extent, and with some help, I have been.

CHAPTER FIVE

Trails of Success

Some days later, I received a very thick, long and heavy envelope from Sam Sharpe Teachers' College. I knew then and there that I got accepted to teachers' college and did not have to go to police training school, to practise to arrest or even murder my biological relatives in the name of the law, even though they had committed so many 'crimes' in my eyes, over the past years. I burst the envelope open which revealed a number of forms and pages. There were all kinds of requirements. There was a form that invited me to do a medical examination and it had even named the specific medical lab that we had to attend to have had it done. This made me panic. What if I was not healthy? Would that mean that I couldn't go to college? What if I had a venereal disease? I had not been behaving myself that well those last few weeks and accidents did happen with those safety rubber nets, especially when one was as inexperienced in its use, as I was. In the latter case, would they have asked me to get it treated then allowed me to do my studies? What did a medical examination have to do with studying to become an educator? Was this yet another way of preventing poor people's children from climbing the socio-economic ladder?

I decided that I would have to go to visit my foster-parents. I was spending time at New Mills when I got the letter. I was certainly going to need a little financial assistance to help me along. Those days, we had no cellular phones and very few people even had a domestic line. So, I had to go to Fort Williams to see the Thompson's, personally. As always, they were happy to help. I would be returning to them later in the week for assistance at their request.

The following day, I decided to go to have the medical done, to get it out of the way. This was where I was going to meet my 'brother', Oliver Nelson. As I approached the receptionist area, there was this very tall and lanky young man who very much resembled me, only taller, but probably not as handsome as I was, at least that was my thought. Yes, great modesty on my part. We had started to have a conversation. I discovered a few things about him, but not too much. He was not much of a talker either. I was better at that too.

"Mr. Nelson, this way, please," the young lady politely commanded.

I started to sweat. I was totally oblivious of what they do at a medical lab. As a matter of fact, I was totally unaware of what they did even at a regular, so-called family doctor's office. I just did not visit those places. Did one have to be denuded as I heard of farmworkers when they go to be tested to work on the North American farms? Did the medical personnel have to examine any private parts, etc.? Were there injections involved and taking of one's blood? I was indeed quite naïve about the entire process. I promised myself that if I got through this impending ordeal, I would make it a priority to visit a doctor, even once a year.

Oliver reappeared smiling. I assumed that it could not have been that bad. Oliver stayed back and waited while I went to have my medical done. It merely involved doing a couple of X-rays and blood tests. There was nothing to it.
"That would be X dollars," the receptionist snorted.

I said X dollars because at the time of writing, I could not recall what the correct amount was. I had read all the documents sent to me from the college but could not recall that it had mentioned anything about paying to do the medical. I had no money. Oliver realized that I was as broke as a church rat and pulled the money from his wallet and paid it for me. Oliver Nelson, not to be confused with my biological brother, Oliver McIntosh, had been my brother ever since. Everyone including close friends, said that Oliver Nelson and I were brothers, even one of my maternal uncles, Uncle Man (James Robinson) claimed that we had to be brothers as we looked and behaved similarly. So, since 1979, Oliver has been my brother and my three children, Kadisha, Kaliese and Michael refer to him as 'Uncle Oliver' and his children refer to me as 'Uncle Joshua', just the same.

That afternoon, before returning to Westmoreland, I decided to walk around for awhile. I went down by Sam Sharpe Square, formerly Charles Square, where I had met Charles Spencer, my father, Johnny, who had come to meet me on that *Morning Star* bus. I remembered the driver screaming, "Charles Square, Charles Square, final stop." I recalled how I was longing to be hugged by my dad, but he just kept walking. I pictured him sitting in the front of the taxi as I sat in the back, heading for the notorious 12 ½ Upper King Street address. I suddenly decided to snap out of my daydream.

I walked and did a little window or eye shopping as I had only my fare left on me. I strolled into an international shoe-store that no longer operates in Jamaica currently. Upon my approaching the store, a well-dressed gentleman approached me and asked If he could help. I said I was only window shopping, passing time until I was ready to leave for Westmoreland. I don't know why he assumed that I did not drive because he offered to take me home or to anywhere, I would like him to take me. I suddenly realized that I was being picked up by a guy. As a 'girls' man', I was shocked and was not sure whether I should have been rude to this gentleman or have been polite. My thoughts returned to what my Mammy, dad, and mother had said about not discriminating against people. That there were different kinds of people in the world, and that we were all equal irrespective of our differences. I looked at him in the eyes and calmly thanked him for his generosity. I then, advised politely, that it would not have been necessary.

I felt quite proud of the way I handled what for me, was a very strange situation. I had never ever had any inclination sexually for someone of my gender. It had never dawned on me that someone of my sex would have had an attraction for me. I wondered what about me that had caused the gentleman to approach me that way. My local homeland was quite homophobic at the time and probably still is, for him having approached me that way, I thought I must have given off some kind of signals that he must have misinterpreted as me being gay, or did I look like someone who might have been gay in his eyes?

I thought about it for awhile. I went in front of the mirror to take a look and felt that I looked like the average Joe; I did not look gay. Then I remembered neither was the gentleman in the shoe store. I began to question the reason I envisioned a gay person to exhibit a certain physique or trait. From whom did I acquire that notion of gayness? I started to question myself as to the reason some individuals were attracted sexually to members of their own gender. I was endeavouring to delve deep down into my being to question whether it was biological or social. That is to say, are gay people born gays, or did they learn to be gay through the media or circumstances, such as a need to belong, or pecuniary challenges? I guess there will always be this debate of its origin and causes.

I don't recall that I had shared this experience with anyone prior. I felt strange about the whole matter. I wondered how I would have been perceived if I should have told someone that some homosexual was asking me out.

All new students were being invited to an orientation process at the college, but I did not attend. I cannot recall the reason for my absence, but I just did not attend. So, the first day that I reported to the college, I knew absolutely no one except for Oliver who I had met at the medical laboratory. We reported in the evening, if my memory serves me correctly, and dumped all our belongings onto the floor of the Multipurpose Hall of the Sam Sharpe Teachers' College, until we were guided to the dorms. The lecture halls and dorms were neatly spread out around, and far away from it – all at the same time. The hall was reasonably spacious. It was adjoining the kitchen. There were platforms at the north end of the building and there was apparently to be some kind of function or concert for us, freshers, according to how it was arranged.

That was how we were addressed by the students, freshers or freshmen. Now come to think of it, I can't recall hearing the term, fresh women ever used. I guess at one time, it was not considered to create that term as women were not expected to attend tertiary or secondary institutions.

We later took our items, clothes, books, and other materials to our respective dorms, and rooms. There were separate dorms for males and females. I wondered the reason for that being the case. I found it ironic that when I was considered to be a minor, I was allowed to share 'dorm' with very attractive, adorable, and sexually-stimulating-to-the-young-male-eyes, females, but now that I was nineteen, the Sam Sharpe Teachers' College administration seemed to have deemed that arrangement of co-mingling its male and female cohorts under the same roof, inappropriate for its institution.

So much so were the extracurricular activities at my former boarding home, that one female student who joined us the subsequent year from New Mills, and related to someone I knew very well, got pregnant and had to drop out of high school. It was also weird that the male student who fathered the baby, then a fifth form student, was allowed to graduate. I thought then that there probably should be some free course in teaching us how either to, suppress this biological urge that overcame us during the period of our high school years or better train us as to how to use that rubbery thing, safety net to prevent us from making mothers of young ladies whose education would have been thwarted. Of course, these male stallions, such as us, would be allowed to have free reign and complete our education. I though it was an unjust system, highly unfair and a very bad approach by these so-called top-notched schools.

I pushed the thoughts to the crevices of my now big-sized head and started to explore the physical structure of my new abode. The dorm had three similar storeys. I was placed in Room A5, at one of the far ends of the ground floor or first floor, probably the northern end of the building. At the opposite far end, there was a room for one of the lecturers who was actually a Canadian. The bathroom, a big open structure with no shower curtains was directly opposite my room. There were several showers inside this big open space but nothing to protect us from the eyes of inquisitive onlookers who would come to wash their hands, just to get a peep at us. I guess the intent was to compare who was bigger or smaller. I was also very uncomfortable when I had to shower in that bathroom knowing that I was not generously endowed as others I had run into, just by mere accident. I recalled running into one of my batchmates, Dannavan Morrison also known as Spratt who was quite endowed. I called down the entire floor to share in the view that day. He was instantly named the 'Bell' or 'Bengaleng' or some such silly name. This was due to the strength of his endowment. There was no escaping the eyes of these voyeurs. It was either that they were going to see your black-you-know-what or my not so endowed front fenders. It was a challenge I, and I imagined others, eventually learned to live with.

Each room had two beds, one to either side of the small room. There was one window, two tables, one to either side, and a closet that each partner of the room would share. Each table also had its own lamp with shade. There was, in addition, a bulb in the middle of the ceiling that could illuminate the entire room if it became necessary to do so. I soon found out that my roommate was to be one Hugh Solomon, pet name, Sala or Hugo. I was surprised to discover that I was about to share rooms with one of the most famous students on campus. He also had his own vehicle. I later discovered that his mother was a school principal and his father, a prominent businessman in Montego Bay. He also had a brother who was big in the national sports fraternity. Hugh Solomon himself, was later to become mayor of Montego Bay. I wondered why they had a young man as poor as a church rat, sharing dorm with Hugo. I later concluded that just probably, it was time that I forgot that poor background thinking and learned to live my new life as a middle class or one on the verge of so being defined.

We started to trickle into the Multipurpose Hall of the college which we had earlier visited. We had stored our belongings there temporarily prior to being escorted to our dorms and rooms. In a few minutes, the hall was full to capacity with students, lecturers, and others. There was music playing and everyone was surely in high spirit. Suddenly, the stereo fell dead and live voices tripped in, and through the air.

"Give it to me, one time, uh. Give it to me, two times, uh. Give it to me, three times, uh, uh, uh."
Arthur Gilling (Leo), Mark Reid, Glendon Lawrence, with the rest of the singing group, sounded almost like the professional

184

Toots and the Maytals whose song they were singing, to set the party off.

The entire first year group of students was up and its feet. They were totally and completely in a frenzy. In general, one Maxine Ritchie was dancing so well, as great as a mad ants! She really had the structured and well timed, organized steps and moves going through. The girls screamed so loudly and jumped so high and wildly, you could not but feel sorry for the plump little bosoms as they weaved back and forth in restrained bras. I quietly wished if only they could have restrained, in the same way, they had restrained their nice-looking bosoms under those air-stifling braziers. By right, only fair. Restrict one, then restrict all, or simply, restrict zero. Let everyone and everything go wild, I thought in my big-sized head.

I listened keenly and realized that they were uttering names such as Pressa, Leo, Farmer-dog, Marko, and Laro. These were, in fact, aliases and pet names. Pressa and Leo were other names for Arthur Gilling, the lead singer. Farmer-dog and Marko referred to Mark Reid, and Laro was another name for Glendon Lawrence. They must have learnt those student-teachers' names during the orientation that was held earlier for all incoming freshers, but I did not attend.

As the show continued, members in the audience were called upon to do their thing. The short, stocky-built Glendon Lawrence reappeared on stage. It seemed he had gathered some more confidence from being part of the opening group. He started to sing. Frankly, I was not one to have given out compliments the way politicians gave out money during the election seasons, but I have to say, the guy sang like a nightingale, and I could not have helped but to acknowledge that fact. Albeit, merely in my, by then, big-sized head.

I suddenly wondered whether those student-teachers should have been embarking on a career of teaching as much as they should have been sharpening their skills to have been professional entertainers. Suddenly, it dawned on me that teachers did need to be entertainers. How else could they be able to capture and maintain the attention of their pupils whose attention spans were usually short, or who probably had no interests in that which the teacher would be endeavouring to instill in their minds? I thought.

I, too, got caught up in the frenzy and excitement. I started gradually to do a couple of my moves. Probably a few of those I had exhibited those years as a five-year old at my father's Hart Street business place. I noticed that I had the attention of a few of my peers. I wondered if they were going to, at least, shout, "Joshua!" or "Ricky!" or clapped or something. I knew by then that I was too old to have been rewarded with candies (sweeties) or given a few cents for my excellent performance. I had also forgotten that I was not at the college's orientation; no one would have known my name, anyway.

I slowed to a gradual standstill to realize that they were yet calling for volunteers to show off their unique talents. I thought about doing my not-too-long-ago written poem, *Daddy*. I imagined reciting it, probably, reading the first stanza:

Daddy, the very word sounds strange

Slipping through my quivering lips, estranged

Endeavouring to escape a child's lonesomeness

Desiring your stern masculine voice

To make me happy, make me rejoice

Daddy just uttering the word, makes me daze

Reminder of a missed phase.

I imagined the females among the group suddenly got damped eyes. I imagined reading on, to the second stanza.

Daddy, you were long gone before your murderers attacked

Forthrightly, the moment you walked out the door

And turned your back

No hugs, no kisses, no rocks

Daddy, I longingly wished that even then, you were back.

I imagined the macho guys started to hurl curse words, questioning, rather, commenting that no manly person should engage in writing poetry. I immediately and suddenly remembered the opposition and struggle I had faced in acquiring a traditional education even though, a mere three years of it. I thought of how, had I given up, I would not have been on a path of tertiary education that would result in my acquiring a worthy profession and career, perhaps later to culminate in my being promoted to the position of principal, just like my Uncle Ben who had enslaved me. An uncle who treated me like something that sounds close to shaving cream. I said to myself that I was indeed beginning to see trails of success, albeit, along a very tedious and rugged path.

I resumed reciting the poem to its conclusion in my head, my big head. My imagination led me to the sounds of a deep and disturbing roar. There were a few well-thinking ones who congratulated me, probably not so much for the quality of the poem, but for my courage.

But what was there of which I should be afraid? I thought. I recalled the great and world-renowned Shakespeare and Charles Darwin, a formidable scientist of his time. Charles Darwin even used poetry to express his scientific theories and findings.

I moved a couple of steps forward to have made my reading/reciting of *Daddy* more than my mere thoughts and imagination but a reality. It was just too late. The show had come to an end.

In retrospect, I was glad I did not start off my college life with the sharing of that poem with my peers. My three-year stint at the institution would have been mired in all kinds of questions and my life would have become an open book as it will now after the publication of this work. Now is the time for it. I am now almost fifty years and do have the mettle to take, endure, and survive the inherent scrutiny that is bound to follow.

Reading that poem would have led to too many things being disclosed too soon. I would have had to explain the reason I wrote the poem. That my father had left my mother. That I was born a bastard under the then Constitution of Jamaica at the time. I would have had also to explain that he was shot and thrown in a pool to drown and later actually died. I can also imagine the numerous other questions that would have been thrown at me like a baseball pitcher to a batter, at a time when I needed all my energy in travelling upon and through this trail of success. These questions, undoubtedly, would have denuded my life among hundreds of prospective teachers.

Today, I think everything happens for a good purpose in life, and maybe, just maybe, there is some truth in this old adage, that it always appears darkest when there is about to be daylight.

Sam Sharpe Teachers' College was a special run institution by Dr. Simon Clarke who, though not being born in Panama, was not merely committed to the institution but was totally and completely committed to Jamaica as well. He had served in various capacities on several Jamaican boards and had even hosted the popular talk show known as *The Public Eye*, on Fridays as well as *Panorama on Education* on Sunday afternoons.

The uniqueness of the institution stemmed from the fact that it was one of self-sufficiency. The student-teachers were all involved in producing most, if not all of what we ate during my stint at the institution. This was something that the Michael Manley Government of the Democratic Socialist P.N.P. was encouraging at the time. Students were involved in rearing pigs, rearing hens for poultry and eggs, among other productive endeavours. Normally, it was the practice that in public, tertiary institutions, students would be hungry or got thinner than when the ate at home, but our experience at the Sam Sharpe Teachers' College was quite the opposite. I was as big as a pig ready to be butchered.

In addition to the above, the principal led by example. He was a role model, second to none. I remember an instant when a group of students, including myself, stood by some sprawling garbage on the ground. Dr. Simon Clarke greeted us politely without saying a word about the garbage, which he proceeded to clean up off the ground. We felt so badly and so much guilt that we all started to help for which he thanked us very much for our assistance. He never commented on why the garbage was there or why we did not see it fit to clean up our property before he arrived.

The college is also located in what, at the time, could have been considered a very depressed area. Initially, the community of Grandville, just outside Montego Bay, viewed the institution as foreign to them and we, the students and lecturers were seen as enemies. I guess we were seen as belonging to rich people's institution in a way. The same views I had several years ago about traditional high schools and tertiary level institutions such as the University of the West Indies, the University of Technology (formerly, CAST), and to some extent, teachers' colleges which, at the time, were all part of the Joint Board of Teacher Education run by the University of the West Indies.

But back to the situation at Grandville and the initial relationship with its tertiary institution in Sam Sharpe Teachers' College. The only difference with my former views and theirs, was that I did not exhibit indifference, nor did I harbour any grudge as to wanting to harm the members of these institutions. I was not like that, probably because I was not raised that way. Dr. Simon Clarke saw an opportunity to change that apparent view perceived by some members of that community. He set up meeting with community leaders and launched sporting events between the Sam Sharpe Teachers' College and the Grandville community. Soon, the perception to the college was changed. The so-called bad guys, gunmen even, would now protect student-teachers if anyone tried to harass us in our commute back and forth between the communities. As the years went by, there were even students enrolled at the college who, like, myself, had come from the dearth and girth of poverty, only that this time the community's name was not New Mills but Grandville. Also, as I knew it at the time, there were no known existence of guns in New Mills. Unfortunately, this was not true for the community in which our educational institution called home at the time.

The college also had a complementary staff, among whom were Dr. Cecile Walden, Mrs. Mighty, Mrs. Stephenson, Dr. Blossom Stokes, Dr. Low, et al.

The college's program of teacher education was quite good. Students had a thorough exposure to contemporary findings and pedagogy and the ways in which children and adolescents learn. There was also great content focus, especially for student-teachers who were reading to teach at the secondary education level.

Sports was an integral part of the college's curriculum. I immediately got involved in almost all sporting activities even if I sucked at it. In cases where I was not a direct participant, I would be around the teams to provide support.

Sport days were the most competitive engagements we had at the institution. The entire Grandville and adjacent communities would come to observe the athletes. I remember on this particular sports day being involved in the 4 x 400 metre relay race. I was to anchor my team. I was considered an underdog. However, the star runner, Glendon

Lawrence (Laro) and others had to admire the back of my sweaty neck, all the way through the finished line as I flew through like a bird.

One very interesting thing happened one year as I was supposed to represent Sam Sharpe Teachers' College at the Annual College Champs held at the National Stadium in Kingston, Jamaica's capital. First, it must be told that I had trained all season for this event. I was told that I would have been running the 1500M, possibly the 800M as well. I trained like a dog. I actually dreamt of me winning this event at the championship. The day before we were supposed to leave for Kingston, our coach, Mr. Jackson, decided that he was going to give me a 'dry run' with a very great athlete called Aubrey Campbell. Aubrey Campbell worked at the then JBC Radio West Station at the time, if my memory serves me correctly.

It happened that during this so-called 'dry run' with Aubrey Campbell, the gentleman had no mercy on me. I thought he would have found out the real reason that Coach Jackson requested of me, and me only, to run in a race with a top-notch athlete as he was. However, Aubrey was intent that he was going to treat this two-man race as if he were competing with eight or more world class athletes at the World's Olympics. He made me look like a fool on the track, doubling me like children wrapping toilet tissues around their arms as they defaecate.

Due to this golden performance by Aubrey Campbell, the coach decided that he was not going to take me with the team. How could the coach have done such a thing to me? Here was a young man who was committed to the task I was asked to do. I put in two hundred percent, but the coach did not see it fit to reward me by letting me go with the team. What about rewarding someone for effort and determination? I thought. My thinking was that there would not have been any athlete at the championship at the teachers' college level who could perform as well as Aubrey. I questioned why he had to use that to determine whether I ran for my college or not. I was devastated! I thought the coach hated me, or he probably was spying on me. He knew that my girlfriend was coming with the posse to see me perform.

That precisely was the big problem here. I had told my new girlfriend who now lived in Kingston, that I would be running at the National Stadium for my college. She had, in turn, invited all her friends to come to watch her boyfriend run. Some of whom had either stopped from school or made great sacrifices to go to see their friend's boyfriend representing the Sam Sharpe Teachers' College. I felt like a fish out of water when the coach stared me in the face to say he would not take me. The entire college also thought that I was going with the team, so guess what I did?

The entire time the team was away, I locked up in my dorm. I hardly breathed because I did not want anyone to know that I was in my room. I understood that my new girlfriend and her posse walked and looked everywhere for me to no avail. I was literally disgraced. To this day, I had never forgiven Coach Jackson for his indiscretion in the way he handled the matter. It should be no surprise then how elated I was when I heard that our team did poorly. The jubilation and utter joy I experienced at the time were out of this world! Today, Coach Jackson is among the 5,000 Facebook friends I have. I always wonder if he remembers this incident.

My years at Sam Sharpe Teachers' College were always quite eventful. I remember one night lying on my back in my room when my roommate, Hugh Solomon, invented, disseminated, and propagated a scandal that has lived with me to this day. Now listen to me. We were both in the room, the ceiling light on, but somehow this guy thought it funny to make up a story. He then called down the whole floor to our room. He told them that I was doing the 'm-word'. I could not believe my ears. To this day, all my friends from the college era, refer to me as 'Fista'. Thanks to Hugo for this name.

There was also another incident while on one of our many trips, to and from a little fun-spot my Uncle Man in Top Grandville operated. We had a serious mishap. The night in question, we had had a few drinks. So, we decided that one of our friends who did not drink, his father being a minister of religion (pastor), would drive us home. My 'brother' Oliver had ridden a motorcycle that night and led the way, as we drove to the different homes dropping off people at their respective homes. Upon approaching a deep corner in a district known as Roehampton, the car just flashed off the road and overturned, sitting on its top. We managed to get out the car unscathed, turned the car back onto its four wheels and went home.

It seemed that college life had brought back the mischievousness that I had from my younger years. During the seventies, there was a group of pre-trained teachers in the system who had not been college trained. This was basically due to the fact that they did not meet the basic matriculation requirements of which I alluded earlier in this book. Again, the government thought that it would give these teachers a chance to be trained. It looked at it from the standpoint that pre-trained teachers were already in the system. The government thought that these teachers might as well benefit from proper training so as to be in a greater position to teach our children.

This was how the ISTETH Program was introduced. Pre-trained teachers of a certain number of years service would now get the opportunity to join the younger people coming straight from high schools. The latter group was much younger and more knowledgeable from an academic perspective.

I can recall that our college took in about four of these candidates the year I was accepted. These candidates were teased and harassed a lot. I don't know how they coped. In general, they also found the work more challenging than the average student. I can recall just staring on one of these new gentlemen who could have been no less than fifty years old and my dad, and blurted out,

"Ancient, why are you looking at me?"

The name had stuck on this gentleman and others of his ilk, that the only names these men were known as were the aliases that we splattered all over them.

It happened that one day, Ancient's wife and grown children had come by on campus to visit him. When they inquired of him using his correct name, everyone on campus said they knew of no such student-teacher. It was a female student who pointed out unashamedly in front of the 'Ancient family' that they were looking for Ancient. I felt very sad that I had started something like that. It only shows that when one is part of a group, one has to be cautious. The group can really cause one to do things of which one would normally not be engaged, had they not been a part of the given social setting.

The first year of teachers' college had come to an end. I, and seventeen others, were sent to the college's second campus in the city and in the heart of Montego Bay. This was where I was to spend my second year of my studies in this institution. I am sure that you will never believe this coincidence. The Sam Sharpe teachers' College had taken over the Pemco Hotel. This is where they were about to send me to begin my second year of teachers' college. It was just incredible. I was going to see and live in the hotel that my dad had worked for years as well as lost his life. I was going to bathe in the swimming pool of which my father's body was dumped just a few year ago. I was going to be looking at the swimming pool everyday, the pool in which my dad's body was recovered floating. I was going to have to put up with this striking memory for a full academic year. How would I cope? Would I go? What would be my end?

September of 1980, all eighteen of us moved into the Pemco Hotel campus now operated by the Sam Sharpe Teachers' College. The building was quite nice and fancy and unlike the Grandville campus, we had a swimming pool. Yes, the same swimming pool in which my dad was found years earlier. We were also in close proximity to a lot of fun places. There was the Overton Plaza, just one minute away by foot. The then Fletcher's Beach was not too far away either, near to a little area known as Lovelorn, close to the Fletcher's Bleach where lovers would go to cuddle. I thought I would really need a lot of discipline in this huge luxury hotel, being virtually on our own if I was going to complete teachers' college successfully. There were just too many distractions, including the bitter memory of my dad being murdered there.

I explored the buildings on the campus the very first day I set foot on it. I am now experiencing some difficulties identifying each building and its use. However, I think I can recall that there were a number of detached buildings outside of the main hotel structure. If memory serves me correctly, one of the buildings had both a pool table and a skittle table. There were also a sort of lecture room and a pantry in one of the buildings where students would sometimes prepare their own meals if they cared to do so. The buildings formed an arc, not too far from the swimming pool, and opposite the main building. The ground floor of the main building in which we would stay, had a nice lounge which was well carpeted. It was also air conditioned as were the rooms in which we would be staying. There were telephones and television sets inside the lounge as well. I also think there was a stereo in this area as well. In our bedrooms, it was like heaven. The shower was clean and sparkly, and we had shower curtains now to protect against the unsuspecting voyeurs' eyes. There was a beautiful balcony on which to sit. It was decorated with chairs all suitable to provide luxurious comfort and to provide us the full view of the external aesthetics of our milieu. This included the buildings described above, and the ironic, beautiful, and serene swimming pool which was to serve as the catalyst of my father's death and the last medium in which he would expend his last breath as a human being. The rooms were massive in my eyes. Each room held two to three beds quite comfortably. My bedroom had three beds, so I shared bedroom with two roommates in Lambert Robinson, now the principal of the Anchovy Comprehensive High School and David Robinson. The two were not biologically related. It is my understanding that David Robinson has now passed. However, I have not personally verified this as true.

The walls of the balcony were made of glass with slide doors. Initially, prior to our getting used to the glass walls, one would think we were playing a new kind of sports called 'Running Into Glass Wall', probably whose aim was to decipher that which it takes to get a pane of glass broken. Would it take a thick physique propelled with lightning speed? Would it take the mass of an elephant-like structure with tremendous force but not as strong as the former in velocity? We would crash into the slide glass every single attempt at going through them to the balcony. For one reason or the other, our rich-people-trained, high school mind, now college, could not figure out how to go through a glass wall, bearing glass door. We had not the genius to have thought that the problem could have been solved simply by leaving the glass slide door open. It seemed that there was some truth to the saying, the more you learn, the less you know. I guess commonsense is not something that can be taught either by rich-people, high school, or college. It did take some time, but gradually we soon got adjusted and avoided those blows.

It is true that which Sir Isaac Newton had postulated some time ago. The fact that, to every action, there is an equal and opposite reaction. The harder we ran into the glass wall, the more pain we experienced and the greater the silly wall seemed to have pushed us back, wanting, perhaps, to break our loins for our dumbness. At first, I didn't know how they did not get broken or us being chopped up like meat for supper. And guess what, it would have been well deserved.

I sat back for awhile to relax and to take in the reality of that which was about to happen to me. I fell in a sort of trance. I imagined my dad walking into his office, with briefcase in hand. He was wearing grey pants, white shirt with probably a plain tie. I saw him sit at his desk. He then got up quickly for a cup of coffee. He eased back in his somewhat easy-chair of his office. He then took a sip of his coffee and made a quiet, covered-mouth burp, looked around, saw no one, so he did not bother to say, "Excuse me." He scanned a few pages, entered a few ledgers, then suddenly, a shadow crossed his path.

"Put your hands up in the air, and don't move, if you want to see your son through rich-people school," one of two men shouted, pointing a gun to the left side of his chest.

The other walked militantly towards him, with what appeared to have been a handwritten note. My dad read it and shook his head. To that response, the guy with the note slapped him hard in the face. He staggered back, somewhat from the blow, partially from the shock. This assault was quickly followed by a spate and flood of Mohammed Ali-like punches and Bruce lee-like kicks in the face, abdomen, and chest.

They then took up my partially dead dad like a loaf of stale bread. They then shot him in the abdomen, grabbed and dragged him quietly and quickly and threw him in the swimming pool.

The manager heard slight screams of cry for help and walked over to daddy's office, but he was gone. However, upon looking over the balcony and seeing the criminals moving away from the swimming pool, the manager seemed to have nodded and winked approvingly at them. Shortly after he called the police.

I suddenly jumped from my daze, even more perplexed and confused. I wondered why I was having a nightmare during the day. I knew my second year in teachers' college was going to be a challenge. I was not thinking so much from the perspective of the academic requirements, teaching practice, and other college related demands. I was thinking to the extent of the mental and psychological strain that would be constantly stirred up in my head, because of having taken up residence in the source of my father's death.

I had never told anyone of my father being murdered at the Pemco Hotel other than my 'brother', Oliver Nelson. However, not even Oliver, my closest friend, knew what I was enduring or my rugged past. I masked all the pains and wounds well, with laughter and by poking fun at everyone, anything, and anyone.

I was a natural when it came to making and giving jokes. In a way, when I made others laugh, it was therapeutic for my soul, my being. No one ever dreamt of the deep pain that I endured deep inside, deep within. No one ever knew the numerous times I cried like a baby in the shower when I was alone, or when the lights were out at Pemco, and no one could have distinguished between the tears on one's face from vaseline on there, to keep it moist. I was constantly reflecting on my life. Why was I born? Was it simply to suffer? Was I a product of retaliation for the wrongs my parents and forefathers have done? Was I cursed? There were numerous questions that constantly permeated my mind. I wondered if it was just mere chance that I found myself living at the precise geographical location that my father was murdered. Was it just simply mere chance that I would be getting this bitter and heart-wrenching opportunity to see, every day, the swimming pool in which my father's dead body was retrieved? I wondered where was the God that my Mammy talked about all the time. I wondered what happened to the teachings that his children would not suffer unbearably. If my suffering was not unbearable, what was? I thought.

One Saturday, we were just relaxing outside, on the Pemco Hotel Campus. Some of us were just lazing in the sun. Others were just talking foolishness as usual. There was one Dudley Jennings, also known as Puss among the group. A few of the hardworking ones must have been working on assignments. David Robinson and Lambert Robinson must have been among this cohort. However, I can't recall for sure whether they were present that day. I sat staring at the swimming pool, some distance away, when I felt a sudden but strange impetus to go closer to it. I had never had that urge before. First, I knew my father died in that swimming pool. That fact of itself, created a chaste feeling toward swimming in the pool, or even going in close proximity to it. The second reason was that I was not a great swimmer. This could have been because of my very close call with nearly being drowned, returning from Stonehenge and walking across the shortcut in Huntley to Berkshire. That close call and experience with the Simon River, had certainly been in the back of my mind for some time now, even though I had swum on occasions.

I suddenly walked towards the swimming pool and shouted to my friends that my dad had drowned in it some years ago. I found it strange that I was making that announcement. I don't think my friends understood what I was saying though. I then suddenly plunged to the deepest part of the swimming pool. Dudley Jennings stared in disbelief and shock. I had on my regular clothes. Everyone thought that I was just being my usual silly, Fista self. Since my former roommate, Hugh Solomon, gave me the name, that was how my batchmates and friends addressed me. I was called Fista. Lo and behold, I was drowning. I started to bob and weave when Spratt (Dannavan Morrison, he was an excellent swimmer, and I might add, cricketer, saw that I was actually drowning and rushed in to save me. To date, I am not sure how to explain what had happened. Had I suddenly gotten suicidal? Was there a spell over me? Was I just being stupid and almost lost my life for it, or did I just need a little excitement and attention?

I had just returned from the Grandville campus to the Pemco hotel campus. I was training and was quite sweaty, dirty, and smelly. I was either dropped off at the downtown campus by my 'brother', Oliver Nelson, in his yellow Falcon, later to be known as the 'Heavy Door' because of an incident with Spratt (Dannavan Morrison) or I had gotten a ride with my former roommate, Hugh Solomon, in his green Fiat. Whichever was the mode of transportation that evening, I was extremely dirty. I was even somewhat smelly from the mixture of sweat, grime, and mud. Upon disembarking from the vehicle with a bunch of equally dirty, sweaty, and grimy batchmates, I saw this very beautiful, Indian lady, about a year or so, younger than me.

"Good afternoon, nice lady. Are you here to see me?" I asked.

The young lady ignored me and kept on walking. I pursued her as she walked towards the lounge, located on the lower floor, outside of the main hotel building. She took a second, or probably, her first sustained glance at me for a full second. She then covered her nose and proceeded to the lounge area.

"Are you here to see one of us?" I insisted to find out.

"What's wrong with you?" she yelled.

The young woman was obviously either full of herself or just being a fool. How could a nice-looking woman like her not being attracted to a sweet, handsome, and educated guy like me? I thought. I shouldn't have to explain anything to this woman. She was on our property, a property of young, educated students but more importantly, handsome, irresistible men, I thought. She was on our property, a male dominated campus. We were young educators, or at least in the making, I continued to think in my big, macho head. Any woman who came on this ground, if they were not relatives to any of us, must be in search of a guy or two, I thought.

I used the towel which hung loosely from my neck, imitating my long, dripping, yellow shorts, to clean away some of the sweat, mud, and grime from my drained face, legs, and arms. I noticed she gave me another glance, but this time the glance was more sustained. I even thought I saw a sheepish smile with her lips pressed somewhat nervously, to prevent revealing two rows of very white, front teeth which she was unable to conceal that time. I stepped back an arm's length, to give her some personal space. I also wanted to lessen the strong stench and odour that were radiating from my adhesive, steam-like skin. I was beginning to imagine the bacteria on my skin, now hoping to take up permanent residence and were fighting each other for a meal or two.

"I am really sorry. My original approach was quite rude and crude," I muttered.

"It takes a gentleman to apologize, especially with friends in sight," she said.

I knew I was getting somewhere. I started to use the towel more frequently around my neck to move little bits of dirt and spots here and there. I looked down on my left leg and saw a bit of dried mud that looked somewhat like the single cell amoeba as perceived under a microscope. I tried to remove it, penetrating through its outer protective membrane into its protoplasm to get to its nucleus. I saw her look at me questioningly, and I came to my senses.

At some point during our conversation, I found out that she had inadvertently come to the wrong place. I told her where she was, and she was quite surprised. I asked her if she could just give me a few minutes to clean up and that I would have been back, probably to show her where she had intended to go. Probably, to sweep her off her feet.

That was the fastest shower I had ever taken. I cleaned up, combed my afro hair, brushed my teeth, rolled on some roll-on, put on a decent pair of jeans and a T-shirt, a pair of sneakers, and down the stairs I ran.

Her eyes lit up like a stadium bulb when she looked at me. This time she did not attempt to hide her admiration of me. I knew then and there that I was not just being a guy thinking the macho way. It wasn't merely me thinking conquer, exploit, but I knew she really liked what she saw in a clean and refreshed me.

She had one of the most beautiful smiles I had ever seen. Her eyes were full, and she was a really sexually appealing lady who exhibited some sporadic quality and signs of intellect and smarts at the same time. Probably a little street 'smarts' as well, perhaps even more than me.

"What plans do you have for the rest of the evening?" I inquired.

She pretended not to have heard my questions. I said to myself, Fista, take it easy. Don't spoil everything now. Women don't like when guys appear to be desperate. Take it easy, Fista, I repeated inside my big head.

It turned out her name was Beverley Ramjeet. She was, in fact, from Montego Bay and resided at her brother's home in the outskirts of the city. Her brother, at the time we met, worked at the Gleaner's Western Office on Union Street, next door to Pemco which was located on East Street. The Jamaica Gleaner is the esteemed national newspaper and was founded in 1834, just about the onset of the Apprenticeship System, which was the start of freedom for former slaves, my paternal fore-parents. They would have become fully free on August 1, 1838 as you learned earlier. Beverley had spent several years in Canada and had returned home to live permanently. I wondered why she would have left Canada, but I did not bother to ask her.

As I looked at Beverley, and at least tried to listen to her sweet voice as I stared at her lovely face, for awhile, my mind started to stray. First, I imagined my maternal grandmother, Adina Topping in our midst, looking on and taking stock. I imagined her feeling proud that I had made an effort to date someone who looked more like her. I said, even though I had not met my maternal grandmother, she would have felt proud that I had made an effort to have her represented in my home. I envisioned two beautiful, mixed children, a boy and a girl. These two growing up to be a doctor and a lawyer, respectively. I also visualized us being upper middle-class folks, and accordingly, our children had no problems acquiring the scholarships to rich-people schools. I also thought of the reluctance her side of the family might have exhibited against us joining the knot. In essence, was my thought, her brothers and sisters could have rightly claimed that they had come way across the globe too, but they had never been labelled the dirty word, 'slaves'. They were a notch up on us, being so-called indentured servants who worked for a stipend (salary).

I jumped out of my deep daydreaming and realised that Beverley had actually held onto one of my hands. I squeezed it gently to let her know that I recognised her affection, we both moved our heads forward, eyes closed, when there were footsteps heard coming towards the lounge. We suddenly rose and walked to the door.

"Ricky, are you going to walk me to the gate?" she asked.

"My pleasure," I grinned.

I walked her to, and through the gate, possibly through to her heart. We ended up that evening in an area downtown Montego Bay that was called the Lovelorn. It was an open area, but it seemed all the lovebirds had gone there to cuddle and do whatever else lovers do. We looked around and found a somewhat secluded spot. We embraced and started to share our experiences. I wondered how I was so open to someone I barely knew. She told me of her parents' death, and I traded my father's death. She told me of her ordeal in Canada, and I returned the story of my ordeal in Jamaica in the hands of relatives and an economic system that was not yet ready to embrace all, with equal opportunities. We cried on each other's shoulders and wiped away each other's tears literally and figuratively. I thought I had found the right lady and she thought I was the only man on the planet, at least that unforgettable evening.

Our relationship strengthened. We were full and complete lovers, and everything was going fine. She would continue to visit me, and we would continue to go to the Lovelorn.

Sometimes, we would even visit my uncle in Granville, Uncle Man (James Robinson). Uncle Man was a very kind and understanding uncle and he would allow us some privacy in his nice little home. He would even prepare meals and send us drinks while we had some quality time together. As the months elapsed, I began to sense some strange occurrences between us. First, the time we saw each other would gradually get less and less. Then when we met, she always seemed to have had other things on her mind. The relationship was just not the same as before. Here were two young people who had had similar struggles. Two individuals who had laid their cards on the table. I had told her everything about me, including my dire poverty. She had told me everything too. We were lovers and dear friends but suddenly things were changing. Days, even weeks, would have passed and she did not call me or visit me at Pemco Hotel. Sometimes, I would be walking on the Montego Bay streets and just run into her by accident. She was usually with other people including guys. She would tell me that they were her brothers' and sisters' friends. I had no way to know. For one reason or the other, she never officially introduced me to her family (meaning her brothers and sisters. I started to think if it had anything to do with the fact that I was black and she was Indian but I never brought up the subject.

Again, one day, I ran into her in a Woolworth store in Montego Bay. She gave me the same old excuse. One argument led to the next. She decided to cite things with which she had grown uncomfortable in our relationship. She finally said that she noticed that I had an incisor that had a small cavity, and that she was turned off by it. I asked her why she had not pointed it out to me all along. She said that was not the only reason. I realized that the love was growing freezing cold, probably, over. Equally as the little cavity of a tooth near to the front of my mouth, must have been getting progressively worse. I turned away with great sadness in my heart and tears in my eyes. I explained to her that I had loved her very much and thought the feeling was reciprocated. I went back to the Pemco Hotel and wrote this poem to express my grief and loss.

Are You Really Gone?

Why did we meet that day we met?

Now only to be left in the cold

I am left alone

Honey, are you gone?

A romance that lightens

And brightens my dull day

A love we shared everywhere

But suddenly my emotions

Are crying out for sympathy

As I have to ask

Are you gone?

How do we compensate

For the wasted days?

What will we do with our few memories?

I guess it's the inevitable

You have got to leave

But still I have got to ask

Are you really gone?

My joys are suddenly flowing

In the sorrow stream

My days are changing to moonless nights

As I watch you gradually

And surely going out of sight

Am I seeing right?

Are you really gone?

Dear God, if it is thy will

So, let it be

But God, help me to remain sane

I am feeling this terrible love pain

Oh God, I have still got to ask

Are you really gone?!

Just three months prior to my starting to write this autobiography (May 2009), I received an e-mail from Beverley Ramjeet. She said she had been looking for me. She outlined that she had a notion to check out the social websites in search of me and ran into me on Facebook. Currently, she resides in Bermuda, she said, and we have promised to keep in touch.

It was now the beginning of my third year of teachers' college. One Maxine Ritchie and I had been placed at the then Montego Bay Secondary School to complete our full year of internship training at this institution. I was going to be teaching Science and Physical Education for the school year while Maxine would teach Home Economics. Even though we taught at the same school, we scarcely saw each other, as we were placed on different shifts in the school. I was on the morning shift and my batch-mate, Maxine Ritchie, the afternoon shift. The country and city had just passed through a rough general election in which over eight hundred people, including children, had lost their lives. The school was not too far from the depressed areas. The October 30 election of 1980 had left some bitter tastes in some people's mouths as well as guns in their hands, adults, and children alike. So bad were the behaviour in the area in general, and the behaviour of some students, not all I must point out here, but a few significant enough, that an armed police officer had to be stationed at the school every school day.

During the third-year internship period, the college no longer was responsible for providing us with accommodation. We had to get somewhere to live on our own. I boarded at a home located at 12 ½ Kerr Crescent, Montego Bay for the first few months of my internship.

This was the home of the Chief Justice of Jamaica's father, Mr. Frank Smith. The then Chief Justice of Jamaica, at the time, was his son, Chief Justice Kenneth Smith. The home was quite great and the food well prepared with fine accommodation. Unlike Mrs. Brown's boarding, here all I had to do was to pay for the boarding. However, I just could not have a life. I felt like I was in a prison. It was difficult to take all my friends or my female associates there.

In passing, let me mention that it was while I resided at this 12 ½ Kerr Crescent address that I met Grace Lawrence, the sister of one of my close friends, Glendon Lawrence, while visiting his home. My friend's sister was also being trained to become a teacher, but it was in Kingston, more than a hundred miles away from where I was living and teaching at the time. Notwithstanding, we developed a very great relationship. We kept the relationship kindled and glowing at first, by writing extremely long letters to each other, and by making extremely long and costly phone calls at each other's shared expenses. We were deeply in love with one another. However, due to religious differences, we had broken off. It would have been many years later that we were to meet again to resume our relationship. Unfortunately, our second effort at love did not last. It apparently was not meant to be. It was all due to my fault. Grace and I, even subsequent to our second break up, maintained a certain amount of platonic relationship but these days, not as much as in the past. I guess, she is no longer interested in a platonic relationship with her old friend. We might have outgrown each other, even though we once had what I regarded as a cherished relationship on a platonic level. I hope she will read these few words and realized that she is still considered a dear friend, and that she is greatly missed.

Dannavan Morrison, also known as Spratt, had met a Japanese gentleman whose name I think was Ike. He was a leader for a religious sect and he and his wife lived at a large home in the Brandon Hill area of the city. Dannavan, at the time, was interested in a place to live. Since he had started his internship training at the Mount Alvernia High School, he had not been successful in finding a suitable, convenient, and affordable apartment in which to live. Ike, apparently had an interest in converting Spratt and whomever else he could, to his faith. He offered free accommodation to Spratt to live at his home which was owned and paid for by the religious organization of which Ike belonged. Dannavan had recalled that I had said that I wanted to move from my then residence at the Kerr Crescent address, so he told Ike about me. Ike agreed that we could move in together which we did. One Saturday,

I was home alone when a young lady came to visit me. Dannavan was not home. I invited the young lady inside our home. The following day, Sunday, I was in my bed snoring and emitting flames as if from hell, when Dannavan awoke me to advise that Ike wanted to speak to us. Ike had a poor command of the English Language. He had just recently arrived from his homeland, Japan whose native language as we know is not English.

"You are boo fire," he shouted.

"What do you mean?" I asked.

"I say you are gone, house, now," Ike tried to explain.

"I didn't gone house," Spratt tried to sound like Ike.

"Spratt just went to play chess at Mount Alvernia High School," I tried to help Spratt explain.

"No, no, no, I mean you fire, boo you, you are fire!"

"Do you mean that we are fired?" I asked.

"Yes, you're fire, boo you, fire," he repeated.

"No, we are not fired. Remember we don't work, we are students," Spratt and I said almost simultaneously.

All three of us were getting impatient that we were not being able to communicate well among us. I wondered what he was trying to say and so was Spratt. I tried to clarify.

"Ike, who told you that we are fired?" I asked.

"Me," he quipped

Ike was actually trying to say that Spratt and I were fired from the religious home. From his 'me' response, I suddenly got enlightened of what was going on and the reason he was firing us. I pretended not to have understood though, as I did not want Spratt to be cognizant of what was going on. I knew Spratt would have been outraged. He had all right to be. Spratt that is, but certainly not Ike, I thought.

"Ike, sorry, we have to go," I tried to be smart.

"No, no, no. Take clothes from house, clothes, shoes, books, now," he uttered.

Spratt had by now understood that Ike was in fact asking us to leave the missionary house. However, what Spratt did not understand at that moment, was the reason we were being asked to leave what I now considered the Convent.

"Ike, why boo of us fire?" asked Spratt, trying to imitate Ike's way of speaking for better comprehension.

"Joshua took girl yesterday, girl stayed long," he replied.

Spratt very light-skinned face turned pink as he stared at me. I wanted the concrete ground on which I stood to swallow me in, but I knew that was impossible.

"How could you have been so inconsiderate?" Spratt screamed, looking at me.

"I did nothing," I defended.

"My friend came to visit me. I did not know that female friends were not supposed to visit me, visit us," I said.

"Don't be smart, Fista. This is not about a female friend visiting you," Spratt remarked.

"What are you saying?!" I screamed at Spratt.

"I am saying that you stayed too long with the girl!" he shouted.

"Now, you Spratt, big time 'swotter', you just be careful how you talk to me," I demanded.

"But look what you have done," Spratt said.

"I did not know I lived in a prison that I had to time how long my visitors stay," I chimed.

I realized that the argument was getting heated and regardless of the fact that I thought I did nothing wrong in having a visitor over my home, who stayed long, I tried to calm down. Our behaviour in front of Ike would certainly not help in getting him to have a change of heart, I thought. I also thought that we were being trained to become teachers, to mould hundreds, if not thousands of fragile, young minds that would be placed to our charges over decades, and yet there we were, unable to settle a little difference, a little fracas, amicably. It was as if Spratt was reading my mind because he uttered that it had already gone wrong and that there was no need to worry over spilt liquid. I agreed.

"Ike can you give us some time to find a place?" Spratt asked.

Ike agreed to give us one week to find a new place of abode. I felt terrible, not so much for me but for my colleague, Dannavan. He had tried so hard to get a place to live since we started our internship training. He had been bouncing around like a sponge ball. He finally got a place, and this was what happened. He could have moved in without sharing the news with me. However, he was kind enough to inform me of a house that we would be living, free. I wondered why Ike was not explicit in the terms of our accommodation at the Brandon Hill address from the onset. Was it as a reason of our communication problems? I wondered how many nations, races, and cultures have had similar conflicts because of misunderstandings and poor comprehension of each other. If not this reason, I thought, was it that initially he had no rules about visitors coming to see us, male or female, who would stay long or short? Was it some other reasons why we got fired? I thought. Did he ultimately feel that we were not convertible material for his faith? Did he feel we were irredeemable? All I knew for sure, was that our landlord must have been a great spy. I had no clue he was home at the time of my visitor's arrival. He must have perched on the roof like a bird, spying, hovering about with steady, unflappable wings. What would have motivated him to do that, I questioned?

I had started to search vigorously for a house to rent for both of us. I eventually found one on Church Street. The house was located at the intersection of Church Street and Dome Street if my memory serves me correctly. The rent was somewhat high, but we took it. Spratt and I lived there for awhile but soon the landlord got upset about too many visitors attending their house and once again, we were looking for a new home. I decided that I would not be sharing with Spratt in the next arrangement. I thought I was being a bad luck for Spratt or vice versa. I soon got a room of a house to rent on Tate Street. I think Spratt must have gotten accommodation at the Mount Alvernia High School, but I can't be sure about this information. The facts with respect to this matter, evaded my mind, at the time of writing.

I settled in well at my Tate Street address. For one, my home was just about five minutes or less away from the Montego Bay Secondary School. It was also near to the house of my 'brother''s girlfriend. His then girlfriend was Beverly. Beverly and Oliver had since gotten married and have produced three very beautiful and handsome children. The two boys, Kirk and Dirk, are now professionals as well as the girl, Olivia or Via. Kirk (Rahim) is now a medical doctor while Dirk is a banker. Olivia works in television.

At the end of my first month of internship at the then Montego Bay Secondary School (currently, St. James High School), I was in for a great shock. While I taught one of my science classes, one of the clerical staff members came to tell me that my mother was there to see me. I said to her that that could not be. I knew for sure that it could not have been my mother, because the previous two years of my college years when

I needed money or visitors, my mother was not among the few who stopped in or sent me even a note of encouragement. I asked the staff member to advise the person that I was unable to leave my class so she should either go, leave a message, or wait until it was break-time which would have come up shortly. She insisted that the individual was my mother because she thought I looked exactly like her. I still did not believe the person waiting was my mother. I thought that it could have been Mrs. Thompson. Mrs. Thompson was of a light complexion like my biological mother and myself. In the past, people sometimes commented that I resembled her as well.

The bell indicating that it was time for break, rang. I instructed my class to line up, of which a few obeyed. After everyone had left the classroom, I packed away my materials and nervously went to see who it was. It was in fact my mother. I could not believe the gall of this lady. She could not have found the time or the will to visit me, or even to send me a dollar while I studied in college, unemployed. However, the moment, she was told that I was teaching at Montego Bay Secondary School, she found me, I thought. I was extremely mad and told her my mind. She walked shamefully down the hill as I watched, refusing to say goodbye, apologize or ask her to return.

A few hours had passed, and I felt sorry for the way I had behaved, treated my mother but I was hurting deep inside. I had remembered how she told Mr. Lovell not to give me money to attend Manning's and now how she had not found me until she thought I was teaching and being paid. The reality was, that I was still an intern. We were being given a little stipend by the college. However, it was only enough to pay our rent, buy food, and probably watch a movie at the cinemas, occasionally. I thought that even if I had money that morning, I would not have given it to her, even if that was her goal.

It was sometime later that a more amicable relationship developed between my mother and myself. I subsequently visited her at her Stonehenge home many times, as will be seen in later chapters.

The then Montego Bay Secondary School as I said earlier was a tough school. Even with the policeman on duty at the main school gate all the time, the few students who had decided that they were going to be disruptive or challenging, continued with disregard for anyone. I remember a male teacher of Physical Education, currently a reporter with the Jamaica Gleaner newspaper, being threatened by a student with a huge gun. The teacher and I were in the staffroom at the time. The student came to the door and called the teacher by name, indicating that my colleague should go to meet him at the door. The student had a big, long bag that hung from his shoulder. He unzipped the bag and asked the teacher to look inside. Upon the teacher complying, he saw a huge gun in the student's bag. He warned the teacher to be careful because, according to him, if the teacher continued to disrespect him, he would have been a dead man. This is an example of the kind of challenges some teachers and other students had to confront at the school at the time. As a young teacher, I was really scared of some of the students. My inexperience as a teacher, did not help much at the time at all.

One day while I was attempting to teach another of my science classes, Joseph, not his real name, decided that he was going to put up a challenge to my authority as a young teacher.

"John, have you ever held a gun, boy?" he shouted across the classroom.

"You can't be talking like that in class," I reminded him.

"Do you think you are my mother?" he asked.

"As hell no! Don't you see I am a man? Do I look like a woman to you?" I asked.

Joseph continued to disrupt the class. And yes, he thought I looked like a woman. I wondered quietly if that was the reason some time ago, I was being picked up by a gay guy, but my thought was quickly interrupted from the constant bickering, chattering, and fooling around by Joseph. Being the inexperienced intern that I was, I continued arguing back and forth with Joseph. I finally decided that I had had enough, and went straight up in his face. That was the first wrong move on my part. Students don't want to feel embarrassed in the presence of their peers. Remember, the reason Joseph was already acting up in class probably had to do with his insecurities. His feelings of inadequacy and his groping for a feeling of importance and attention. My approaching him in his face, challenged that desire to be in control and the kind of powerhouse star that he wanted to reflect to his peers.

Joseph immediately swang his fist at my head and I just managed to elude its contact to my tough, big head. I wondered had it contacted, what the result would have been? Would it have resulted in Joseph acquiring, yes, acquiring, a broken arm and swollen knuckle, or would the contact knock me out flat, like my having just faced a Michael Tyson in a heavy weight showdown? The student cheering on the great Mike Tyson for the Knockout or better yet, the situation being viewed as a David and Goliath confrontation; a big, grown, masculine teacher and probably, one also seen as a bully, being slaughtered by a young student.

He pushed me away, probably to regain his personal space. I hung onto his arm. He flashed away and went outside. There was a sudden calm for about sixty or so seconds, and I felt that I had taught him manners. As of today, I thought, no student would be messing with me. Then suddenly my students screamed almost in unison.

"Mr. Spencer, duck, duck, duck, Mr. Spencer!"

Joseph had gone outside and had gathered enough rocks, tall enough to build the CN Tower. He was throwing them at me in the classroom like he was timing himself how quickly he could dismantle his well-built tower. I had to hide under the table and chair. I discovered that not only did I have excellent reflex and body flexibility under that table, jumping like a frog from each quick and scattered splash of rocks, but I was quite flexible and a lucky man in general. Quite a lucky teacher, indeed, I thought I was.

The noise had gotten quite loud and a teacher or two, might have overheard and/or seen the commotion and sent for both the policeman at the gate and the acting principal. Joseph had left the school when he realized that the acting principal and the police officer had both arrived at the scene. I related the incident to the acting principal with the police being present.

Joseph lived with his mother alone. However, it turned out that his father was a police officer who had been separated from his concubinage relationship with Joseph's mother. I also realized that Joseph's father was someone I had met before at a couple of functions. The acting principal thought that Joseph should have been expelled for his disrespect for me. He inquired how I felt about his plan and I suggested that he should invite his parents to the school to have a discussion re the matter. Subsequently, and during that same day, a general assembly should be called where Joseph would read a public apology to me in the presence of all the students of our shift. My suggestions were implemented, and the matter resolved with all parties very satisfied with the outcome.

My internship had come to an end. Many of my intern friends had acquired permanent teaching positions at their very prestigious schools. For example, Glendon Lawrence and Dannavan Morrison stayed on at Mount Alvernia High School to teach Spanish and Science, respectively, after completing their internship. I can't recall whether Maxine Ritchie had stayed on to teach permanently at the Monegot Bay

Secondary School or whether she had acquired a position at Montego Bay High School or Mount Alvernia. She currently resides in Canada like I do, but at the time of writing I felt ashamed to contact her to confirm the latter piece of information. I also wanted this book to be a surprise to her. The true reason though, was that we have not been in the habit of communicating with each other for awhile. However, I decided that I, for sure, was moving house. I sent out a couple of applications after checking the Jamaica Gleaner for available, advertised teaching positions. My first response came from the principal of the Maud McLeod High School in Darliston. The Principal of the school was one Mr. Noel Monteith who was to go on to become a formidable Jamaica Teachers' Association (J.T.A.) president, and later a senator and the Minister of State in Education. This was the district, years ago, that I had to run from New Mills to Darliston for the onset of the new life, to write my entrance exam to high school. I had thought that I would have been late after all the other students had left me, even though I was told the driver would have returned for me. I felt very confident about getting this teaching position though. I don't know if it had to do with the fact that my first, big success had been started in that community, but I just felt confident.

I contacted Mr. Monteith to confirm my interest in the position and for an interview date and time. Upon arriving at the school, I was quite impressed with the plant. The school was fairly new and was built by the M.P. for the then South Eastern Constituency, Mr. P.J. Patterson. Mr. Patterson had later gone on to become one of Jamaica's prime ministers. There were various departments, Mechanical Engineering, Agriculture, Science, Electrical Engineering, plumbing and Welding. Physical Education was also a big thing at the institution. There was a national volleyball team of which Maud McLeod was its home and the coach was Mr. Noel Monteith. Many team members played all around the world including the U.S.A. I remember one of its prominent players was Colin Hitchman, who was also a teacher at the school during my time there.

I walked into Mr. Monteith's office and noticed the various diplomas and certificates on its walls. I glanced at the diplomas, awards, trophies, etc., which revealed that this was a quite accomplished man academically. I also observed that he had read for both his Bachelors and Masters' degrees in Canada. I wondered why such an accomplished man returned to Jamaica. I concluded that he must have been quite committed to his country. I liked him very much for that reason. However, that was not the only reason that I admired the man. He was so calm and down-to-earth. I felt like I was just with the ordinary Joe. He smiled readily and was quite amicable. There was no scare tactic as some people of power usually employ to pitch an air of importance. All that kind of nonsense was non-existent with this man.

Mr. Monteith pulled out my application from a high pile, but neatly packed bunch of documents.

"Joshua, Mr. Spencer, I have an opening for a Science position for grades 9 through 11. This position will be available for two years only, initially, but one cannot be sure what will happen in two years," he said.

I made direct eye contact with the gentleman and sat uprightly, trying to appear confident and to appear intelligent. I thought it was a pity that I was not wearing glasses then. I had always heard that glasses make one look more scholarly. I nodded in approval to his statement.

"The regular teacher for this Science position will be pursuing further studies at the U.W.I. and will not be able to be at both places at the same time," he said.

I thought that this guy was funny. I started to feel so at home with this gentleman, that I started to think of him as just a guy, my buddy that I had just met.

"We have a great Science lab and the students will move to you there. You don't have to go from class to class. They come to you," he repeated.

Since this was my first teacher's interview, I started to think that interviews were like the breeze. This is what happens when one goes to an interview to get a teaching job, I thought. The principal tells you about the former teacher of the position, and what will happen when you get his or her position. That was cool and easy I continued thinking.

I started to think why there weren't more individuals of my backdrop being promoted to the so-called middle and upper middle class, as teachers were considered then. It was not so hard I was thinking, when suddenly Mr. Monteith took me all off guard with a question.

"So, Mr. Spencer, why should I give you this job and not all the other people who have applied, as you can see in this pile?" he asked.

I started to sweat. This man is a trickster, I thought. He had me in his office talking so leisurely with me, so cool, but suddenly now he was turning up the fire under my tail like mongoose being slammed under its rear parts by a hard, tough metallic trap, I rumbled in my perplexed mind, trying to come up with a decent answer.

"I don't know anything about the people in your bundle, sir but I know that I am a dedicated worker who will work to the best of my ability when you give me this job," I managed to say.

I was endeavouring to read his body language. He seemed not to want to disclose his feelings at the moment. However, I got a sense that he was quite impressed by my response. Frankly, I was impressed by my response too. I had not thought about this question prior. As a matter of fact, I had just gone there believing that my getting that teaching post at Maud McLeod would have been as easy as my passing the G.N.A.T. which I had, many years ago.

"What, if anything, that satisfies you most about teaching?" Mr. Monteith asked next.

I was now beginning to hate the gentleman. This man is a real con artist. He had given me the impression that there was nothing to do at an interview and I would be in the classroom in September but now, all these tough questions. I took a blank stare then suddenly looked him in the eyes.

"Teaching a child, to me, is like farming. You have a few grains of corn and peas and the soil is always tough, grassy, balky and bushy. However, if you go to work little by little, seeking the help of your neighbours when necessary, then gradually, you can start planting. Pretty soon you start to see corn and peas growing beautifully or whatever product, sir. This is what satisfies me most about teaching, Mr. Monteith, the ability to move students from the rough and tough to growth," I said very confidently.

Mr. Monteith was now forgetting his pretence. He liked my analogy with the students being corns and the soil being the situations that teachers face everyday. He liked my response and was smiling at it.

I was, however, once again, taken off guard by his next move. He handed me my application to scrutinize.

"Mr. Spencer, look at your application that you mailed me, any comments?" he asked.

I was confused. What was it he was trying to say? The application was handwritten, as were most, in those days. I thought he was talking about my very poor penmanship. I knew I wrote very close to the paper.

"I am sorry I write so badly, sir. I am going to blame my grade one teacher for that," I joked.

"I could read it. I have seen worse. I wanted to point out that you misspelt 'Darliston'. You wrote D-A-R-L-I-S-T-A-N," he remarked.

I sat quietly for a moment then said I was sorry for the error.

He pointed out that he almost did not bother to call me when he saw the spelling error on my application. He said for one reason or the other, he still decided, ultimately, that he would give it a shot.

He shook my hand shortly thereafter, and said he hoped I would not only make him feel that he had made the right decision, but I should enjoy my job come September and shouldn't make silly errors.

I left the Maud McLeod school quite elated. I whispered to myself that this was just a silly error. I remembered all the trial and crosses I had gone through. The exploitation by my own biological blood. I thought of it long and hard and said to myself teaching at Maud McLeod could not be more challenging than all the tortures of life that I had overcome. I thought that I would have been able to realize at least two of the suggestions of Mr. Monteith. I was going not merely to make him proud of his choice for the teaching position of which I was hired, but I was going to have fun as well. In a way both goals were to have been achieved for a significant portion of my five year stint at Maud McLeod but the factors that had propelled me to the decision to resign for another school, had not totally left my psyche, not even today,

August 20, 2009, 2:39 A.M., as I type this sentence. You could deem the circumstance that had led me to take the decision to resign from Maud McLeod, one of my big, silly errors.

Maud McLeod was a great school, probably still is. My first of three wives and mother of my first two children, Kadisha Spencer and Kaliese Spencer Carter, had, a few years ago, retired from the school as a guidance counsellor. When we met in the nineteen eighties, she was a teacher of English and five years my senior. I remember upon meeting her at the school, feeling very attracted to her. For one, her surname was Robinson, the same as my mother's maiden name. She was, probably still is, of a light complexion like my mother was, and hailed from the parish of St. Elizabeth where my mother's parents had roots, though she grew up in Mandeville, Manchester with foster-parents. In so many ways, she reminded me of me. I wondered secretly, to myself, whether we were related but I did not bother to say this to her as I had other plans.

Merfelin used to take care of me at the school. She would share her lunch with me and even invited me to her home for dinner.

Remember, I was just about twenty-three years old. Here was a woman, who had already taught five years at the school, I got my first teaching job, inviting me to come to supper. What else do you think a young man would think? Yes, I thought Ms. Robinson, as I called her then, had romantic interest in me. You could only imagine how stunned I was when after eating her lovely food and made advances only to be treated like a kid or her little brother.

"Ms. Robinson, you're a very sweet person, I like you very much," I said.

"I like you too, as a brother," she responded.

Upon hearing that response I moved quickly to her side, ignoring the 'as a brother' portion of the statement but was pushed away, bouncing my big, numbskull head on the wall. I thought in my big head whether women were insane or something. I was wondering the reason that a woman would invite a man, a nice, handsome, young, virile, stallion-like, young man like me to her house, and did not expect me to make sexual advances to her. Even though she was five years older, we were both in our twenties, and she looked really attractive and was quite intelligent.

"I am sorry if I hurt you. But I thought you were a gentleman," she said, after she shoved me into the wall of the house.

I wondered what Merfelin meant by hurt, whether she meant physical hurt or psychological or both. I guessed it did not matter too much what she meant as anyway one looked at it, I was hurt by those words and blows. Thought I was a gentleman? I rumbled in my big head. What did she mean by thinking I was a gentleman? That I had no manhood at all? That nature would not give me that urge when a beautiful woman invited me to her home and treated me like a king?

The truth be told, being a new and young teacher at the school, I thought that I had to be successful at my pursuit. I had an ego to massage and have massaged here, people. I needed to have my entire being, physically, and psychologically, massaged. I wanted to demonstrate that I had what it took to do what apparently the other virile, almost as handsome men as I was, could not have achieved. "Ms. Robinson, I don't understand you. A nice sexy lady like you, without a man, invites me to your house and you don't expect me to want you?" I asked.

"Young man, do I look like an infant killer to you?" she beamed.

I felt really crushed with that utterance. I don't recall whether at any time she had asked me my age. I knew I looked some years younger than twenty-three years as well. Even if she had changed her mind that night and had decided that she was merely kidding, my manhood and more, would have been gone. I would not have been able to stand tall as a man would, under the circumstances. She had just told me that I was a baby. No woman had had the audacity to say something so unmanly to this stud since my sixteenth birthday.

I tried to change the conversation and when I was successful in doing so for say, about ninety seconds, I bade her goodbye and thanked her for her lovely meal.

We continued to have a great platonic relationship. I would continue to visit her. She would even stop by my little one bedroom, near to the Darliston Police Station sometimes, when she passed by my home. I continued to think this lady was weird. I couldn't touch her physically or otherwise, but it was obvious that she enjoyed my company. What about me she enjoyed so much? Were we in fact related and it was just a mere biological attraction? I questioned myself, in my big head. Did she have some information about our being related of which I was unaware, I thought?

One weekend, late in the night, I was drinking and stopped at her house on my way to my home. She was shocked that I was calling her up so late, but I was not fearful as I had been drinking. All reservations were gone.

That's why people should not drink. It gives you a false sense of security that could put you into big trouble, especially if you are not lucky, but I was lucky that wonderful night. I did not get into any trouble.

Upon talking to Ms. Robinson, I discovered her female roommate, Ms. Blake, also a teacher at the Maud McLeod School, had gone home to Manchester for the weekend. I said to myself in my now big, drinking head, it had to be then or never. She opened the door. She invited me to sit on the couch and she sat at the far end. She asked whether I wanted something to eat. I did not feel for that sort of meal, but common sense said I should say yes, so I did.

Ms. Robinson was quite different that night with me. I said what a difference a few weeks could make with a couple of drinks with a woman all alone and lonely. Our relationship took on a new horizon and direction, starting that night. We got married the following year on August 20, 1983 in Kingston, Jamaica. My 'brother', Oliver Nelson not only was my Best-man, but he also served as my Chauffeur to Kingston and to the church where Merfelin and I got married. Note, as in previous important events, no biological relatives on my side of the family, were in attendance at my wedding. Soon after, we had our first daughter, Kadisha Spencer. Kadisha was born at the Cornwall

Regional Hospital in Montego Bay, Jamaica. Again, my 'brother', Oliver and I were constantly at the hospital the night I was supposed to become a father. Those days, I was a chicken and did not have the guts to watch my then wife give birth, but as soon as the baby was delivered, I was there to see my lovely daughter. I was the happiest and proudest father anyone could have found. When my daughter was born, I noticed one of her legs was up in the air like a fig tree branch, unable to lie flat. I panicked, grabbed the leg and lowered it to the floor. I was concerned that she might have had a physical handicap, but it probably was just being squeezed in the uterus or some such thing. Today, my daughter is a grown woman and a high school teacher, with fine legs. No disfigurement whatsoever. No legs cocked up in the air like a fig tree branch.

My second daughter, Kaliese Spencer, was to be born three years later. She was born in Darliston and by the time of her birth, my wife and I had already broken up, due to an indiscretion on my part. It was a real heart breaker for all of us concerned. I started to develop all sorts of headaches. It was quite difficult at first, as my then wife and I taught at the same school. Kaliese, like Kadisha, attended my old school, Manning's. Kaliese, as I write these lines, is currently representing Jamaica at the World Championship Games in Berlin,

Germany. A few days ago, she came fourth in the 400M hurdles for women. This race was won by her close friend, training partner and compatriot, Melaine Walker with a time of 52.42 seconds. Kaliese did a time of 53.56 seconds.

After our marriage, my wife and I had moved into her home. When we broke up, I moved back to my little one bedroom, near to the police station. I, as a result, developed great relations with the Darliston police. When a police officer was transferred, we would still maintain contact with each other. As a result, over the years I had grown close with a number of Jamaica's police officers. Sometimes, I would even go out on duty with them. The drug men sometimes either thought I was a cop or a police informer. The truth is, I was not a police informer. I just enjoyed driving around with the officers and observed how they operated.

While living in Darliston, I met one Norman Buchanan, the nephew of Mr. Noel Monteith. His mother, Mrs. Joyce Buchanan was also my colleague and worked as a guidance counsellor at the Maud McLeod School. Norman Buchanan later became a medical doctor, and we became very close friends. He introduced me to the People's National Party Youth Organization (P.N.P.Y.O.). He was elected as Chairman of the Westmoreland P.N.P.Y.O. and I was elected as its Parish Secretary. I was also elected shortly after, as the then South Eastern

Westmoreland P.N.P.Y.O. Chairman, replacing Dr. Norman Buchanan who was then elected to the Political Bureau of the P.NP.Y.O. We had been involved in organizing a number of sporting activities with other members of the P.N.P.Y.O., such as Cebert McFarlane, now a Parish Councillor, Errol Graham, and many others. Mr. P.J. Patterson, Constituency Chairman and M.P. who was later to become prime minister of Jamaica, was quite effective and supportive in our drive to get the constituency's youth engaged in sports and education, politically, and generally. We ran football, and cricket competitions. Milton Buchanan, at the time a Cornwall College student and Norman's young brother, would travel around with us to these games that we had to supervise, to ensure that everything was running smoothly.

Norman Buchanan had left Jamaica to pursue studies abroad at Yale but later returned to serve his country politically and as a medical practitioner. Unfortunately, shortly after he was nominated and voted by the constituency's delegates to have been the person to replace the then, retiring Prime Minister, The Honourable P.J. Patterson, he died suddenly from a blood clot. When I read of the death of the late Dr. Norman Buchanan via the online versions of the major Jamaican newspapers, the Jamaica Gleaner and the Jamaica Observer, I was in utter shock. I thought I was dreaming. The following day my daughters confirmed his death. This led me to write the following poem in his memory immediately.

Norman

Norman, the Gibraltor

Norman, the innovator and leader

A people person and champion of the poor

But our Norman is now, no more.

Why should the good hearted

Be snatched away?

Even before he gets a bay?

We'll never know

But Norman Buchanan will always be remembered, as our champion.

His captivating, smiling face lit up the darkest dungeon

Inherently endowed with a steadfastness, uprightness, and drive

To keep the disadvantaged and underprivileged alive

Ignited and energized, his sole motivation to survive

To succeed and nurture the feeblest and weakest of the human heart.

Oh Norman, we'll remember you always

The days you coached us to be our best

And all the rest

With all the challenges and the tests.

The greatest hurt we feel

Is how disappointed you must be

For not having the chance to let the poor and the weak, have their jubilee.

But who knows, Norman?

The Beyond must have a plan

Probably had we the insight, we'd understand.

Later when Norman's funeral was arranged and was to take place, I was unable to attend because of serious pecuniary challenges that I had been experiencing, which will be shown beginning in chapter 6 and onward. My frustration in not being able to attend my close friend's funeral in Jamaica, even though I resided in the so-called first world Canada, led me to pen my emotions this way.

Couldn't Have Been There

My friend died and at his funeral

I couldn't have been

Oh, what a grief and burden I feel

Oh, what pain I squeal

For to me, this is an awful deal

My good friend died and I

Couldn't have been there.

Oh, Norman and relatives

I indulge your forgiveness

How could it have been

That at this your farewell

Your friend and comrade bestows his absence?

My good friend died and I

Couldn't have been there.

Oh, my good friend died and I

Couldn't have been there

My pecuniary slides

Cause me to this land, to be 'immobiled' and

abide

Had me tied to Canada

I couldn't have been at your graveside

Oh, my good friend and comrade died and I

Couldn't have been there.

Norman Buchanan and relatives

Oh, I ask your understanding

Norman, you were a great individual

I should have been strong

I should have stood up to the bangarang

Be in Jamaica

Be in Lennox, Bigwoods, Westmoreland.

Be at your graveside

Bearing your casket

Giving you my last respect

Oh, I am sorry

There can be no excuses

Your friend and comrade

Joshua Spencer should have been there.

My daughters told me

How much our acquaintances lament and comment

"Where is your dad?"

"Where is Norman's friend?"

"Is he sick or didn't he get the news?" they mused.

My good friend and comrade died

And I was nowhere to be found

My good friend died and I

Couldn't have been there.

I just couldn't have responded to this call

I cried, I bawled

When I read of his death

My daughters in Jamaica did not call me yet

I said to myself, I must have been sleeping

Oh Beyond, I only hope I have been dreaming

But the dawn of day, shoved my hope a bay

My good friend, Norman had really passed away.

I remembered at my wedding, in ninety-two

My friend, Norman, now dead

Sent me a speech and said

I am abroad but my brother

I must come a yard

To Jamaica, to your wedding

To increase your happiness, my presence I must bring

But my good friend died, and I couldn't have been there.

I decided, in 1987, to resign from the Maud McLeod School and went to live in Savanna-La-Mar, Westmoreland. While living there, my two daughters, Kadisha and Kaliese would visit me regularly at my new home. Even though I had a rented three-bedroom house on Rose Street at the time, I felt really badly to let them sleep alone, so I usually have them sleep with me in my bed. Usually, it was quite emotional for me to see these very nice children growing up without me being there to share in the physical and emotional aspects of their growth. Whenever, Merfelin told me that they would be coming to spend time, I would put away all other matters. No matter how beautiful the woman was or the amount of fun my buddies and I had planned, everything would have to be placed on hold. I committed myself, one hundred percent whenever they were with me to be a dad and nothing else.

I must say that I am happy that both of my girls have turned out well. I was really concerned and beat up on myself several times because of our broken marriage. If they had turned out worse, I would not have forgiven myself. Even when little problems occurred later, I always deep down felt guilt and said it was because of my indiscretion that they had those difficulties or problems. It had only been the last two to three years that I stopped from thinking in this way.

Like myself, both my daughters attended the prestigious Manning's School, Jamaica's second oldest high school which was founded in 1738. Kadisha, as I said earlier is a teacher. At the time of writing, Kaliese was a university student and a world known athlete. On August 17, 2006, she acquired the world championship in the 400M in hurdles for juniors in the Beijing World Junior Championship Games and as I said earlier, she is, as I write, representing her country in Berlin, Germany where she came fourth in the 400M hurdle event.

While I lived in Savanna-La-Mar, I met a lady who was to become my sister-in-law and the introducer of my second wife, Cherry. Note that Cherry is not her real name. I had taken a brief break from teaching to sort my big head out. I was working with a private company known as Courts Jamaica Limited. Here I met this lady who found out that I was not dating anyone. She told me that she had a friend who was a British-Jamaican-Canadian who was living in Canada. She told this person about me and gave me her information and the lady started to communicate with me.

Let's explain this complicated British-Jamaican-Canadian scenario. The lady who was to have become my second wife on July 25, 1992, my grandmother, Mary Spencer's birthday, had complicated roots. She was born in England on November 2, 1958 of Jamaican parents. She, however, arrived with her parents and siblings for a few years to Jamaica and attended the Rusea's High School in Hanover, Jamaica. Shortly after graduating from fifth form, her parents, she, and the rest of siblings, emigrated to Canada where she currently lives. Her parents had returned to Jamaica a few years ago to retire.

CHAPTER SIX

Another Attempt at Love

The year was about 1989. My to-be sister-in-law introduced me to her sister, Cherry (not her real name, as I said earlier) who lived in Canada. At around the time that the relationship started to take on some telephone line and letter steam, I left the private company with which I worked briefly, to return to teaching at the Frome Technical High School in Westmoreland. At Frome Technical High School, I taught Science to the CXC level as well as to grades nine and ten. I also served as the teachers' representative on the School's Board of Governors for three successive years. After my teaching at the school for one year, one Mr. Neville Vickers (Neville), the then Head of the Science Department was promoted to one of the school's vice principals and I acquired the Head of Science portfolio which I held until the time of my emigrating to Canada on December 20, 1993.

The Frome Technical High School was a great institution. The only negatives were that while I taught at the school, we had two colleagues who died. The principal, Mrs. Morgan, a very sweet and gentle lady and later, one Mr. Lawrence. Interestingly, the night prior to Mr. Lawrence's passing, he and other colleagues, including Mr. Vickers and myself, played dominoes almost all night. Upon my returning to school, the next school day, Monday, and he was not there, I found out that Mr. Lawrence had actually died the following day after we played dominoes, quite suddenly. It was quite shocking and the whole school was extremely saddened by the passing of this very excellent teacher of Mathematics. From the moment I stepped on the school's campus that gloomy Monday morning, I knew something was wrong. Mr. Lawrence had not only never been absent in his twenty-odd years at the school, he was always the first teacher to be at school with his brand briefcase. That sad Monday morning as I entered the school's compound, his absence was pronounced. He usually stood by the gate where he would smoke a cigarette or two. I am no doctor, but I think that alcohol and cigarettes might have played progressive and important roles in his early death.

The Frome Technical High School was very good at football (soccer) and was involved in the inter high school competition of western

Jamaica known as the DaCosta Cup. In the eastern section of the country, was the equivalent Manning Cup. It was fun. None of the games would miss me. When the matches were away from Frome High, I would travel with the team and the coaches on these trips. I would be the loudest supporter at these away games. During the home games, I would be in charge of collecting the money to enter the games' playfield. It was during my time at Frome Technical High School that the school had collected the most money at the gate. As a consequence, I started to receive a small 'salary' at the instructions of the late Mrs. Morgan in recognition of the very efficient way in which I conducted events at the gates during a match and for the volumes of cash I usually collected.

I think my knack for handling money stemmed from my involvement with my mother's shop at a young age. It was just natural for me. The entire school would always marvel how I managed to collect so much funds at the gate compared to prior years, when I was not associated with the process.

It was at Frome Technical High that I gradually became more relaxed and did not feel as stressed as I was in earlier times as a result of my failed marriage. I started to feel loved and that my colleagues, male and female alike, really liked me. I was well respected. I also started to write regularly to the Jamaica Gleaner and almost every month would have my commentary published as what the paper deemed, Letters of the Day or even better, I had two very popular pieces published in the Jamaica Sunday Gleaner's Education page section. I became even more popular at the school, as a consequence.

There were two foreign teachers who were part of the staff during my four-and-half-year stint with the institution. The female's name was Ms. Alison Curtis and the male's was, Mr. Robert McTiernan or Bob. Bob was in the Mathematics department and Alison was in my department. These two teachers became very close friends of mine. So much so that there were started to be rumours that Ms. Curtis and I were intimately involved. The latter had lost her fiancé missing in action during the Gulf War of the nineties. She had travelled to Jamaica to just cool her brain a little as she later confided in me during the course of our platonic relationship.

Bob was my very close friend too. I remember the first weekend that we went for a drink. I noticed that he was gulping down the Red Stripe beers too quickly. I warned him that he should be careful.

"Joshua, do you know where I am from, sir?" he questioned, dismissively.

"Bob, what do you mean, by that? You told us you are from New York," I said.

"That's exactly the point. New Yorkers can't get intoxicated," he uttered, confidently.

We drank beers upon beers until I decided to change to something stronger. Being the New Yorker untouchable that he said he was, he too, had to change to something stronger. To make it brief here, let's just say we had to take him home like a two-day-old baby or an unconscious patient on a stretcher. He knew nothing. He was just knocked out by the alcohol, like Mike Tyson had him for a brief minute or so, in one of his thirty-five-second matches. He was completely down, down, down and really out. His snores were as course and heavy as those of the tractors of the Frome's West Indies Sugar Company (W.I.S.C.O. factory, just a few yards away from the school. Luckily, he was with responsible friends. Who knows what could have gone wrong?

It is important that one be careful when imbibing alcohol. The good rule is to take it if you have to, only when you are at the age of majority and don't endeavour to compete with anyone. You could end up destroying and disgracing yourself if you fail to adhere to these golden rules.

At Frome High School, one Mr. Perry, Mr. Knott and myself got our students involved in

261

the Debating Club Competition for high schools in western Jamaica. We won the competition on one occasion and did well in subsequent ones.

I seemed to have in fact found new, probably lasting love, albeit via phones and through letters. Cherry and I wrote so many letters to each other, along with making numerous phone calls. Sometimes letter would cross in the mails. Sometimes we would not be sure who owed who a response. As the mails and the questions were coming at us like lightning, at least the strength and the speed of Jamaica's Usain Bolt at the recently held Olympic games (Summer 2008) and the Berlin World Championship (August 2009), I felt so relieved of the amount of stress that had previously piled up in my brain and my heart when I taught at Maud McLeod School and lived in Darliston. I was still missing my family, however, it was becoming a little more bearable.

In early 1990, Cherry said she had to come to meet me personally. She had actually bought her tickets for the summer holidays. She worked at a university in Toronto, so the summer was suitable for her. She could stay in Jamaica for a few weeks. It was also quite convenient for me as well. The only hiccup was that the vice principal, Mr. Vickers and I had committed to doing a free Chemistry course at the U.W.I., sponsored by some international organization that had an interest in improving education for our local students in Science. It was during the early part of summer that we had planned to do this course. The course would have started in July and Cherry would be in Montego Bay with relatives the last week of July. The U.W.I. is located in Kingston, approximately one hundred miles away from where Cherry would be staying in Montego Bay. This was with the hope of us getting to know each other more and to decide whether we wanted to take the relationship to the next level or simply be friends or just regard each other as obnoxious snobs. My Chemistry course would have been completed the first few days in August, if I recall correctly. So, with the U.W.I., I had a Chemistry course going and at the same time when I was speaking with Cherry, I had a chemistry with her via phone. Would this chemistry be extended, and be in existence when Cherry and I would have met in August 1990?

Cherry arrived in the country and every day we would call each other. I would call her using the public payphones on campus.

"Hi Cherry, honey, so near yet so far away," I said to her.

"I can't believe I spent so much money to come to see my sweetie, and this is all I can get, a phone call," she laughed.

"Who says life is fear?" I chuckled back.

"Ricky, have you been behaving yourself?" she asked.

"I always behave myself. Remember everything one does is a behaviour. If you just sit still that would be behaving as well," I tried to be philosophical and academic.

"You stop playing around with me. From those pictures, you're one handsome guy. I know the Jamaican girls are aggressive," she explained.

"What do you expect to get?" I asked.

"Why does a woman date a man, to tell your friends you have a nice, hot-looking man who hopefully you'll have, to decorate your house like furniture?" she asked, laughingly.

Her voice sounded so Jamaican, probably too Jamaican for someone who spent a mere four years in our wonderful country. I always questioned myself whether this lady even knew England much more to have been born there and left when she was almost twelve years old. I remember having a few cousins in England, and one of them in particular, after having resided there for less than four years, whenever she speaks you would think that she was Queen Elizabeth, deep, so-called rich English, well complemented with the British accent. My experience speaking to Cherry was that I was speaking to one of those country girls in a deep, rural part of my beautiful country, Jamaica.

It was not merely Cherry's accent and language that I found remarkable, neither British nor Canadian as I said earlier, it was also the pictures that she would send me. I remember receiving a score of photographs in the mail that should represent her. However, I was left confused as to the looks of this woman who I was dating via telephone and letters. Every picture that I observed seemed different and depicted contrasting features from picture to picture.

There was a picture, one that I really liked, that was apparently taken in her basement. She seemed so calm and attractive that the plumpness of her physique took backstage to her overall beauty and sexual appeal. Then there was another where she seemed very thin, almost washy in her face, but of a lighter skin. The picture seemed to be the precise opposite of the first one I described. However, the dates the pictures were taken shared the same year. I wondered if this lady was a witch or something. How could this lady change her appearance minutely like that? I thought. I wondered if my woman was sort of a sorcerer who had more powers than the iguanas I used to watch as a child.

I would be sitting under a breadfruit tree or just walking along the New Mills grounds when I would suddenly lay eyes on a big, fat, and green iguana. Being the mischievous boy that I was, I would throw a stone or two in its direction. Not to hit it, mark you, just to scare it. It seemed the iguanas always knew I was just fooling around because instead of crawling away, it would just stay there and start to change colour for me. At the early stage of this colour metamorphosis, it would change to a light blue. The more I teased it, it would gradually change darker and darker, until it was jet black. Then as I started to move away and look back in the tree, you would behold a beautiful green iguana, just as it appeared minutes before I disturbed it. I always said to myself, such actor, you are Mr. iguana.

I usually wondered why the iguana chose to turn black or dark to scare me. Apparently, the angrier it became, the blacker, it became. There was a direct proportion between being angry and being black, I thought, and it just did not make sense. I wondered why that was the case. I questioned why I had not been lucky to see an angry white iguana, or yellow or pink, even Chinese shades or that of an Indian shade. I thought that nature was interesting and sophisticated, or was it just downright biased, I questioned, in my solidly, firm, and big head.

I remember an incident where my grandmother advised me to stop teasing the iguanas. That the iguanas were ghosts and that the iguana I was constantly teasing was the same one or the same iguana that was giving the illusion of being more than one. Irrespective of whether I saw it crawling on the toilet seat, on my dining table, the breadfruit tree, mango tree, it was the same iguana, she advised. She said the iguana lived on that breadfruit tree for a reason. She said the breadfruit tree belonged to my father. She pointed out that as a child, my father used to climb the breadfruit tree just to relax in there. She assured me that it was my father and that she was not joking. She concluded that she who felt it, knew it. She gave birth to Johnny, my father, Charles Spencer; she knew him when she saw him, she reasoned.

I wanted to comment that I did not know that she gave birth to a ghost, but I held myself back. I remembered our several clashes on subjects such as religion and politics, and the reasons that people think and believe the way they do.

I recalled that it only put our relationship farther apart the older and more educated I became. There was the argument about people landing on the moon. My grandmother got quite irate and said no one could ever go to the moon. That was God's only place and that's why it was in space with no oxygen. I tried to convince her that it was possible by asking her a number of pertinent questions. I was even surprised that my grandmother believed that there was an element known as oxygen. I was certainly pretty shocked and wonderfully relieved that she believed in one Science fact. I started a series of Socratic questions to show her that her views were in fact simplistic and lacking.

"Mammy, ever heard of meteorologists?" I asked her.

"Ricky, what fool you think of me? I hear the meteorologists every day. The weatherman, I hear them all the time," she uttered.

"So how does God let them know that he is going to flash lightning, roll thunder, and flood out the place, but can't let us know how to go the moon?" I questioned, provokingly.

"Ricky, I don't have time for you and your stupid questions. You just put everything in God's hands. That is what you must do," she concluded, and walked away.

There went my attempt at applying Socratic questioning to my grandmother, I thought. One, no matter how eloquent, could not, or would never win an argument with my grandmother. If she felt that her point was being threatened by logic, she would just walk away or concluded that it was God's business and that we should not ask any questions. I thought how ingrained, was the power of indoctrination, every single time that my grandmother and I had these conversations.

Cherry's various and apparent changes of appearance even in build, had brought me right back to my childhood days. I focused some more on a third picture. In this picture she stood and was well-dressed. She looked like a real professional and quite sophisticated woman. I wondered whether she changed her accents and level of language in that picture to match how well-dressed she was, or to match the occasion for which she was so well-adorned. I looked closely and it appeared that there was a little toddler in the far background. I wondered how she could have been so careless to have taken such a beautiful, professionally done picture, yet had a stranger's baby in what appeared to have been diaper only in its background. I wondered if she was that careless in the way she went about conducting her business or that if the photographer should be blamed for that problem, not her. I went through the pictures one by one until I apparently fell asleep.

Mr. Vickers (Neville) and I were having fun doing our summer course on the Mona Campus of the University of the West Indies (U.W.I.). We would read over our notes quickly and do any assignments we had. The rest of the time was ours to socialize with the other teachers, in particular, the women. I remember meeting a very nice lady who liked me at first glance. I said to myself, why couldn't I have met her before Cherry and I got so far in our telephone-love-letter affair? She was getting quite forward with me, if you understand what I am saying here. This newly found, on-campus friend, that is. I told her about my position, relationship-wise, but she either thought I was joking, did not mind playing second fiddle, or probably had hopes that after I got to know her really well, she would have come out the winner to play first fiddle or the only fiddle there would have been around to play. So, she would come over to my dorm at nights and we would share in just about everything, our backgrounds, our experiences. I discovered that she was of the real so-called upper-class stock. As the years had gone by, I had begun to realize that upper class people were not significantly different from individuals of my background. In some cases, because they have more money to carry on their antics dubiously, they could even be worse than us and even, wilder. So was my newfound, on-campus friend but I liked her style. I really did, to my heart.

One evening after classes, she spent some time with me, then looked me straight in the eyes and said she wanted to drive me over to meet her parents. I asked her if she was on drugs or something. However, the fact is this lady was not on drugs and she was not joking. I told my colleague, Mr. Vickers (Neville) what was going on and he suggested that we should all go to see her parents.

I told my female friend the condition upon which I would go to meet her parents. She decided that it was fine. All three of us drove over to her parents' home. I was shocked to see the mansion in which they lived. The place was secluded with a nice, white wall and a huge, iron gate. The place just seemed out of this world. Massive! Huge and luxurious. I noticed that we were well-received by her parents, particularly her mother. Even the big, wolf-like dogs were welcoming of me even though I felt uncomfortable as they seemed to have fallen in love with my socks more than they did with me.

It could have been my feet in the socks though, but I would never know. I could not take my socks off. However, there was something there that attracted them. I noticed that I was being treated even better than my friend. I wondered what was going on. Was my perceived better and special treatment as a result of something she had told them about our relationship, or was it because I was of a lighter complexion than my colleague or both? I questioned myself. Slavery was abolished in Jamaica in 1838, however, like many other places in the world, some individuals have been mentally brainwashed to see and believe that the lighter the skin shade, the more superior is the person. This meant that the more one had a closer appearance to the planters of slavery days, the clearer one's skin is, the better that person was deemed, was their nonsensical logic.

I took a tour of the house. I had never been in the White House in Washington, but I am sure this was giving it competition. There were antique items all around. The living room was spacious and luxuriously adorned with all the conveniences for entertainments. There were libraries, two or three of them. I was shown the bedrooms, the guestrooms, and more. I started to think, why did I have to meet this young lady so late? Almost every room in this palace had a computer and a television set in it. The chandeliers hanging overhead, as I stood still one moment to think through what appeared as a nightmare. As I pondered, it seemed everything was there to beckon me home. I shook my head and said I could not do that to Cherry. I walked toward my on-campus friend and whispered gently in her left ear, to inquire whether she was ready. She nodded.

That night we had a very upfront and deep discussion. She had actually told her parents that I was her boyfriend. I thought it was ridiculous of her, but it gave me a strange, good feeling. There I was, a man from Spencer Hill in New Mills being loved by not merely the only child of this very wealthy family but this very affluent family seemed to love me too. I was confused. I wondered if I should call Cherry waiting for me in Montego Bay, to say it was over. I thought about my two young daughters. I wondered how they would have felt if what I was considered doing at the time, was being done to them, when they grew up and fell in love via telephone, on-line, in person, or through love letters, or all the above. I tried to put myself in Cherry's shoes. Empathize. She had come to Jamaica to see me. She must have made a lot of sacrifices to have realized this trip, to find love and to give me love. I started to think of Kadisha and Kaliese again, and decided that I must stick to my telephone and love-letter love affair that I had found in Cherry. What if they had met two guys and then travelled abroad to meet these persons and then suddenly upon landing on the airport, the guys said, sorry? I was no longer interested. It kept being repeated in my mind. I realized then and there that my new, on-campus friend and I would be just that, friends. We would share whatever friends can share but there could have been nothing more, and nothing that would cause one's heart great pain.

At times, notwithstanding the foregoing realization, I tried to find a good excuse to stick to my new, found on-campus love at the U.W.I. campus and to forget about the love letter Cherry. I thought, well, Cherry and I had not even met. At least, I knew the woman on campus, knew her background and her wealth. To make matters worse, at the time Cherry was getting into the picture, a former love and I had also started to rekindle our love life but she had left to study at a Canadian university with the hope of returning home to me. I was completely and fully confused.

Cherry and I would have our telephone talks as usual. I would continue to talk to her from the U.W.I. campus and she, at her relatives' home in Montego Bay, awaiting to meet me as soon as the course was over. I was not as sparkly on the phone as I was prior to meeting my new, on-campus friend's parents. I started to feel as if I was actually falling in love with my new friend as well. It was very hard to attend to, at that moment, but I was convinced that irrespective of my ambivalence, the right thing, had to be done. That is to stick to the evil that I did not yet know. It was a strange scenario but that was how it had to be.

Cherry might have felt the difference in attitude and behaviour too. She told me the second day of our conversing via phone, and after my having met my friend's parents, that she would be coming into Kingston the following day. She said she found the information of a female high school friend whom she had contacted. Her friend would receive her and take her to the U.W.I. to meet me.

I told my friend and colleague, Neville (Mr. Vickers that Cherry would be coming on campus to see me. I also told my friend that I would not be able to see her again as my friend from Canada would be staying there until my course was over. She was quite disappointed, to say the least.

One interesting bit of information that needs to be said here, is that neither my newfound, on-campus, female friend nor Neville knew that Cherry and I had never met. Neville thought I had met her before and that we had dated. I probably had told him so in response to questions he had asked me in the past. My on-campus friend also assumed that this woman, Cherry, was in fact someone I knew, probably dated in high school. How else could I have told her that I had a girlfriend who lived in Canada and was there waiting in Montego Bay for me to finish my course? How else could I have been giving up the known for the unknown? How else would I have fallen in love, and sensed the flesh and blood of the giver but yet, must gamble all that for the uncertainty in my love-letter-telephone-line Cherry? The questions were many but as per usual, the answers were slow in coming, and downright, when the few came, they did not make much sense.

The strangest thing had happened. Cherry's friend, Cherry, and one other female companion had come to see me. It turned out that when they came to the area that I advised Cherry she should, upon arriving on campus, the only person they saw to inquire of me, was my on-campus, female friend. She came to get me, and Neville and I went to meet them. Upon our seeing the three ladies this was what occurred.

"Joshua, which of them is Cherry?" Neville asked.

"Wow, it's been awhile that we met, but I know for sure it's the one in the middle in jeans and black T-shirt," I said, uncertainly.

"She is nice," said my female, on-campus friend.

"So, I have taste, don't I?" I asked.

I began to get extremely nervous as I approached the three women. As they moved closer towards us, I prayed the Beyond had helped me to have guessed correctly. How embarrassed I would have been if my guess was wrong? How would I have explained this to Neville, my colleague, but more importantly, my female, on-campus friend whom I had put on the backburner because of Cherry.

My heart suddenly calmed down when two of the women suddenly stopped and one continued to walk towards us, the one I had guessed was Cherry. I thought how lucky I was. I thought when a man was lucky only Satan could stop him. I thought about that thought and corrected it to, 'only God could stop him'. I knew my grandmother would have preferred the latter. It made me sound more of God, more in tune with God's teachings as my grandmother understood it.

"Ricky?" she asked.

I noticed that the voice was Jamaican, but it did not sound like the one I was accustomed to hearing on the phone. However, I did not linger on that recognition for long.

"Sweetheart, you're looking gorgeous!" I screamed.

"I am not Cherry," she shot back.

I wanted the earth to take me in but quickly put my brain in process, despite having pointed her out as Cherry before.

"Why would you say that? You are drop-dead gorgeous!" I repeated.

"I am Cherry's high school friend at Rusea's," she explained.

"She told me," I declared.

I wondered what kinds of games these ladies were playing with me. I thought I was not going to make any further fool of myself. I also wondered the reason that my female, on-campus friend would not move on. Why did she want to stick around with me and my girlfriend? That was what I kept thinking. Nothing made sense to me then. I thought women were the strangest creatures under the sun, and that might not have been an exaggeration at all.

Whatever I did next, I thought, must not further reveal, and confirm to my female, on-campus friend and Neville that Cherry and I had not met in the past. I knew I had erred in identifying her in the distance but that could have been a result of my being so far away, I thought.

"Cherry, why are you standing so far away, come and meet my friends," I said.

"Cherry had always been a shy woman, especially when she was meeting someone for the first time," Cherry's friend disclosed.

"I can understand that, but she can at least come over to meet me, I am no stranger," I managed to say.

Cherry's friend finally realized that I did not want the others to know that we had not met.

"That's true, come over, Cherry," she commanded.

Of the two women who had been left behind, had I to guess which of them was Cherry, I would have been dead wrong again. Absolutely none of the pictures I received from Cherry looked like her. She was a good-looking woman, but she was no model. She gave me a little squeeze, smiled widely showing beautiful white teeth between extremely dark gums. The contrast created between gum and teeth, made the teeth even more beautiful and the gums more pronounced. I had dated a few ladies but had never been so lucky to date a woman with such a beautiful set of teeth complemented with lush, healthy-looking, black gums. Mark you, I had had ladies with beautiful teeth, and yes, I had had ladies with beautiful gums. But to have had a lady with beautiful white teeth and black gums all in the same mouth, was like winning the lottery to me. I thought of the few people who did not believe in, or support interracial marriages, if they could just take a glimpse in Cherry's mouth, they would have had to have a change of views, of heart. To see it the way I was seeing Cherry's teeth and gums, complementing one another, could have resulted in nothing less than love for integration whether between white teeth and black gums or white folks and black folks, or any other combinations. Each of the two anatomical structures just brought out the best in each of the structures, if merely in appearance, in this case, making a wonderful end-product, mouth, and that was my thinking.

My guests continued to intermingle with my friends and me. While we conversed, I continued sporadically, to observe my woman. I looked at her legs. They were covered in jeans, but they were quite well shaped. I was quite attracted to them. They reminded me of the well shaped mortar stick that my grandmother and grandfather had made out of pimento wood, to use to beat the corn for corn porridge or pudding, or cocoa seeds to make chocolate, only that its texture would not have been of wood. Probably more of wool. The chocolate prepared from the mortar, would later be grated to make the hot chocolate beverage. The very thought of it got me thirsty. The chocolate that is, not the legs. I looked up at her stomach which quickly pulled my eyes to a protruding and attractive chest. I started to imagine all sorts of things but pinched myself out of the thought.

"Ricky, are you going to show us your dorm?" Cherry asked.

"Sure," I said.

My on-campus, female friend took that as a cue that Cherry probably wanted some time with me alone.

"Ladies, it was nice meeting you all," she said as she walked away.

I tried to see if there was any sadness in my friend's steps or general body mannerism that betrayed her confidence. She walked briskly, head up with a little rhythm in her hips, her bottom seemed to have taken on a weave every two seconds or so. It was something I had not observed in my friend before. However, probably it was her permanent walk and I just didn't stop to notice it in the past. I wondered whether my friend was hurting deep inside but was putting her best foot forward, along with her best walk to protect her heart. I felt very perturbed inside. I knew I had feelings for my female, on-campus friend, maybe more so than I did for Cherry, but I had to be committed to an assumed, verbal contract of sticking to my new, telephone, letter writing friend whom I had met just moments from the time of my thoughts. At least, until I had good reasons to rescind on what was an assumed contract between us, there was no alternative. That was my inner thinking. One that probably I would live to regret, painfully.

We moved in the direction of our dorms. We walked pass through a narrow passage that led us to our building. There were a few teachers, who like me, were doing the summer course at the U.W.I. or permanent U.W.I. students hanging around. One couple seemed as horny as a rooster flirting around a bunch of peacock-like hens, but I won't describe that scene here. I want children and all to be able to share in my life's journey. We proceeded to my dorm.

Upon starting the course, we had been originally placed at the Theological Seminary. That is the part of the U.W.I where they trained students to become ministers of religion. I always wondered the reason that these young men and women were being described as being trained to be ministers of religion. They were merely being trained to be ministers of Christianity. That's what they would do when they graduate from college. They would tell you about Jesus and his work to save sinners from Satan and hell. They would tell you about Moses and God's sacrifice in allowing his son, Jesus to be crucified so that we could earn eternity in heaven. They would even tell you about Joshua. This thought gave me a great thrill. Even in church, millions of peoples all over the globe were mentioning my name. That he commanded the sun to standstill. That's what they were trained to do. Even if Islam, or Hinduism and Buddhism and the others were touched in their curriculum, it was merely from a perspective to show how superior a religion Christianity was. So, I was having some contention in my mind about the idea of these biblical scholars being trained to be ministers of religion when they should correctly be described as ministers of Christianity. I was getting quite worked up about the whole thing and had to say out aloud, "Calm down, Joshua, simmer down." I might have listened to myself because I did calm down. If that had not worked, I was planning to count backwards from twenty, even fifty, to one, if there was a need to do so. If that would not have calmed me, nothing would have, I thought.

I recalled when we just moved into the holy dorm, that we heard sounds, strange sounds similar to the ones associated with the private acts between married couples, but I quickly pushed that to the recesses of my mind and went to sleep for the couple of days we stayed there.

From the holy dorm, we were transferred to the more ungodly, Taylor Hall. Here I guess, we felt a little less holy and freer to indulge a little in-the-not-so-righteous acts and here was where my on-campus, female friend usually visited me and my friend, Neville. Neville's dorm was just next to mine. We had requested that arrangement which was fulfilled. All five of us now stood on the verandah-like section of our dorms. I pointed to my room and everyone marched in, to my verbal command, most sitting on the floor. Cherry chose to lie on the bed, and she seemed sleepy. I apologized for not having anything to eat.

Friday and Saturday evenings, Neville and I used to go to Papine. There we would buy roti or jerked pork or chicken. We would then wash it down with a few beers and good music. We shared this information with the ladies, and they decided that we should all go there. So that was what happened.

Cherry and I got really acquainted and re-acquainted through the loud music and the drinking of beverages. She did not drink any though. She said she did not drink alcoholic beverages.

Cherry had decided that she would stay over the night with me if that was okay and would not get me in trouble with the university.

"There won't be any problem, Cherry.You stay if you feel up to it," I said.

"I don't want you get kicked out of the place because of me," she said, somewhat concerned.

"Cherry, it's not like I am a student here. It's just a course I am doing to better teach my pupils when I return to Frome Technical High school," I reassured her.

The girls dropped us back on campus. I noticed Cherry went to whisper something to her high school friend. She nodded, and they left with Cherry staying back with me. She cleaned up a little bit and I did the same. I changed into my pyjamas, that is to say, my underwear. I never liked pyjamas. I still don't. They give me the feeling of being an old man, even now that I am old. What irony! I noticed Cherry changed into a very thin night wear with frills like the spectrum of light at its helm. It reminded me of the spectrum of light I learned about in my third form Physics class at Manning's. The white light being split into red, orange, yellow, green, blue, indigo, and violet with invisible infrared rays at the spectrum's edges. The nightwear had left nothing to my imagination. There was a beautifully-laden underwear that sucked on skimpily to her adorable body. I took a quick glance at her bosom to confirm my earlier thoughts as we chatted outside earlier. She reached for the light switch and jumped in the bed, taking me with her. I said to myself that Cherry was a very clever woman. She was just pretending all along. She knew exactly what was going to happen and what she needed to do, to have it happened. I thought that being a part of that two-person party, I was indeed quite lucky, and I was.

Neville came to awake me the next morning because both Cherry and I had overslept. He came knocking at my door, screaming, "Joshua, Joshua."

I jumped up and remembered that I had company. I asked Neville to give me a minute. I had to rush. It was almost the end of breakfast time. If we missed that, then we would have to go to buy our own. This Chemistry course of which we were partaking, was free, being paid for by some international organization or the other, if my memory serves me correctly.

We left Cherry in my room. I took her breakfast first and then returned to get mine. She told Neville that it was fine for him to join us, so Neville came inside our room.

"Cherry, where in Canada are you from?" Neville asked.

"I am not from Canada," Cherry retorted.

"Joshua, why are you such a liar? You told me your girlfriend was from Toronto," he admonished me.

"I am not lying. She lives in Toronto," I said.

"So, Joshua, are you saying that Cherry is a liar?" he questioned.

I now wished that Neville would stop asking so many questions. The next thing, I thought, was that he would be asking her where we had met, how long, and all that kind of information. Cherry and I had not yet discussed those questions. We were too tired last night and went to sleep. If I had had an opportunity, we would have discussed all the possible questions to anticipate and what the established responses would have been to such questions. I now wished we had not invited Neville in the room in the first place. Worse, I regretted that I had come on the course. First, I would not have met my beautiful, new, on-campus friend and Neville would not have been there poking nose, hands, and tongue into my business and about to cause trouble, I thought.

"Joshua is not lying. I live in Canada, but I am not from Canada," she clarified.

"Joshua gave me the impression that you were not a Jamaican. However, the moment I heard you talk, I knew you were a Jamaican," Neville responded.

I wanted to stuff dirty cloth, worse, faeces in Neville's mouth. He was talking nonstop. Either he was going to embarrass me, or himself or Cherry or all the above. I was trying to use body language and other cues, to stir the discussion in a new, more progressive direction but my colleague insisted that it should remain on his track, no detour. I felt very uncomfortable. I did not know Cherry well enough. I was not sure where the conversation was headed either. I wondered if he could talk too much and revealed our little secret with my new, on-campus friend. At one point, I said if that slipped from his lips, it might have been a good thing for me. I was now having the same feeling for both women. I had now met both women, and knew them equally, very well and thought I liked them very much, equally.

"How do I talk?" Cherry asked, calmly.

I thought that question would have put Neville on his guard, but he paid no attention to caution. I prayed deep down that Neville would choke or anything to have gotten him to stop his line of questioning. Cherry had shown some real patience. I wondered if it was because I had mentioned that Neville was my good friend and that he was a really, smart, and intelligent person and a vice principal. She must have been giving him the benefit of the doubt, but I wondered how much longer that kind of control and patience would have lasted.

"Your being abroad has not changed your accent from our lovely, Jamaican accent," he said.

"Thanks, Mr. Vickers, I am so happy that I have a Jamaican accent. That's my goal, but I am of Jamaican descent only," she explained.

"So, you are not Jamaican?" Neville queried.

"As you know, Mr. Vickers, by the stipulations of the Jamaican Constitution, I am a Jamaican, with all the rights and privileges that our locally born Jamaicans enjoyed," Cherry said.

"I am assuming that you were born in Canada, Toronto, perhaps," Neville said, sounding a little stunned.

"No, I was born in Birmingham, England," she declared.

Neville finally seemed tired of asking questions or he might have felt a little off track.

I was glad that the bout of questions had come to an end and our relationships were still intact.

Cherry's high school friend had returned to pick her up. It was just about 10:30 A. M. Saturday, but to me, it felt like we were there talking all day. She gave me a little squeeze in the same manner she did last evening when we first met. I wondered if she wanted to pretend to her high school friend that things were moving more slowly than they had. I smiled wryly and bade them goodbye.

I told Neville that I was returning to bed. He muttered something when I said that, but I did not hear clearly. I lay on my bed and the last thing that came to my mind was sleep. Sleep was as far away from my mind as the former Soviet Union was away from the U.S.A., literally and politically, I thought. I started to think about the strange life that mother nature had handed me. From the time I was born, enjoying the bird faeces in Albion, Montego Bay to my trip to all the various places I had lived and gone to school in Jamaica. I thought about the G.N.A.T and I thought about the Common Entrance Examination. I wondered whether I could have been a doctor or a lawyer or someone even more upper class than a teacher if I had the guidance and family structure as a child. I said there was no need to feel small as a teacher. A teacher is the foundation of all professions. I thought about the Simon River and how I nearly lost my life. I wondered how Mr. Lovell would have felt had I been drowned with that crocus bag of food that he gave me to carry on my head from Stonehenge to Berkshire over nine miles, while he rode his bicycle home. The Simon River also brought in focus my narrow escape in the Pemco Swimming Pool. I remembered Donald battering my mother, squeezing her by the neck, my mother running out in the middle of the night with me, her only child then, stuck to her side, as she ran for her life on her then slender and frail legs, often barefooted.

I could not forget the time when I lived in Berkshire and my friend and I would play marble. I remembered how I usually went there to play. That at times, he wanted to come and play but there were rules to follow and he could only come out at certain times of certain days. I also recalled his obsession with the sun. I thought that was great. The sun being the source of life should be observed and taken seriously. I could not block out from my mind, the way my mother treated my attendance at school with scant regard. Her saying that I should leave for my father if that was what I wanted. However, thinking that such a lust for an education on my part was tantamount to exhibiting a sense of ungratefulness. I was being perceived as being a sell-out to my humble background, to aspire for big things, to dream dreams and have visions. I remembered the agony my own Uncle Ben had put me through. The isolation. My being given a wash pan in which to bathe while my uncle, his wife and two children, my biological relatives, used the bathrooms as much as they pleased. I recalled that the only time I could use any of those bathrooms was when I was going there to scrub their dirty scum, that they carelessly and deliberately left for me to wash. I remembered seeing what appeared to be my father one late night when I was left alone on the back verandah to wash all the dishes used by their party friends. He must have seen what was happening to his child and had come to take me away to his home. Wherever that was, was a question of which I still could not be sure. I remembered having to walk several miles barefooted to run away from slavery at King's School. Having had to sleep with complete strangers in a gas station. I was lucky, I thought, I could have been molested.

I also could not forget my first trip to Darliston when I nearly outran the taxi. I remembered the joy I felt having been the only candidate who was successful in the G.N.A.T. I also remembered my second trip to Darliston and how, as a consequence, I had acquired a profession and family that I had soon lost. The days my children spent alone, and their sorrows inundated my imagination. I remembered moving to Savanna-La-Mar, taking a break from the profession I love so dearly. I remembered meeting this woman who told me that she had a friend in Canada with whom she wanted me to communicate. I thought about how I returned to the classroom and the successes I had at Frome Technical High School. I questioned why I had not met the new, rich, on-campus friend before I had met Cherry. I questioned whether destiny would have been kind to me. I turned on my belly and felt great emotions. The tears flowed freely down my face like the Simon River I nearly drowned in years ago. I wondered what was in store for Cherry and me now that we had spent some quality time together. I resumed a position of lying on my back. I felt really, really uncomfortable. I went on my side. I must have fallen asleep, shortly thereafter.

Cherry came back just about the same time she had, the first time she had visited me. We continued the same routine until it was time for us to leave for Montego Bay. In Montego Bay, I was introduced to some relatives who, like Cherry, I had not met before. However, there was a female cousin of hers who worked at the Sangster's International Airport whom I had seen quite frequently even though we had never spoken.

Cherry and I would drive to Negril, Ocho Rios, and other tourist resorts in beautiful Jamaica. I also introduced her to my friends and family members with whom I was in touch. The holiday had flown by so fast and it was almost time for her to return to Toronto and time for me to return to school. She said that she wanted to spend a couple of days with me alone. There should be no friends, no relatives, no distractions. I agreed.

"Ricky, it has been quite awhile that I have not felt this way about any man," she said, rubbing her hand lightly along my face.

"I feel strongly about you too, but we need to take things slowly," I said.

"What do you mean by slowly, when you meet someone, you know if this is it or not, no?" she asked.

"Possibly," I said.

"Do you love me?" Cherry questioned.

"What is love? I don't know," I said.

She kept quiet, staring at me, wanting me to say more. I felt like I was in a courthouse testifying and that the lawyer was asking questions. She was also using the power of silence to suck out my every thought and to assess my mindset.

"Cherry, I feel quite strongly about you," I repeated.

"You would never know. Canada is a lonely place," she confessed.

"I have an idea. I have two aunts who live there," I said.

Cherry went on to say that she hated to sleep alone in her big king-size bed. That she was not getting any younger and that she felt that it was time that she had settled down with a decent man. She thought I was that person, that decent and handsome man. She went on to say that she worked good money and she was
employed with one of Toronto's universities.

My head started to hurt. I sensed that this lady was moving extremely fast. I was falling for her. However, I was not certain that the arrangement she had in mind would work for me. I was still married to my wife and had not even considered seeking a divorce. Furthermore, I was sensing she would not move to Jamaica. She would want me to move to Canada. I had absolutely no intention to live, not even visit Canada. I had actually tried to obtain a visiting visa to the U.S.A and was turned down, but Canada, no, that country was the last on my mind at the time of our conversations.

"Ricky, how do you feel about coming to live with me in Canada?" Cherry asked.

"I don't know about that. I heard Canada is hard and I would have to do factory work," I said.

She was once again quiet. Using her technique of silence just as I had imagined that female lawyer doing to me in court. She looked at me and I returned the favour. I was sure that it was now her turn to speak and that I was not going to speak out of turn. I said in my head that I was not going to get all loose tongued here. I was not going to get manipulated, worse tricked by anyone, foreigner, or local, I said to myself.

"Ricky, you're right. You would not be able to teach immediately, but I could help you with that," she said.

"I don't want to be dependent on any woman, plus I don't want to leave my children so far away," I said.

"You have already left your children. Whether you are in Jamaica or Canada, it's no different, you have already left them," she uttered.

There was so much truth in what she had just said but I felt very angry when she said that. I felt like telling her to go about her business and to let me be. To hell with you woman, I thought of telling her. I kept quiet. She saw that my countenance had changed.

"Did I say or do something wrong?" she asked, genuinely.

I told her that she had, when she mentioned about my children. I told her that I realized that what she said was true, but it caused me great pain because I loved my children so very much. I continued to say even if there were no children, I would not be comfortable going to Canada where my Aunt Almena (Aunt Minna and Aunt Lucille lived and had already told me how tough the country was. I thought it would have been silly of me to have walked away from my daughters, my friends, my government job, to go to Canada to leave all my hopes and future in the hands of a woman who I barely knew.

"Ricky, I can get you into university easily and tuition-free," she almost screamed.

"I am too old for university now," I said.

"Don't be ridiculous! You should be in Canada to see old people with cane still in school," she said.

"That's them, not me!" I slammed back at her.

Cherry pointed out that if I changed my mind, she would take care of my divorce, sponsor me to Canada, get me in the university of which she was employed, without it costing me a cent. She said her benefits would cover my tuition. It started to sound exciting, but I still needed time to think about everything. I started to question why things seemed to have been changing positively, yet so quickly, for me. I started to think about the whole idea but was yet undecided.

"When I return to Jamaica next year or during Christmas this year, let me know how you feel about my proposal," she demanded.

I felt like a piece of meat on which a price was being placed. I wondered the reason, that of all the wonderful, handsome, and educated men in Canada, why Cherry did not choose one of them. Why me? Would it not have been easier for her to marry a Canadian, no divorce to pay for and also the possibility of one marrying her merely to travel abroad, would have been nil in that scenario. I started to reason that either this was ordained by God to happen to me, or two, something was wrong with this woman, mentally ill, perhaps, or she was hard to live with, and so could not find a man.

"Ricky, I am not going to force you to do it if you don't want to, but I know you would be better able to take care of your children if you accept my offer," she said.

The rest of the holiday was spent with Cherry and I travelling Western Jamaica. She took me to visit relatives and I did the same. I remember taking her to New Mills to which she whispered in my ears that if my relatives abroad could not have helped a little more than was evident. She thought the house was just short of being a hut. She also thought there could have been electricity or a private generator to supply the rundown structure with a little light on the perch of Spencer Hill in New Mills. She even suggested that she would see if she could get a cheap generator to donate as a gift to her future in-laws. I thought that was very fine of her and wondered if that generosity was a trap to hook me.

After leaving the Spencer Hill of New Mills that day, we left for Negril. At Negril, the Thompsons operated a supermarket (Save-A-Dollar Supermarket and a hotel (Bar-B-Barn Hotel. The Save-A-Dollar Supermarket had been closed since, but the hotel still remains at its Norman Manley Boulevard location at the time of writing. I did not want to introduce Cherry to Mr. and Mrs. Thompson as my fiancée as I was not sure where the relationship was heading. Secondly, I thought it was too soon to do so. I also found out that she too, had some reservations in meeting the Thompsons. On our way to Negril, she advised that once one of her cousins who was alleged to have been stealing animals from the Thompson's property was fatally shot on site. She claimed that the accusation was false and that she was afraid that she might have been recognized as related to the alleged thief. It was the first time I was hearing of the incident. To this date, I had never repeated this information to anyone, including the Thompson's. I guess it took a book on my life to have me repeat this information said approximately nineteen years ago.

I drove our rented car onto the Save-A-Dollar driveway, located in the Negril Square, and parked the vehicle. I was hoping that I would meet Mr. Thompson (Mr. T.) there. He usually stayed in the supermarket while Mrs. Thompson (Mrs. T), stayed at the hotel as I recalled. We decided that we were going to do a little shopping together and if we ran into him (Mr. T.), I would introduce her as a friend. She agreed. In that way, I thought, if we got serious about this marriage plan, it would not be a complete shock to them or seemed as if I just ran across the street and picked up a woman and then married her. I wanted to, at least, appear as if I had some good judgement still left in my big head, despite my indiscretion a few years ago. An indiscretion that cost me my family. I knew that Mr. and Mrs. T had a lot of respect for me. I just could not let them down after just having fouled up my first marriage. They would now have all the evidence to conclude that I lacked good judgement. I couldn't afford for the two people who saved me from the ghetto to have come to such a conclusion about me. Hence the reason that it was extremely important to me, that they knew of Cherry, one way or the other. Yes, even if it meant hoaxing a shopping spree at the Save-A-Dollar Supermarket.

We went inside the supermarket but did not see Mr. T. We, however, proceeded to do our shopping. We went from aisle to aisle. Cherry picked up one item, squeezed, felt, squeezed, felt put it back on the shelf or the freezer as the case might be, went to another aisle do the same ritual, then returned to the original aisle to retrieve the former rejected item. I started to get very tired of it and felt like screaming but I could not do so. For one, we were in public and I might have been recognized as the young man who Mr. and Mrs. Thompson helped to attend high school and college. Secondly, Mr. T. might have been around watching from some safe spot and third, our relationship was too young for such minor disagreements and quarrels to fester into a public brawl in a supermarket, no less than that of my foster parents.

While I pretended to have had interest in an item, Cherry walked away. We got lost briefly. I was about to ask her why she did not tell me she was ready when she left, for a new aisle when suddenly I heard a familiar voice.

"Joshua, what are you doing, shopping?" he asked.

"My friend, Cherry is shopping, sir, not me," I explained.

"Where do you live, Cherry? Never heard of you until today," Mr. T. remarked.

"Oh, I don't live here," Cherry responded.

"So where do you live?" he continued.

"Canada," Cherry said softly.

"Canada?" he inquired

"Yes, cold, freezing Canada," she said, with a smile.

"Joshua, I did not know you travelled to Canada," he joked.

I tried to read into Mr. T's comment. What was he trying to say? I thought quietly. Was he saying that it might have been early days yet for me to be shopping with someone whom I obviously just met? I wondered, how would he have reacted if I should have given him the whole story? That we had done a little more than shopping together. How I met her through a sister who first claimed she was a mere friend. How we started to send love letters and call each other so often that I wondered how the phone bills were paid. I wondered what would have been his reaction had he realized that Cherry came to see me all the way from Canada, then to the U.W.I. and right away decided that it was okay to stay overnight. How would he have reacted if I had met a nice, wonderful, and educated, local Jamaican during my Chemistry course, who loved me, took me to meet her parents, but I settled for a complete stranger instead, whose parents nor sisters I didn't know but for the one who introduced us? How would he have reacted, I thought, that already marriage was being negotiated, at least by one of the parties? For some reasons, I thought he would not have been too happy or pleased about most, if any of it.

"Mr. T., even though, it's not too long, we make each other so happy," I managed to squeeze the words from my vocal chords and through my nervous lips.

He looked at me. I wondered why he looked at me like that, after I had said those words. I remembered that sometime ago, I met a nice fashion designer girl. She was opening a bar and club in St. Elizabeth and wanted me to share in the business. I had gone to the bank to procure a loan. The bank had agreed to give the loan if I had a reliable guarantor, surety, or security. I had gone to Mr. T. to play that role for me.

"Joshua, if it was you alone opening the business, I would give you the money, myself," he said.

I stopped and waited to hear the rest of his statement. The statement seemed to have had something missing. I waited, and waited, and waited but the wise Mr. T. said nothing. I finally relented and gave in.

"Why is that?" I asked

"Joshua, remember you introduced me to that girl? That girl is a rich, sophisticated woman. She will be gone out of your life as soon as she gets the money. Gone!" he exclaimed.

I thought his judgement was wrong, but after all, this was the gentleman who had taken me out of rags and gave me not exactly riches, but an education. I did not have the audacity to argue with him about his judgement. I too had the world of respect for him and his wife. I silently agreed to disagree and bade goodbye.

The reality is that the lady of whom, Mr. T. spoke was not that way. She had actually taken me into her home, let me drive her car everyday while she took the bus in-between hours. I would go to pick her up at work at her fashion design business with her own car. She would sit their patiently and wait until I got there. We were not planning a marriage or anything. We had never even used that word in our vocabulary. However, she was quite a genuine soul. She was more than a girlfriend to me. She was a caring human being. I was the one who moved out of her house during one of her many vacations in the U.S.A. Her sister who lived in the lower floor of our home had tricked me into believing that my girlfriend had a boyfriend in the U.S.A. I, in my rage, got the company truck, the company I worked for briefly at the time to move me and my belongings out of her home. I later found out that her sister was merely jealous of us. She was lonely. Since her sister and I met, we would go everywhere together she was usually left alone at home as her boyfriend, a police officer did not allow her to come along with us.

"Joshua, how do you define happiness?" he laughed

I thought that Mr. T probably definitely thought I should try and work out things with my wife than trying to pursue love elsewhere. He, however, did not know that I had tried on several occasions after my indiscretion, but she refused to forgive me. Neither was Mr. T. aware that I had even brought a good friend of ours, one Corporal Moore, a police officer and close friend of both my then wife and I, to convince her to forgive me but instead, the goodly police office received dirty water being splashed in his face instead.

"Mr. T., I am not sure," I relented.

Someone called Mr. T.'s attention and we bade goodbye and promised to talk soon.

Cherry and I were a bit quiet the way back to Montego Bay. We spoke very sparsely and sparingly and when we did it was to the point. I wondered what was going on in her head. Was she giving up on us? First, it was me not wanting to leave my children and to take the risk to start a new life in a foreign country. Now, she was probably reading between the lines as to Mr. T's implicit statements. I was secretly hoping that she would have considered us forgetting the whole thing. I knew though that it would have been hard for her to do so. I had written some really powerful letters to her. Letters that I knew had touched her heart, soul, and body. I knew what I was good at doing. This was my gift. I can express words creatively on a page. I wondered what would have happened had there been no trees, and subsequently, no paper. Half my being would have been subdued, I thought. I changed my thought to my friend, Grace, in Canada, the university student. I had told her what was going down. I could only assume that she was hurting too. She did not say much on the subject. Probably, she was more focused on reading for her Education degree. Maybe, I thought, I could get her to forgive me. If that did not work out, I still had my newly found, on-campus friend's information and could contact her, if merely to meet one or two of our physiological needs until, we could decide the direction we would be taking. My head hurt and it was a big head too.

The days had passed quickly, and it was time for her to depart to Canada. I drove her to the Sangster's International Airport in Montego Bay. She warned me to be good and I uttered the same sentiments. I watched her walk away, I felt a cold, longing loneliness. I watched to see if she wouldn't look back, and yes, she did look back, and gave me one full smile. The integration of her black gum and white teeth rekindled my former thoughts about racial integration. I thought about what Canada would be like with her, with us, with my children hundreds of miles away, over waters, and my big head hurt, even more.

CHAPTER SEVEN

Marriage, What a Trip!

I called Cherry the moment I thought she had reached home. We chatted for about an hour. The discussion was more lively and flowing this time, unlike the one we had on our way from Negril to Montego Bay, on our last, out-of-town excursion. At first, she reintroduced the need for us to be together. We spoke of how we just hit it off like that. She spoke of herself being quite lucky to have found love in someone as nice and intelligent as I was, and I echoed her views right back at her, straight in her face via the telephone. We laughed, she cried. Already, she had begun to make plans for her next trip to Jamaica to be in the arms of the man she loved and I, too, was beginning to make plans to receive her. We were fully in love at this point, or so I thought.

"Ricky, I am so lonely," she said.

"I understand," I responded.

"No, you don't!" she screamed.

"Canada is such a lonely place when you're alone," Cherry said.

"Everywhere is a lonely place when you are alone," I uttered back.

"But in Canada, it's worse," she insisted.

"There are so many things one can do to avoid being lonely," I tried to encourage her.

"That's true, but once all that engagement comes to a rest and one lies in bed all alone, the loneliness persists," she explained.

"I guess it's the weather there. At least here, you can go out, even with your naked butt any time you want," I declared.

Cherry laughed and asked me not to bring back memories by talking about naked butts. She figured that such discussions would not merely get her lonely but would get her you know what. I laughed once again and was happy that a lady who worked in a Canadian university was in love, or so fascinated with me, a poor Jamaican man who came from a background of dire poverty and deprivation. I said to myself, there must be a God smiling down at me or some Beyond, how else could one explain this situation with Cherry and me? I was in deep thought.

She brought up our meeting at the U.W.I. and thought it was strange that she stayed over the very first time we met. She said it was the first time she had met someone for the very first time and felt so helpless that she had to know him better then, and there. She spoke of how she felt badly in the eyes of her friends, but she just could not help her desire to be with me, and all the time, once she had set eyes on me the first time. She confessed that when she stayed with her friends in Kingston, even when they went shopping, she could not get me out of her head and her heart. I wondered why Cherry had chosen to tell me all this during a telephone conversation. We had been together many days and nights in Jamaica, and she said nothing of the sort. I realized that she was somewhat a shy person or probably quite lonely.

"Ricky, this is what I am going to do," she said.

"What?" I interrupted.

I interrupted partly because I was anxious to hear what she wanted to do. I also wanted her to know I was still listening and not falling asleep on the phone while she spoke. It was a little while that we had been talking. She had also asked me to call her collect. I was wondering, how she could afford all these long distance, overseas calls.

"I will be coming down to marry you in 1992," she said.

"Okay," I heard myself saying.

I must have been tired or was falling asleep. I couldn't believe that I had actually agreed to her proposal to marry me in 1992. I wanted to say that I was joking when I said I agreed but I knew that would have probably caused an argument. I started to sweat profusely and continuously asked myself, what in the heavens had I just agreed to? I wondered if I, too, was lonely and just held out all along as I wanted to be manly. I thought Cherry was also clever and uniquely smooth. I thought she was like a salesperson. She just cleverly got me comfortable. As soon as I got comfortable and not focusing properly, she made her move. She got me to agree to getting married to her just like that. Just like that, I thought.

"Ricky, honey, I am going to call Cousin Jacky (not her real name) tomorrow and tell her that we are going to get married on July 25,1992," she said excitingly.

"Okay," I said.

Cherry was going to have her cousin do the arrangements for the wedding. She would send her money to cover all the costs, cake, location, everything. She would be coming down December of 1991 to put on the finishing touches. She was also going to send me money to get a lawyer to file and complete my divorce so that by July 25, 1992, the day she had in mind for our wedding, I would be free to be hers on that blessed day, to be not so free, once again. I thought that was a strange arrangement. That is, the idea of divorcing to get 'undivorced' once again. All logics told me that was a ridiculous and nonsensical act, but I guessed I had already gone too far. There was no turning back. I calmed myself in saying the whole affair with Cherry and myself had been strange, not just the act of me getting divorced to get married. This was not a normal relationship. But then again, so was my entire life, not being normal.

She hung up the phone and I could not fall asleep. I questioned myself as to whether Cherry had just put a spell over me. Could I find the courage, maybe the following day to say, that I was dozing off when I said 'okay' to her proposal? I said that would crush her too much. After all, she was a fine lady. She had already outlined that she was going to ensure that my children and myself were going to be fine. That in Canada, my suffering would not be long. As a matter of fact, there would have been no sorrow or suffering. She would use her benefits from the university she worked to provide me with a free university education. An education that would enable me to continue, as I had for most of my Jamaican, adult life, being a teacher. I started to feel a little excitement in my heart and mind. I started to work out the foreign exchange difference, which was about one Canadian dollar to eight Jamaican, at the time. I thought that I would soon be a Jamaican millionaire working in Canada and that I would have been able to sponsor my children to Canada in no time.

The letters and phone calls continued between us. They became even more intense and emotional the more the months passed. Cherry had come to see me in the summer of 1990, the first time we met that summer at the U.W.I. The next time I was going to see her was in December of 1991. This would have been the second time we would be meeting each other. Yet the third time we were going to meet in the summer of 1992, would be for what was to be an extravagant wedding. I just continued to think the whole thing was just too crazy, too wild, too bizarre. I even found it stranger that this lady would not even allow me or my family to contribute anything to this wedding. She and her parents were doing it all. It was just incredible. I had never seen anything like that in my thirty-one years, at the time I was thinking about the whole insanity.

This day in question, I had a strange discovery about my-to-be bride. As we continued to talk about our upcoming wedding and how it would be done, two very important shockers emanated. These two observations should have served as striking red flags with respect to my marrying this woman. During our conversation that day, it took the strangest spin and revelation.

"Ricky, honey, I love you so very much," she said, softly and romantically.

"The same here," I replied.

"I was wondering what roles my two children are going to play in our wedding," she said.

I wondered if I heard her correctly. I said she was probably referring to my two children, Kadisha and Kaliese but she wanted to show me how much she started to assume a motherly role now that we were about to be husband and wife.

"My son is only a little over one year old, but my daughter is almost nine," she continued.

I was utterly stunned. It was not because she had two children, I love children. It was the fact that no mention had ever been made about these children until a few months before our wedding.

"Cherry, I did not know you have children," I tried to say calmly.

"I hope that's not a problem," she responded.

I wanted to say the children were no problem but the way they were just being introduced, certainly was not great. I bit my tongue once again and said nothing. I just could not understand this woman. She had two children but did not think that that was an important piece of information to give to her future husband before marriage arrangements were made. I was deeply disappointed in that arrangement now. Had I not told my friends, mother, foster parents, and siblings that I was getting married, I sure as there is a hell, would have called it off right then and there. However, I couldn't, too many people had learnt that I was going to marry this rich Canadian woman, then go off to teach in Canada and to work the big bucks. I just had to bear my disappointments and would go along with our plans. Just about anything and everything that she decided to pitch at me like a baseball, I decided to, at least, swing the bat at, just in case it made contact.

The second matter that amazed me was the fact that she was considering having her children take active roles in our wedding but my two girls, Kadisha being just about the same age as her daughter, Kaliese three years younger, were not mentioned. Kaliese, my younger daughter, was much older than her son, who she wanted to take part but again no mention of my kids. I felt some resentments, but I bit my tongue and bit it even harder each progressive time.

As she talked on the phone, I listened attentively as she expounded on all the negativities about her children's fathers, how they were no good. I questioned myself, as I always do, the reason I had gotten into this trap, this trip. I genuinely hoped and thought that I was doing this for the right reasons, love, not the trip but I had begun to question my motives. I genuinely thought that my heart was overpowering my head and so was my pride, but I was not sure. How could I have called off the wedding? I thought. Everyone would think the Canadian lady walked out on me, was my reasoning. I never liked to come out looking as the loser. I had a lot of pride and determination. I had always been a fighter and in all situations, I ultimately always, always triumphed.

Cherry sent the money to set my divorce proceedings in motion. The moment I got it, I went to seek a competent lawyer to get this moving quickly. I heard about one Mr. Don Foote of Savann-La-Mar who I had actually met in the past. He was said to be a good lawyer. I also liked his mannerism. He was a real, cool, down-to-earth individual and he was about my age, at least that was how he appeared. I felt comfortable to sit down with him to discuss my dilemma and the urgency that I needed to be divorced to get married once again.

"Well Mr. Spencer, if your wife does not contest the divorce, it could take a mere couple of months, depending on the amount of work on the books," he said.

I wondered what he meant by if my wife does not contest it. From the context, I thought that he meant that if my wife agreed to the divorce. I thought about this long and hard. I said to myself, what if my wife does contest this divorce, what would happen next? My wife to be, Cherry, had invited to this wedding, virtually the whole of Canada, including downtown and parade of their Canadian cities, I thought. There were the bridesmaids, all Canadians, some of whom would have been visiting Jamaica for the first time. There were also going to be her parents who, though they were Jamaicans, had not travelled to Jamaica in eighteen years, I started to tremble.

"What if she contests the divorce, does it mean I wouldn't be able to get divorced?" I questioned Mr. Foote.

"It does not necessarily mean that you would not be able to get divorced, but it would be much harder and more time consuming," he explained.

I trembled even more. I kept questioning myself as to the reason I had got caught into the trap and trip of Cherry, the marriage idea. I would have been disgraced if this divorce did not come through on time for me to get married. First, the minister getting us married must get a marriage licence on our behalf. In procuring the licence to get us married, it would have been revealed that I was already married. He would not be able to do it. Even if he could, I would not have been taking the risk of breaking the law and committing polygamy. It would have been an utter catastrophe. I imagined all the Canadians, including Cherry's mother and father, being down in Jamaica, relaxing in their hotels; I had to go nervously knocking door to door, explaining that there would be no wedding and the reason was that I was already a married man. I imagined them chasing me with guns, cutlasses, and machetes. I, running and screaming like a toddler being chased by strangers. I imagined going to Cherry's parents' room last. When they discovered what had happened, they had heart attacks, sprawled out on the floor like dead frogs. I panicked and jumped over the balcony, to my ultimate passing.

I calmed my thoughts by thinking there would be no sense in my wife doing that, unless out of spite. I had already attempted to make it up with her and she refused, I thought. However, to play it safe, I said I would not send the invitations for my children to the wedding too soon. Just in case it gave my wife some ideas. I also said that if the worse should happen, I would ask the minister to take a donation from me to fake a wedding. When no one was looking, he would then destroy the signed documents. This, surprisingly, gave me a contingency plan as well as lowered my blood pressure somewhat to normalcy.

Mr. Foote set to work to prepare the divorce papers and had them sent off to Kingston. From there, everything would be out of my control. He was paid a tidy sum to see to it that the paperwork was done quickly and not just sit on some desk in Kingston. My wife would be informed of my intention and if she did not contest, violá, I would have been a single man once again, albeit for just a few days.

Almost everyday that Cherry and I had a discussion via telephone, the first thing that came up after reassuring each other of our love, was to inquire of how the divorce was proceeding. To each time that this question came to the fore, the response would be the same. That is, I was not sure. Cherry was becoming a nervous wreck over the whole matter, and so was I.

It was December 1991 and once again, Cherry was in Jamaica. This time, she brought her son and daughter. They were very cute children. However, there was a problem. Whenever, the little boy was around, I could not touch his mother. He was one of the most jealous men I had ever seen. If Cherry and I wanted to go out, one of us had to leave first and then the next would tiptoe to catch up with the other. We could never be together in his presence, no touching, holding of hands, no romantic connotations. He was a quite cranky and rude fellow too. His sister was the opposite, calm and loving and she liked her new dad. I wondered what would happen after the wedding when I went to Canada. I wondered whether I would have had to sleep on the floor or worse, the kitchen or bathroom, and leave my wife with his possessive son.

Unlike her first visit to Jamaica to see me, the second visit was no fun. We were always busy. She, getting everything done. My role was simply to get a best man, a Masters of Ceremony, and the liquor for the wedding reception. I asked my 'brother', Oliver Nelson to serve as my best man, but he flatly declined to do so a second time.

"I am not going to be your best man twice in one lifetime," he said.

I understood his reasoning. He was my best man for my first wedding. In a way, he could have been my bad luck. So, I moved on to get another dear friend in my batchmate at Sam Sharpe Teachers' College in the person of Dudley Jennings. Hixwell Douglas, a good friend of mine also, and a genius of sort, was to be my MC. He was also blind and had served as our college's student council president. The last time I heard of the now Dr. Hixwell Douglas, he was a chief education officer. The term education officer is synonymous with the term superintendent used in North America. Desmond Jackson, also a batchmate of mine at the Sam Sharpe Teachers' College would assist in acquiring the alcohol beverages at discounted rates. He worked with the Desnoes and Geddes (D&G) at the time. He would buy the goods directly, so I could benefit from the discounts. Desmond had sadly deceased a few years ago.

Cherry was in the country some two weeks before the July 25th date. Most of her entourage was down since the Monday of the week we were to be married. They were sprawled all over Western Jamaica awaiting the big day. I met my in-laws. They were just marvellous. I got a sense that they were extremely happy that their daughter had ultimately decided to settle down to marriage. Cherry left me with her father briefly upon our first encounter, and I became quite uncomfortable. I hoped deep down that he was not that kind of questioning type. What if he started to ask me too many questions? I was not sure what Cherry had told them about me. I knew for sure they were told that I was a teacher, so I started to talk about school and education.

"So, I understand in Canada the students have a lot of facilities in the schools," I said, a little conscious of my Jamaican accent.

"Yes, the governments have the schools mostly well equipped," he shot back.

"I wish that were the case with most of our schools," I said.

"I know. I attended school in Jamaica before emigrating to England," he said.

Cherry came back in the room and I felt somewhat relieved. She took over the conversation and it went back to the wedding.

It was just the Thursday, prior to the Saturday that my wedding was to be held, that I got a call from Lawyer Foote that he and I had to go to Kingston. I told Cherry that my lawyer had just called and requested that he and I had to go to court in Kingston. I did not ask Mr. Foote too many questions on the phone as I was too scared to get the wrong responses. I thought, oh my gosh, what was I going to do if my wife really contested this divorce? The shame, the disgrace, the lost of my pride. How was I going to face my colleagues and others who were all invited? Even though I had the contingency thought of faking the wedding in such a circumstance, I still, at some point, would have had to attend to the reality that Cherry and I had not gotten married. It was hard thinking about it, not to mention how nerve wrecking that thought had been.

I went over to the lawyer's office in Savanna-La-Mar and we rode into Kingston. All that was required was for me to sign some more documents. The notice was sent to my wife that I had filed the divorce and she had not responded. However, they had to wait a certain time period before the marriage could have been officially dissolved. That Thursday was the minimum time that they had to wait. The situation was outlined to me. We arrived in court, in what seemed a private chamber, a few hours before the official waiting period had elapsed. I had to wait. Every female shadow that stepped through the offices' doors that day and hour, caused my heart to skip a beat. I was still thinking that my wife could have decided to contest this divorce which would cause me great hell. Suddenly the hour had passed. I rushed to the bathroom to relieve myself and to wipe the tears that had begun to roll down my face from my burning eyes. I had a narrow escape, I thought. Once again, I triumphed, I said calmly.

The wedding was to take place at the Lucea United Presbyterian Church in Hanover. Hanover was just a few miles away from Montego Bay and Negril where most of our foreign guests had stayed in hotels. After the incident with my mother during my internship, we had put that behind us and she was also invited to my wedding, along with my siblings. As a matter of fact, I was often in the habit of visiting her in Stongehenge even to sleep over. Interestingly, some of the acts of my indiscretion that had led to my wife and I being separated, were done at their home in Stonehenge and with their full knowledge of what was going on. After the separation with my wife, as I did not take any furniture or appliances from the matrimonial home in Darliston, my mother even loaned me a bed that I used for a long while and which I gave to my sister Georgia only some long time later.

It was a real gloomy-looking day. The wedding day that is. By the afternoon had arrived, there were heavy rain and floods. I was concerned that many of our local guests would not have been able to make it. Hixwell Douglas and Dudley Jennings were no problems though. They had come early. My 'brother', Oliver Nelson was busy quite early, transporting the alcoholic beverages from Montego Bay to Hanover in his father's pick-up truck. I had also made arrangements with my former colleague of Maud McLeod High School, Colin Hitchman, to transport my daughters, Kaliese and Kadisha, to and back from the wedding and wedding reception. Colin Hitchman lived in Darliston at the time, so it was not inconvenient for him. He was also one of the persons chosen to give a toast at the wedding reception. My long-time friend, Norman Buchanan, at the time a medical student at the Yale University was also in attendance. Mr. T. had advised that as Custos of Westmoreland at the time, there had arisen an emergency meeting with the Justices of the Peace and others. He probably would have been late, he had advised me. However, he expressed that if it was merely to attend the wedding reception, he would certainly have been there.

The rain continued to pour heavily throughout the afternoon. However, by the time the wedding had gotten started, the rain had ceased to fall, and the sky cleared nicely. Initially, only a few people trickled into the church for the ceremony but as the minutes progressed, the church was full of people, from all walks of life. However, when I pervaded the whole area, apart from my beautiful daughters, there was not even one biological relative of mine in attendance. There was not Mr. T. either but I did not feel too badly about his absence. After all, he had a reason not to have been there. He had gone through the trouble to explain it to me. I had received no explanation from other relatives. I felt like a fish out of water when I saw how well represented Cherry was and the blatant absence of my own family. Her entire family and relatives, most of whom lived abroad, some visiting Jamaica for the first time, were all in attendance. I thought about my life and how rocky it had been. The more things changed I thought, the more they had remained the same.

The 'Here Comes the Bride' song rang through the air to the melodious rumblings of the organ. I heard a loud cry from the front. I realized it was my jealous stepson, crying. The father gave his daughter, my stepson's mother, to me and I thought what my stepson was going to do about that now. We went through the marriage rituals and I suddenly realized that within two, short days, I had had two women as my wives.

The reception went well apart from an incident with some of the workers who were stealing the liquor and who got caught by my friends. Several speeches were made. My best man, Dudley Jennings, currently a principal at a Montego Bay school, spoke highly of me and how I was the most sociable and determined person he had ever met. He described how I was involved in a race and how even when he saw that I was out of breath and soon, my life, on the verge of dying, I would not pull out of the race. He said, he had run along and advised that I should fake injury, but I refused, he claimed. I responded to all in the audience, that my friend was really creative but a great liar, nonetheless. The audience all laughed. Hixwell Douglas, my blind, genius friend punctuated the whole sessions with incredible jokes. At one point when I pointed out that my friend was in fact blind, no one believed, including my newly wed wife whom I had managed to keep the secret from as well.

It was while I was on vacation during the summer of 2008 that my sister, Georgia, advised that they had not attended my wedding on July 25, 1992 as on their way via train from Stongehenge to Montego Bay, they got involved in some commotions and were arrested. That was the first time I was being made cognizant of the reason for their absence from my wedding. It did make me feel somewhat better, but I thought that that information could have been communicated in a little more timely fashion.

The wedding had taken place. Cherry, her parents, and siblings had all returned to their respective homes. Some lived in the U.S.A., others mostly lived in Canada and England. Immediately as Cherry returned to Canada, she started to put in motion the filing procedures so she could have me in Canada at the shortest, possible time. Within the end of the first week of her returning to Canada, she had advised that she had completed her end of the transaction. She said everything was now up to the Canadian Embassy and its Immigration Department. I returned to work.

We continued to talk via phone and to communicate for the first few days of her return to Canada. However, during her immediate return and the period in question, I began to sense some changes. I did not feel that spark in our conversations as we had prior to becoming married. The phone calls were not happening any longer, and the letters had almost come to a standstill. When I attempted to call her, the phone would ring on and on, but no one would answer it. The answering machine was also no longer attached to the phone. I found it extremely strange. Consequently, I wrote her a long, very explicit letter that outlined my concerns as well as disgust, over the situation that was gradually evolving. I also wrote her this poem which I enclosed with the letter.

Your Love Keeps on Healing Me!

I often falter on the wayside

The challenges and the woes of life

Keep nudging at me

At my optimism

But the knowledge of your love keeps on healing me.

The glory of the morning's sun

Brings along with it

The ironic sorrow and doom.

In the night, a pale and changing moon evolves

Around which life

My life, seems to revolve

With an equal paleness

And I retire to doom

To a feeling of nothingness

A vacuum of hopelessness

And just then

The knowledge of your existence

Frees me of the stench

And I'm made strong.

The youthful minds

The youthful beings

Yearn for hope, for knowledge, for eternity

For future strength

And are put to my charge.

The responsibility is great

The task is nerve wrecking

And at times, I shiver as if I'm quaking

Wanting to die, to succumb

To life's rough way

To society's onslaught

To society's torture

To nature's pain.

But I take a break and I sigh

And you become real as the sun is to day

I'm lifted! Uplifted

You are the one

Who makes me tick along

As your love keeps on healing me.

How discouraged I become sometimes

The loneliness

The frustration

The sorrows

The usually long, lasting illness of a relative, a mother and a friend

Even death!

And always as I decide

To hang up the hammer

You I remember.

A sudden hope oozes

In the vacuum spaces of my thoughts

Like a sudden rush of wind on a summer desert

Which envelopes my being

Engulfs my pessimism

And makes me merry

Your love keeps on healing me.

I realize how precious you are in my heart

And for every negative vibe

That inundates my soul, my being

I'm elevated and re-inspired

By you, through you

You, baby . . . your love has got a hold on me

I'm inspired to greater thoughts, positive energy

Your love has made me well

I'm healed.

Shortly after I got married, a number of relatives of mine died like it was a domino effect. First, it was my mother. She had just found out that she had bone cancer. Within weeks of this knowledge, she was dead. Shortly after, it was my Aunt May May (Mavis Robinson) who lived in England followed by my Uncle Man (James Robinson) and my paternal grandmother, Mary Spencer who had actually raised me for a significant portion of my early life in New Mills, as you will recall. My grandmother was ninety-two years old at the time of her death. All these deaths happened within months, even weeks of each other and in the year 1992. Yes, the same year I got married. To make matters worse, shortly after my mother died, one of my brothers got mentally ill. It was devastating. When my mother died, I advised my wife in Canada of her death, but she said she was sorry to hear and would not attend her funeral. I thought that she might have been somewhat offended because they did not attend our wedding which I thought was becoming a funeral of sort, as well. I also remembered while talking to Cherry that the first time when I introduced her to my mother, my mother commented that Cherry was the darkest woman of whom she had ever seen me being intimate. I could tell my wife was quite offended by the remark. I knew my mother had some influence of mental slavery still in her veins, but to have said that out loudly to Cherry, I was not expecting that at all, and it had taken me completely off guard. I was quite offended of what I thought was a racist remark, but I did not want to start a heated argument among us, so I let it be at the time.

My mother's funeral was kept in Stonehenge, St James. I told my friends and colleagues at the school I taught. A number of them attended the funeral. My good friend, Christopher Suban, I called him 'Roomie', lent me his car to drive to my mother's funeral in Stongehenge. Christopher Suban is actually the brother-in-law of Oliver Nelson.

When I thought that my wife had gotten my letter and poem, I tried to call her and within the third ring she picked it up.

"Hello," she said, barely.

"How are you honey, how are you?" I asked.

"I am a little under the weather," she said.

"Why is that? Do you miss me?" I asked.

"I don't even have time to think. I just came home to a bunch of bills," she ignored the content of my question.

I knew that things had changed drastically since we got married and a few days after she had returned home to Canada. I started to wonder if all she was interested in was to get married. Since she had now achieved that goal, there was no longer any shine or excitement in her bones. I started to curse myself. I called myself stupid, idiotic, and simplistic. I wished that when I was in school, my students would see the simpleton in me as well, then yell, Stupid! Naïve! Simplistic! I was, I thought, too naïve and that I had gotten used by a woman and I deserved it. It still did not make sense to me that all that had happened in such a short period of time. I wondered whether my marriage was already over, even before it got started. I even wondered if her earlier talk about sponsoring me was just chat and she did not do anything about it. I wondered if that was the reason that she had said she had done all there was to have been done from her end. That would mean, if I did not hear anything, it would not be her fault. My migraine immediately started to act up on me. I thought I was going to lose my mind. Even though the wedding just cost me the value of liquor, I felt that I had wasted my money and time and worse, got married to a complete stranger, a completely, mentally, unstable individual, those were my feelings.

"Cherry, is there something that you want to tell me, dear?" I questioned.

"Not really, but I was just remembering all you had said before, about coming to Canada," she said softly.

"I had said so much. What specifically are you talking about?" I queried.

Before she could even say the next word, I started to get a very uncomfortable feeling inside my stomach. Who was this woman, I questioned? What was she capable of doing, was my next thought? Why did she come to Jamaica to cajole me into marriage, and now sounded like she had absolutely zero interest in either marriage or me, I pondered? She sounded like someone who was rather intoxicated for a few months and had suddenly gotten sober, only to realize that she had done something, getting married, something that she had no intention of doing. Worse than that, she gave the impression that someone, me, had held a gun to her head, a rope taut around her neck, and dragged her to the altar. I just could not understand the sudden change. It was driving me crazy.

"Joshua, I think you probably were right. Maybe you should stay in Jamaica a few years first," she said.

I could not believe my ears. I tried to touch and squeeze my flesh to ensure that I was not dreaming. I was able to squeeze and touch my arms, my legs, and just about every body part that I felt comfortable touching and squeezing. It happened with ease. I realized I wasn't sleeping or dreaming at all. I also noticed that the last time, she referred to me it was as 'Joshua', not the affectionate, 'Ricky'. "Woman, are you kidding?!" I screamed.

"Why are you screaming, Joshua?" she asked.

I felt like hanging up the phone, but I counted backward and tried to remain calm. I said, if I were to do that, I would not hear the full story or decipher for myself what was either going on in Cherry's mind or her life. I started to listen.

"I am beginning to feel that you should stay for awhile in Jamaica as you wanted. I just need some time to sort myself out," she explained.

"Cherry, are you in your right mind? I told you I had no intention to take a trip to Canada. You forced me! Why the sudden change?" I exclaimed.

"I need to move out of my parents' basement, and I need to get a car for you," she explained.

I told her that she should have thought about all those things before she forced me into marriage. I told her that I was not interested in a long-distanced relationship and that I would be going to Canada the next day after the papers got finalized.

Cherry got quite indignant and loud. I had no idea she could have been that brawling. I really could not believe the whole matter. Here I was talking with a woman who first failed to disclose to me that she had two children until we had agreed to get married. A lady who had talked me into getting married because she was lonely and was being tired of living alone. A lady who, to my argument that I did not want to travel abroad, in particular to Canada, said that she had the wherewithal and I needed not to worry. She could get me qualified to the level that my qualifications would have me teaching in a few years, upon my arriving in Canada. Now all that had changed. I was very hurt. I said that I could not stay in Jamaica after everyone expected me to travel abroad. Fly high or low, I said, I was going to be in Canada if she had actually filed for me.

"Cherry, you're a bigtime fraudster!" I screamed, slamming the phone down.

Cherry and I had virtually stopped communicating with each other, even though I pretended to others that everything was fine. When I wrote letters, she would not respond to them. I attempted to get her via telephone a couple of times but to no avail. Accordingly, I was quite surprised when about the first week of September 1993, I got this letter in the mail.

Canadian High Commission

Immigration Affairs Branch

30-36 Knutsford Boulevard

P.O. Box 1500

Kingston 10

Jamaica, West Indies

File No. B0246 90632

Date: September 2, 1993

Dear Joshua Spencer

I am pleased to advise you that your application for permanent residence has been accepted. Your Canadian Immigration Visa which is enclosed, is to be presented at a Canadian port of entry. You should not mark or alter your visa in any way. Every holder of an Immigrant Visa must also have a valid passport on arrival in Canada.

Please note the date of validity of your visa. You must arrive from outside of Canada at a Canadian port of entry on or before the date shown.

If there are any changes in your marital status, or changes in your immediate family (such as a birth, marriage, divorce or death), before you leave for Canada, you must inform a Canadian Visa Officer at the High Commission in writing. The Visa Office will tell you when you can leave for Canada.

On arrival in Canada, you must be "landed" by an Immigration Officer at the port of entry to become a permanent resident. This status may be lost if you reside outside of Canada for a total of one hundred and eighty-three days (183) in any twelve month period. If at some future date, you wish to remain outside of Canada for extended period without forfeiting your permanent resident status, you should apply for a Returning Residence permit at a Canadian Immigration Centre before your departure from Canada.

Vaccinations are often required for students. Parents of school age children should obtain copies of the children's records of immunization from their family physician, school, or national health service before departing for Canada. Evidence of immunization for diptheria, tetanus, poliomylitis, measles, rubella, and mumps will be required for children enrolling in school in Ontario and New Brunswick. You should check with your local school board in Canada about correct inoculation requirement.

Enclosed is information including "advice to Immigrants" which you should read carefully.

I would like to take the opportunity to wish you future success.

Yours sincerely,

Counsellor

Encls.

Please Note: the above file
number must be provided on
all future correspondence or
inquiries directed to this
office.

I—I

(06/92)

I had until the end of January to take up the
offer, otherwise the Immigration Department
would deem my visa null and void. After going
through all the hell, I decided that I was going
to leave the country on December 20, 1993. I
sent a letter to Cherry advising that I had
received the visa and that I would be submitting

my resignation effective December 31, 1993. School would have been out before the December 31, 1993 resignation date. In making my resignation effective at the end of December, it was merely and simply to guarantee my full month's salary which I had actually left for my daughters, kaliese and kadisha. There were also some Government Bonds that all teachers had at the the time. I had also left instructions for that money to be made in monthly instalments to my two girls. I knew that probably I was about to face some tough times in Canada, but it was a risk I was willing to take. Later all the appliances and other materials I had were sold and also given to my children.

Fay, my cousin, had visited Jamaica from England to attend our grandmother's funeral. I had outlined to her my dilemma. She subsequently gave me six hundred pounds which I used to purchase return tickets to Canada at the cost of eighteen thousand Jamaican dollars, if my memory serves me correctly. I just wanted to be cautious. Just in case she had told Immigration that we were separated or did not come to receive me at the airport. I also contacted both of my aunts in Canada and advised that they meet me at the airport in Toronto just in case Cherry did not turn up.

I tried to make a last contact with my wife. I was lucky. She picked up the phone.

"Hi Cherry, did you receive the good news?" I asked.

"What good news?" she asked, coldly.

"The news that my papers were finalized to join my wife," I said.

"What's so good about that?" she asked.

"When I used to say there was nothing that exciting about Canada, you painted a nice picture," I said.

"Things and time change, Joshua. Nothing in life remains static," she responded.

I really could not understand my wife and what had actually got into her. I felt like crying like a baby. However, I held myself together.

"Cherry, will you be meeting me at the airport?" I asked.

"I said it does not make sense that you come now," she said.

"But Cherry, I must come. There is an expiration date on the visa. What's the difference between coming now and January?" I asked.

She was quiet for awhile. It seemed she did not realize that I had a deadline to reach with respect to the visa. She said she had to go, and she hung up the phone.

I wondered if I should still travel abroad after all. I became quite ambivalent about the whole matter. I lay on my bed and began to think so hard that I thought a blood vessel would burst in my head. I said that I must go. At least, I would get a deeper sense of what was going on.

I thought that she must have misrepresented a number of things to me. I wondered if she really worked at a university as she said she did. I wondered what was her real motive in her wanting to marry me. I remembered how sweet she was when we just started our telephone love affair. How romantic our letters were. I remember how she couldn't wait to have me in her arms and in her home in Canada. The loneliness she said she was experiencing. I wondered what had caused the sudden change. I was dying to find out, and I would.

There were about three teachers, including myself who would not have been returning after the Christmas break to Frome Technical High

School. The principal and staff of my school planned a send-off party for us. There were lots of big speeches and people stating how nice we were and lucky to have been going abroad to a first world country. I tried to appear elated but deep down I was in great pain. I danced and received gifts. I knew I was loved by the Frome Technical High School staff, but I did not know it was so solid. Some teachers even cried when they spoke about me and how I made the place so jolly and productive. I felt the tears dripping down my eyes as well, and some glimpsed them. However, they would have never known the real reason for my tears.

I was really thinking of how my colleagues appreciated me so much, cared and loved me, even more so than my wife. I was thinking that I actually knew, and that I was more associated with my colleagues than I was with my wife. I knew from the start that something was amiss. That something was just not right. However, I resisted this built-in safety guard which I think every animal, including human beings, possesses. I must warn that one should always listen to this in-built safety net with which nature or God provides us. If it does not feel or seem right, believe it, it probably is just not right.

I felt when it was my turn to speak at our send-off to say what was really going on in my head. That I was not happy going to Canada.

That I was probably going to be living on the streets in a few weeks. That I might never ever have the liberty of moulding young adolescents' lives as I had, since 1981, my in-training years at Montego Bay Secondary School, now known as St. James High School. But I resisted the urge and started my acting role.

I opened my mouth and started to say that I really and truly loved them all. That was not acting. That I appreciated their gifts but more importantly, the way they accepted me at Frome for the past four years as if I had always worked there. That too was genuine stuff. That it would be great if they would keep in touch. I gave them my wife's address and phone number, but I deeply hoped that they would never call. That was acting me. I did not even want them to call me at Cherry's home. I knew it was a meagre chance that I would be living there with her, at least not for long. Would I have been right?

The night of the 19th of December 1993, my 'brother', Oliver Nelson, drove me to Darliston to say farewell to my daughters. It was really tough for me and for them too, especially Kadisha. She was really my little pet, being my first child but I loved them both, equally. Kadisha was also with me until she was a little over three years old so there was a greater bond between us than my little, sweetie, Kaliese. Kadisha would have been ten years later that month. Kaliese would have been seven years in May.

We drove into the yard. I tried to exhibit a happy face. I did not want them to see any tears coming from their father. It's a pity they did not know that they had a really emotional, 'cry cry' baby man as their father, I thought. I took my two daughters and held them very closely and let them know that I really loved them. I also told them that I would never forget them. As a matter of fact, I had taken my daughters to do the medical with me to travel to Canada as well. It was my hope that I would be able to get settled soon and then sponsored them into Canada, the same way Cherry had done for me. Would it ever happen? Would I be in a position to realise that dream for my two little girls?

It was the hardest night I had ever had in all my thirty-four years. I sat in the back of Oliver's car when it was time to go. When I turned around, I saw Kadisha crying. I felt so hurt inside. There I was. I had already done them wrong by living elsewhere, albeit the same parish and country. Now, I was on my way to an overseas country. I thought that they would never forgive me for my actions and promised that I would repay them handsomely, one day.

December 20, 1993 had arrived. I did not sleep well the night before. I was with my 'brother', Oliver Nelson who took me to the Sangster's International Airport. I don't remember if I had told him of what was going on with Cherry and I. Probably I did, probably I didn't, but it was truly hard leaving my friend, buddy, 'tightpiece' and brother, coupled with my children, Kadisha and Kaliese. The uncertainties that were ahead of me did not help much either. Oliver helped me with my luggage, and we bade goodbye.

The plane was virtually empty. I was able to move from seat to seat. After all, it was December 20. Everyone was heading away from Canada to get rid of the cold, not approaching Canada to meet the cold. I thought about that too. I questioned why it is that my life always seemed to be going in the direction of a Canada when it should have been going towards say, a Jamaica, or Florida or Cuba. Why was it always headed for the cold? I said to myself that there had been warm days though. There had been those days that I danced as a five-year old for the customers at my father's establishment on Hart Street in Montego Bay. There had also been those days, that I felt so lucky to share the friends that I had, especially those whom I had met during my years at Sam Sharpe Teachers'

College. I thought also about those warm days, when it seemed I was heading to a tropical country when Mr. and Mrs. Thompson came into my life. I said, yes, there have been some warm days. Warm days when I met my newly found, on-campus friend who took me to see her parents, and some warm days and temperatures when I met my sweetheart who was now studying in a Canadian university. Even Cherry, initially, brought the thrill of warm days. However, those warm days had suddenly transformed into a blistering weather condition, leaving me with a runny nose, itchy throat, and a persistent chronic cough coupled with the chills. Would the environmental condition of my new habitat change for the better or deteriorate? Only time would tell, I thought.

Notwithstanding those times when I found myself travelling towards a Mexico, a Cuba, Trinidad and Tobago, a Guyana, even though I had not travelled much before this day, I could mostly picture me going to an England, an Iceland, a Canada. I had indeed travelled to some sub-freezing temperatures and countries. It did not seem that that would have been changing soon, at least not on December 20, 1993. But I had hope and an inherent determination to succeed, if only for my children's sake.

I landed at the Pearson International Airport Toronto, at about 5:30 P.M. I was out of immigration about 7:30 P.M. I looked around nervously to see if Cherry had come to pick me up for my new abode, but she was not there. I was about to use the telephone booth to call my aunts when I saw one of them, Aunt Almena also known as Aunt Minna or Sis, then the next, Aunt Lucille. They were both with their husbands in separate cars. I asked them what they thought I should do, since Cherry did not seem to come to receive me. They said I should try to go there. If I did not, she could call immigration on me and I could have been deported, was their argument. That would have messed me up big time, I thought. My hopes of travelling abroad to North America or Europe or any other foreign jurisdiction, for that matter, would have been nil if that should have happened to me, I thought.

Just as I was about to board one of the cars to take me to my wife's address, I saw my brother-in-law drive up. He shouted my name. I wanted to return the favour, but I could not remember his name. We had only met at the wedding and he was a reserved guy. I introduced him to my aunts and uncles without

352

using his name, packed my stuff in his car and he sped off to Cherry's home.

Upon my arrival at the house, I noticed my brother-in-law seemed to have been in a hurry. He helped me with the luggage and sped off. I was directed to the basement of the house. That's where my wife lived. Upon my seeing Cherry, I walked towards her to hug and kiss her, but she pushed me away. She went to the bathroom, had a shower and went upstairs.

I started to cry like a baby. This act was becoming quite regular and ordinary for me. I started to ask myself the reason my life was taking a retrograde step. While I was there thinking, I noticed my wife came back downstairs and got dressed. She went back upstairs and shortly after, I could here her car rolling onto the street. Her son and daughter stayed upstairs. I was just by myself. Not even my in-laws came downstairs to see how I was doing. I felt abandoned. I started to think that God hated me or worse, that there probably was no God. I asked, why else would all those things have been happening to me? I knew I had a good heart for human kind. I knew that I worked hard and that I did everything that I possibly could to move out of my quite humble origin, one that was inundated with all manner of evil, struggles, and setbacks. However, I thought I had overcome all those obstacles and that I was well on my way to conquering the odds so blatant in my earlier experiences. I just could not understand why things were once again going downhill with me, with me having no control. I felt a very heavy heart. I thought that I had made two many mistakes in my life. If only I had stuck to my girlfriend studying in Canada or to that young lady I met on the university campus in Kingston, Jamaica, or best, not indulge in my youthful indiscretion during my marriage to my then wife, Merfelin, the mother of my two beautiful daughters, I would not have found myself being taken for granted and treated like the garbage in the bin at the door I stood staring through. Those were my unflinching thoughts.

I got a shower and changed into some clean clothes. The television was left on, so I just flicked the remote control aimlessly. A couple embracing and being in a romantic mood, caught my eyes, on one of the channels. So, I lingered there briefly. I thought I would have been in the position that the couple was in now that I had carried out Cherry's original wishes, but it was obviously not meant to be. I was getting too emotional and lonely by the carrying-ons of that channel, so I continued clicking up and down, the same way I thought my life was. I ran into a wrestling match on another channel, it too reminded me of my life's struggles and my current situation with my second wife. I continued clicking. I eventually just dropped the remote on the table and left the television to play. Psychologically, I was doing the same with my life, if even for the rest of the night.

I remembered that my 'brother', Oliver Nelson had made me a few bottles of rum punch for me to take to Canada, so I reached for my luggage. I got a glass, rinsed it out and poured me some of it. I drank it and it calmed my spirit a bit. I kept drinking until the bottle was empty. It was about 12:30 A.M. By then, my first night in Canada was a real lonely one. Once again, the tears rolled uncontrollably down my wretched face like a car out of control. I was all by myself and I had no idea where my wife was. She just stepped out and drove away. She did not as much as say bye, dog, I would be back. I thought I was going to die. The rum punch had helped me some. I lay my head on one of the pillows and fell asleep.

For some reason or the other, I woke up about 2:00 A.M. At first, I forgot where I was then I remembered that I was in the powerful first world country of Canada. While I lay in the dark, I noticed that there was a light flashing in the dark room. I remembered the light that flashed in my bedroom as a child at King's School and my thoughts went to my father, briefly. However, now I was much more mature.

I got up to trace the source of the light and realized that it was coming from the phone. The phone was actually ringing at 2:00 A.M. But my wife had deliberately turned the ringer off before she left.

"Hello," I said, somewhat unsure of myself.

"Who is this?" the male voice asked.

"Who are you?" I asked.

"Who the hell are you?" the man raised his voice angrily

"What do you want?" I asked politely.

"Is this 1234567?" he asked.

"Yes, this is the number," I said.

"So, who the hell are you?" he wanted to know.

I gave up. We seemed to have been asking each other the same questions for more than two minutes, so I relented.

"I am Cherry's husband," I said.

"What, you're what?" he asked again.

"I am Cherry's husband," I repeated.

"Cherry is married?" he questioned.

"If I am her husband, what would you conclude?" I asked.

The irate man slammed the phone down in my ear.

I started to see why it was a problem for me to be with my wife. I felt not only cheated but I felt like I deserved better than what I had just realised I had been handed.

My investigation revealed that the reason Cherry was so anxious to get married was simply that her son's father, even though in a relationship with her, had moved in with another woman. She was merely trying to spite him or make him jealous by getting married. I understood that she had been intimate with this guy for years, even prior to my stepdaughter's father being in the picture. I was also made to understand that no matter what happened between them, relationship-wise, Cherry would always return to him.

I stayed at Cherry's home for approximately two weeks and for those two weeks I was there, she did not exchange a single word with me. We did not touch each other. She had eggs and bread, etc., in her refrigerator, so I used them to make my breakfast or snacks. Sometimes, I would go upstairs to talk to her parents when they were around. Otherwise, I was just a little boy in her bed and basement. At the end of the two weeks, I called my Aunt Almena to come to take me out of my misery and she did.

It was early January 1994 when I moved into my Aunt Almena's home at her Annamore Road address in Mississauga, Ontario. It was obviously a middle-class area. At the time I moved there, my aunt was the only black family in that little area. The rest of her neighbours appeared to have been Italians or of Italian extractions. There were also two or three individuals who spoke with a British accent. I wondered why my aunt would choose to live in an area that had not a single person who looked like her or spoke or shared in her culture. I did not have the audacity to ask her the reason for that though.

My aunt was retired by then and so was her husband. Almost all her six children except one male and a female had moved out and were living on their own. Her son who lived at the home, occupied one of the four bedrooms upstairs. He was employed and had his own vehicle. He was a very quiet and reserved person. I hardly ever saw him for the eight months I was to live at this home. He would be there for a week or more, and you would not even know. He did not even come to the dining-room to eat with the rest of us. My female cousin lived in the two-bedroom basement with her three children. She was unemployed at the time. I often wondered how she was able to sleep so much. I thought she stole all my sleeping ability. Every time I went to the basement, she would be fast asleep. I could sleep no more than three hours nightly. The few hours she was awake, she would spend most of that time shopping. My female cousin was very kind though. She would take me in her mother's car to get a hair cut frequently. She would buy me shoes, clothes, etc. I said to myself, Canada was not that bad. If one did not have to work, have three children, and could spend so much money, have all the gadgets that one can think of, Canada couldn't be that bad after all. I started to feel hopeful, even amidst my sorrow and trepidation for the future.

I occupied one of the rooms upstairs and my aunt and her husband occupied the master bedroom. I felt very uncomfortable living at my aunt's. She treated me well, but I had a very bad feeling. The first reason was that all along they had told me that Canada was tough. I therefore felt like a big jackass to have ignored their advice, at least in their eyes, and now had to end up being a liability at their home. The second reason was that when I needed help to attend high school in Jamaica, they did not help me or they said they did not have any money to do so. However, now I had to depend on them for food and shelter. I was actually living in one of their homes. I wondered how they thought about that arrangement whenever they were not in my presence. It made me feel quite uncomfortable, indeed.

My aunt was, and still is, a very religious person. Every morning at 4: 00 A. M., no matter how soundly one slept, one's sleep was going to be cut short beginning that hour, seven days a week. She was involved in what was called telephone prayer. With her, appeared to have been a whole bunch of her church sisters and brothers screaming in prayer in their respective homes, all at the same time. She would scream to God on the top of her voice and talked in what they described as tongues. I found that practice quite unusual but had to learn to like it over time. To live with it. I was a guest or a tenant who was not paying rent. I had no say in that matter.

After my first month at the Annamore Road address in Mississauga, I enrolled in a computer programming course with the International Correspondence Schools (I.C.S.). As a part of the course, I was provided with a computer. This was how I got introduced to computers and how to use them effectively. I was totally ignorant about the operations of computers until I started that course. I am really glad I had enrolled in that correspondence course. The first time I had used a computer, I was about twenty-nine years old and that was for a brief time.

I started to check the advertisement pages of newspapers, in search of work. I applied for all types of jobs, including factory, and was unable to land a job. I was virtually running out of cash. That made me quite nervous. I used to give my aunt some money weekly for food, but I was getting broke. I told her my situation and she advised that I should seek social assistance. I had no idea what that was. However, she explained to me what it was and how it worked. She said that in my situation, I might not have qualified for it as my wife had just sponsored me. My wife was legally responsible for me, was responsible for taking care of me for the first five years or so, until I was in a position to do so myself. However, I decided to go to the Social Assistance Office, notwithstanding.

I went to the office and spoke to a very polite lady. I had always heard that Canadians were quite polite. However, I did not make much of it until I met this lady. She explained to me how the program worked and how one might be qualified for what I considered easy money.

Where I came from, if one did not have a job, dog would eat your supper. You would have to sell soup on the pavement or find some other means. Getting free money was therefore quite a surprise for me. I started to question why my relatives had said it was hard in Canada.

The lady, whose name evaded me at the time of writing, said under normal circumstances, I would not qualify. She, however, was going to take up my case at some meeting or the other. She took my information and said she would contact me in a few days. She advised that there was no guarantee that it would be approved and that I should continue to search for work. She added that even if I should get approved, I would still have to be job hunting five days a week. I thanked her and left the office.

I began to worry and wonder if I had done the right thing. I wondered if my approaching the welfare organization could lead to me being deported as my wife and I were now separated. I worried for all five days before I got the call. The lady told me that I was lucky. That I got approved and would be receiving social assistance until I could find some kind of employment. I was elated. I could not believe how lucky I was and easy it was to get free money. I collected my first cheque and gave my aunt my little contribution to help with food. I was also able to get my hair cut with my own money and bought a few other items as well. I felt proud of myself for having been able to succeed in collecting social assistance.

One day, one of my cousins and I were driving around in Mississauga. We went to a supermarket and he remarked that he could tell that the guys standing on the corner were losers and were receiving social assistance. My cousin was not aware that I was now collecting this money, and I did not know that one was being looked down at if one participates in such a program. I felt extremely ashamed. I felt like calling the office and tell them to remove my name, but I could not. I had no other way to survive. I kept extremely quiet until my cousin returned me home.

As of that day, I worked twice as hard at getting a job. I applied for dish washing jobs, factory jobs, supermarket, just about everything that anyone could do, but I came up with absolutely nothing.

One day in July 1994, I got a call from a former college friend, Glendon Lawrence (Laro). You will remember Glendon as the singer at our inception at teachers' college. At the time he contacted me, he lived in Winnipeg. We had a discussion and decided that we were going to rent an apartment jointly in Toronto. He had a friend who got us a job at a Supertest Road address in Toronto. Our job was to make Christmas decorations. I had never done anything like this before neither had Glendon, but we took the job. I was able to move out of my aunt's home in August and out of welfare. Glendon and I moved into our two-bedroom apartment at 1010-2677 Kipling Avenue, Toronto where I was to live for three years and even got married for a third time while I resided there.

Glendon and I were paid six dollars and eighty-five cents per hour. That was our gross pay. Our apartment was about seven hundred fifty dollars per month. The work was hard, and the manager and owner, was a true slave driver and he was very strict. For each eight-hour shift, we were entitled to two breaks of fifteen minutes each. One day, I can remember having gone in the resting area. I was just about to leave when the boss came in.

"Joshua, did you know you are one second, late?" he asked.

I could hardly believe this man. I thought he was joking at first. However, when I looked at his face, I realized he was very upset as I had stayed one second too late.

"It is now three seconds!" he yelled.

I rushed to take up my factory position drawing some kind of straws or grassy materials from a machine to make Christmas decorations. My friend was even more unlucky than I was with our manager. He was actually fired a few weeks later. This was for some small infractions in the eyes of the manager. I wanted to lose my cool too. However, I realized that both of us could not manage to lose our jobs at the same time. We had rent to pay.

My friend had contacted a Jamaican friend who worked as a supervisor at the then Chimo Hotel, later to become Holiday Inn Hotel in the Woodbine and Steele area of Markham, Ontario. This lady was the supervisor of the House Keeping Department of the hotel. Glendon started to work in the department. His job was mainly to fold towels. He also told her of me. I subsequently was hired as a houseman in the same department. My job was even more menial than Glendon's. My portfolio, yes, portfolio, was basically to clean the elevators, the windows, sweep the hotel compound, including getting rid of the leaves, remove the garbage. Our shift was from 2:00 P.M. to 10:00 P.M. Remember, Glendon and I were teachers for all our working lives, until we arrived in Canada.

The job was very hard, and I thought I had to go back to school. I reasoned that this kind of work was not utilizing my skills and abilities. I decided that I was going to apply to university. I was also to meet my third wife at the Holiday Inn.

CHAPTER EIGHT

Life's Fluctuation

I started a full-time, houseman position at the then Chimo Hotel, later to become the Holiday Inn, located at Woodbine and Steele, Markham, Ontario. This was in early 1995. At the same time, I had either sent out, or was about to send out applications to the universities in Ontario via its Ontario University Application Centre in Guelph. I found my jobs not merely very grinding and mundane but unbearable. I knew I could not continue to do these kinds of work indefinitely. I had no idea how I was going to get out of this rattrap but I thought that acquiring a Canadian university degree might have been a good way to start the process, to get out of what I considered slavery, contemporary slavery. I hated all the jobs I had done in Canada up to this point, with all my life, with all my soul, with my entire being. Like all the other jobs I had acquired since my arrival in this wonderful, first world nation, the Chimo Hotel work was quite routine, dirty, hard, and monotonous. At least in my view, those were my perceptions, anyway. My significant disgust with the kinds of work I was doing, was even more so, as I had not been in the habit of doing manual, or what I considered menial work until I arrived in Canada. The hours at the Chimo Hotel were from 2:00 P.M. to 10:00 P.M. I was also required to work weekends. I got my days-off during the weekdays. Nothing in that arrangement was in line to what I had grown accustomed in my little, third world country. I really could not understand why people were leaving their, very exciting, tropical, third world nations albeit impoverished, to these so-called first world nations inundated with depression and solitude. Countries where it seemed, to me, that slavery was rampant but had only taken on a contemporary camouflage.

I had also recalled my uncle, the school principal, packing and moving shop, so to speak, and emigrated to the North American jurisdiction, running from what he said was Socialism at the time. I also recalled that he had also ended up working in factories for the first five years or so, in the U.S.A., until eventually he hit the jackpot in the real estate business and became a United States millionaire. I wondered if my Canadian university degree was going to give me the opportunity to acquire the kind of financial success that my uncle had eventually acquired overtime.

My duties at the Chimo Hotel basically involved my cleaning the yard, taking out the garbage, cleaning the elevators and windows, cleaning the restaurants, bars, and bathrooms, and so on. I was required to carry a walkie talkie or pager or both, at all times. This was to ensure easy access to me by management and supervisors. The slave must have the shackles around his ankles even if it carried a different name and was positioned differently, I thought. The contemporary slave driver was quite clever in his approach. They were quite good at masking what was going on, I observed. When one travels from a country such as the one from which I came, to one such as my current, it was easy to see how the masses, the ordinary people, were so brainwashed to work for nothing to build and perpetuate the status quo. Sometimes, I smiled at what great experts the powers-that-be were at what they do. I thought that at the Chimo, for example, where we were provided with pagers or walkie talkie, this was also to ensure that we could not just find a little area and hide away or take a well deserved break. Canada is a capitalist society, its vast wealth relies upon burning out every ounce of cheap labour out of its unsuspecting labourers, especially those new immigrants who come to these countries every year. I wondered how these new arrivals could not spot the trick and the craft and trickery at work here. They, observingly, depicted a sense of importance walking around with their masters' pagers and walkie talkie. They also felt so important when they could buy all the junks with their credit cards and drive a car, even if it meant that they would have to do six jobs just to manage to keep up with the payments. It did not matter whether they were able to enjoy their 'properties' or not. They got all caught up in this psychological game being set and played by the establishment, the powers-that-be. However, I saw it as soon as I disembarked from the plane at the Pearson International Airport. It was so blatant. Unlike my original thought of the country with the social assistance program, I truly and really concluded now, that nothing was free. Someone had to pay for what had appeared free to me at first. Now I was paying for all that so-called free money and more.

The job was hard and tedious for me. I can remember during the autumn I was constantly being called upon to sweep up the leaves outside the building. However, every time that I would sweep them up, the wind would just blow with vengeance, as if it was teasing the new slave boy in town, and the entire place would, in seconds, get all covered in dry leaves once again. One of these windy sessions, I had been called five times for the day to clean up those loose leaves. The sixth time I was called to do so, this was what occurred.

"Joshua, did I not tell you to clean up the leaves at the front of the hotel?" my supervisor asked.

"Yes, and I did it five times," I said.

"Do you take me for a fool?" she asked

"You ought to know if you are a fool or not," I said.

"You know you have no respect. Glendon would never speak to me like that and imagine, he was a teacher," she said, getting a little upset.

"Do I look like Glendon to you?" I queried.

"Joshua, I am not going to argue with you. You go and sweep up the leaves now," she ordered.

"I am not going out there to make a fool of myself with those leaves. I cleaned them up five times already, and they keep reappearing," I insisted.

I told her to ask the front desk staff the number of times they saw me there sweeping, if she did not believe. She said she was not going to ask anyone anything. Her job was to ensure that the place was clean, and it was not. It was obviously dirty and that I should go to do it summarily. I walked off and stated that slavery was abolished long time ago. I went about my business, grabbed a rag, and started to clean the lounge windows

Deep in my heart I was very worried. There I was shooting off my mouth. However, if I got fired, I would have had absolutely nothing on which to resort. I was just getting fed up of my life and with the whole situation in which I had found myself. I was on the verge of breaking. I sincerely hoped that I would not snap, and someone got all my built in and fully stored anger and pain. I prayed that it did not get uncontrollable to overflow like a bomb in any of my so-called superiors' faces.

Sometime later that year, I met one of the female colleagues who was a cook at the hotel. I found her quite attractive and started to pursue her, but she had no interest in me. I guessed the reason was one that everyone whispered, that she was a virgin and had no romantic interest in men. I also thought that the fact that she was from the Philippines and I, being a Jamaican, now a floor cleaner, were contributing factors to her non-interest in me as well. However, one day during my break, she was also at break and we started to talk. I made some references to the difference in behaviour and attitudes of Canadian children compared to the students I taught in Jamaica. Immediately I said that she looked up at me.

"Were you a teacher?" she inquired.

"A high school science teacher for approximately ten years," I responded.

Our break came to an end but not our relationship. I noticed that although she expressed no interest in me romantically, she would now acknowledge my presence by saying hello or nodding or something. She would never pass subsequently, without expressing some form of acknowledgement of my presence.

"Laro, there is a cook in the kitchen, man. I like her," I said.

"She is nice man," Glendon said.

"I heard she is a virgin, and that she does not have a boyfriend," I said.

"That's what I heard," he said.

I continued to endeavour to create interest romantically, but it was too slow in coming. For a few weeks, I kept trying to get her romantic interest but to no avail. So, I decided to use my best weapon at my disposal. That was my ability to express my thoughts, and my ability to communicate well, through the written word. I went home and constructed a letter. Basically, I expressed how beautiful she was, how despite my previous challenges and disappointments with women, that I was deeply attracted to her. I also gave her a brief synopsis of my background and what my goals were in Canada.

The next day we met on the outside. I slipped the letter in her right hand. She took it and I noticed she went downstairs. In moments, she was back upstairs. I realized she had simply gone to put the letter in her locker. I thought after she got an opportunity to read it, our relationship would never be the same again, and I was correct.

I was cleaning one of the restaurants of the hotel when I overheard a conversation among three of her kitchen staff colleagues.

"Did you know that Joshua and Reflor are having a relationship?" one of them said.

"I think she could do better than him," the second said.

"I don't believe it's true though. What would she see in that guy? I just don't believe it's true," the third said.

I continued to mop the floor and one of them walked across. I stopped briefly to avoid my mop touching her. I said to myself, how ironic that situation was. Here were a few, probably, high school dropouts, looking down at me as being equal to the work I did; mopping the restaurant's floor. I thought had I been in my homeland, they would refer to me as Mr. Spencer but right then they could only see me as my job, a floor mopper. I said to myself, mopping floors was neither me nor my job. It was just simply something I had to do temporarily. I remembered one of my aunts saying that Cherry thought I would end up working permanently in a menial job ambience, for the rest of my life. The more I thought about the gossips of the kitchen staff and Cherry's alleged comments, the more I felt the desire to prove them wrong.

Within months, I received an acceptance letter from the York University to study there, full-time. I would have been attached to its McLaughlin College. I got accepted to an Honours Degree Program. The honours program was a full-time four-year program, at the end of which I would get an Honours Bachelor's degree, which would amount to one hundred twenty credits. That is to say, I would study for thirty credits per year. However, while I studied at the university, I had a conversation with a professor during my third year, who outlined that to teach in Ontario, all I needed was a teaching diploma and a three-year degree. Upon hearing that, and because I had some problems, financial and otherwise, I decided to graduate after three years with my BA degree majoring in Psychology, without the honours. During my study at Canada's third largest university of 55,000 students, I pursued several courses in Psychology, as well as many others. Some of them were Science, Spanish, African Studies, Philosophy of Law, and many others.

Towards the end of 1995, I decided to resign from the hotel. I got a part-time job at a No Frills supermarket at the Dufferin Mall in Toronto. Reflor and I continued our relationship. Some way along all this, I had applied for a divorce to an attorney-at-law, Mr. Joseph S. Farkas. His office was located at 3089 Bathurst Street, Toronto. Unlike my first divorce, there was no tension or stress in my second official divorce from my then wife. It happened really quickly and without hitches. I just had to pay five hundred Canadian dollars to get it done. It was hard finding this money, but I made the sacrifice once again, to be divorced, yet to get married once again as I did before. Some may think that I was a fool. However, I am not. It's just that I believe in structure. A structured family life, probably of which I yearned when I was a child, running from home to home, like wild animals running around in the woods.

Reflor Graciano Tominez and I got married on August 23, 1996 at the Toronto City Hall. My first wife, Merfelin and I were married on August 20, 1983. For the first time, I had biological relatives at my wedding in the persons of my Aunt Almena and her husband, Uncle Beresford at the Toronto City Hall. Reflor and I had our only son, her only child, Michael Spencer, in February 1998. In 1996, I had also acquired a support worker job with an organization known as N.A.B.O.R.S. (Neighbours Allied for Better Opportunities in Residential Support). Its office was located at 2 Carlton Street, Toronto, Ontario. Its Executive Director at the time I started working there, was one Beth French. A Year later, she had moved on to another organization. Sherri Franklyn succeeded her as Executive Director. This was a non-profit organization attached to the Ontario Ministry of Health. There were twelve adults attached to this program. Each adult had its own staff and a coordinator. Each adult who was either physically or mentally challenged or both, was provided his or her own home and a small staff, run by the coordinator. The coordinator's role was basically to ensure that the adult who was put to his or her charge was fully integrated in society. That is to say, the coordinator had to create a full plan that would meet all this adult's needs, including finding voluntary work for his client. It was also the coordinator's role to assist in the interview of individuals to serve these physically and/or mentally challenged persons acquire suitable staff. Within six months, I was promoted to the coordinator role of my unit. I was to continue in this role until the end of 1999. This was not bad. I was earning about twelve dollars an hour in a short time. I was able to lease a 1998 Toyota Camry in 1998. When I leased the car, the salesman said it was a lease to own arrangement. I asked him whether that meant that at the end of the four years, I would own the car, to which he responded in the affirmative. The monthly lease was three hundred seventy-three Canadian dollars. I was happy that things had appeared to be moving forward.

Notwithstanding the above, I must point out that during all this period, I had serious financial problems. There were times when I had to use my credit cards to pay my rent. There were times that I had no dental care and was unable to attend a dentist until in 2005. As dental care was, and still is, very expensive in this country and not covered by the Ontario Healthcare System, I had no coverage until then. I remember having fillings in some of my teeth. These were fillings that were done while

I lived in Jamaica. When I got in Toronto, I was unable to see a dentist between December 1993 to September 2005. My menial jobs and the not-so menial ones, thereafter, had no benefits that would take care of this problem. I think at N.A.B.O.R.S., I got some benefits that actually covered a certain portion of my dental care. However, the problem was that in that case, I was required to pay for the cost up front and then my employer would reimburse me. I just could not find the money. The result was that my teeth started to get very bad and some that had lost their fillings, got broken off while I ate the junk food that I could barely afford most of the times. As a consequence, many people I met thought I was shy or that I was too serious an individual for my own good. Little did they know that I was one of the most jovial persons who had ever been born. It was just that I had something to hide. Something to hide in my mouth. Now that I have fixed my teeth, I sometimes still forget that I can go ahead and skin my teeth like an angry dog. Every time that I feel like laughing like my old Joshua, Ricky, Fista self, and start to squeezing my lips together, I have to force myself to let them show, to let them glow. In fact, I was stressed and upset but I was unable to smile before, not so much because of my stress and challenges, but because my teeth were gone or were going bad and I could not fix them.

I remember having gone to a dentist's office at the Sheridan Mall in the Jane and Wilson area in Toronto while I worked with N.A.B.O.R.S. The dentist had me lie on his chair to examine my mouth. He then said that I was required to pay nine hundred dollars to start the work. I told him I had insurance but was told I had to pay up front and then my employer would reimburse me. He said I could use my credit card. However, my credit cards were all to their limits. I had to apologize and walked out with my head bowed like an embarrassed dog.

So, the reason I always appeared to have been serious was not a result of my personality. I was a very congenial person who loved to laugh as I still do, but I had to protect my mouth. In a sense, I had to protect my status or completely trick everyone in that regard. I could not let the world know that I had hit rock bottom in Canada. How could that have been? I kept asking myself over and over again. I had passed through the schools of successful folks in my homeland. I had been fortunate to have met so many successful women who had serious intimate interest in me and, I had already been married to two of them. I could not reveal or deny the reality, that the more things changed especially with respect to me, the more they remained the same, or even deteriorated.

In August 1998, when my son, Michael Spencer, was only six months old, I visited Jamaica to see my two daughters, Kadisha and Kaliese as well as my siblings. I was always in touch with my girls. I missed them so much but because of my financial bind, I was not able to do much or visit them prior to this date.

In addition to my work with N.A.B.O.R.S., I had also started part-time work in a restaurant in Etobicoke, Toronto, where I washed dishes after school sometimes. At times when I left the restaurant, it was five in the morning, just time to have had a shower to get ready to go to classes at York University. Now that I think about it, I don't know how I survived.

In about 2001, my daughter, Kadisha Spencer, came to Canada through a Students' Exchange Program between the Government of Jamaica and the Canadian Government. She was in Newfoundland, so I was unable to see her. We communicated regularly via phones and e-mails, however. I even helped her with some of her homework via e-mail. Fortunately, at the end of the program, her flight stopped off at the Pearson International Airport. I went to see her. I was happily surprised to see the lovely young lady whom my daughter had grown up to become. It was really hard for both of us. We were both in the company of her friends and others, so not much affection was shown between us. I also wanted to take my three year old son, Michael Spencer, to the Pearson Airport at the time, but my wife and I were involved in one of our many fights; she did not allow me to take Michael to meet his sister. I think most of the fights and challenges between us had been caused as a result of the financial challenges that we faced, especially after we got married and began to live together. I was also a fulltime student as you know. There were other challenges of compatibility and cultural challenges, and so on. However, the strain and financial burden might have contributed significantly to our many conflicts, more than any other variable.

Talking of conflicts between us brings me to this disclosure. January of 1997, my wife and I were involved in a domestic situation. The letter below, provided some time later in 2005, by me, to a potential employer, will illuminate on the matter in a nutshell.

Dear Sir/Madam:

January 1997 my wife and I were both charged with assault, and assault with a weapon. We were both fingerprinted as a result of these charges. Both sets of charges were subsequently dropped on November 6, 1998. The weapon being referred to, was a spatula which my wife had hidden in the bedroom closet. She took out the spatula during an argument and I grabbed it from her. This latter charge was summarily withdrawn.

I have been recently offered a teaching position with a school board. Its background check has resulted in a police document being forwarded to the board and a copy to yours truly, depicting these charges. These charges had been dropped approximately seven years ago and legally, should have been expunged from your data base. I have contacted your department via telephone and was advised to scribe this letter for this request to be effected summarily. I also request, kindly, that you forward a new, updated record to the school board in question.

My full name is Joshua Spencer. My date of birth is October 31, 19--. My social insurance number is 123 456 789. I currently reside at—. At the time of the alleged charges, I resided at

1010-2677 Kipling Avenue, Etobicoke, Ontario
M9V 4P1.

Thank you.

Sincerely,

Joshua Spencer

Shortly after returning from Jamaica in 1998 from my vacation, I was no longer working as a coordinator with N.A.B.O.R.S. The client, Paul Popwell of whose care I was the coordinator and was responsible, had transferred to another program. As a result of being out of this full-time employment, my financial situations got even worse. I had also got upset with the poor treatment that was being meted out to me at the supermarket I worked as a shelf packer on a part-time basis at the time. I walked off the job after telling the then manager my mind and what I thought about him. I was left with only the dishwashing job.

In the year 2000, I met a manager from one of Canada's major banks. He was an associate manager in its insurance department. I soon discovered that he was born and grown in England but that his parents were Jamaicans. We had a long discussion and he offered to recruit me into his unit of which he was the manager. To do so, he was going to need references and conduct a background check. When he revealed the latter, I told him frankly that I did not have a criminal record but that in 1997 my wife and I were involved in a domestic situation which led to both of us being charged which was later dropped. However, my police record might still make references to the dropped charges as a certain number of years had to have passed before it would have been expunged from the police data base.

"Mr. Spencer, let me tell you the truth. If I mention anything about dropped charges, the branch manager will not approve my hiring you," the associate manager said to me.

"I guess it's my bad luck then. I had to tell you the truth," I said.

"No, no, no. You did the right thing," he assured me.

"If you were to commit a crime and you sought a lawyer, you needed to tell the lawyer the full truth," he said.

"What do you mean?" I asked.

"I am now your lawyer. Leave everything up to me," he said.

I felt so elated and relieved, all at the same time. I felt like getting up from my chair and give him a big hug, as well as bawl as a baby, let the tears flow, but I kept my composure. The associate manager gave me some booklets to study so I could go to write the qualifying exams which are requirements to get licensed. He said that he knew that I did not have to go to the branch for lessons. However, he advised that I should do so in order that the branch manager would see me around and get familiarized with me. So, I read through both booklets. One was based on Accident and Disability Insurance, the other was Life Insurance. To get the Ontario Level 1 licence, a candidate had to score a minimum of 75% in each exam. I did the exams and was successful.

I was officially hired as an Insurance Sales and Service Representative by the company. My role was to sell insurance to the company's customers as well as to everyone else. I also had the job to service current accounts. It also involved making numerous phone calls daily and travelling to the homes of clients and potential clients throughout Ontario. I was paid by commission. That meant, I was paid a percentage from the sales I made. However, if I sold a policy and it lapsed within two years of being written to the client, the full or part of the commission would have to be deducted from my future commission payments, depending on the length of the time of the two-year period that the policy was on the books. That arrangement even worsened my already dire financial situation. The first year I did well, but soon the policies started to lapse. It became so bad that months upon months, I had no income. I started to owe the company money that grew into thousands of Canadian dollars as the months progressed.

While I worked in the bank's insurance department, I used my opportunity at the company to study, successfully, a number of financial courses. I studied and completed successfully, the Institute of Canadian Bankers' course, the Investment Funds in Canada security course. This course gave me the legal instrument to conduct business in Mutual Funds in Canada and I assume elsewhere in the world as well. I also used the opportunity to complete successfully, the Canadian Association of Insurance and Financial Advisers courses; 101-

IFATC 1, 102-IFATC 2 and 103 (B IFATC 3. In each of these courses I acquired marks above eighty-three percent. The bank paid for all the courses that I wrote successfully. I was quite proud of my achievements in my new-found home. Even though my financial constraints continued and there was a huge struggle to sell successfully, life insurance, I had started to see some hope in the future. I had always been a hopeful, positive person and I thought things would get better. I set out to work, and in all my daily activities and interactions, with that thought process in mind.

Notwithstanding, the period 1995 to 2000 was to begin one of the toughest periods I was to have encountered in my new home. I had become afraid of answering the phones. There was always one credit card company representative or the other at the other end of the phone. In the latter part of this period, the call would also include and relate to my student loan payments that were always logging behind in payments. I would constantly make arrangements to pay by the next two weeks, but when those dates arrived, I was still unable to meet my financial obligations. As a consequence, I started to develop bad credit. Some of my loans and credit card outstanding amounts were beginning to be handed over to collections organization. This was not good. In a

388

first world environment, one needs credit to survive. If one's creditors should sell their debts to collections organizations, dog would virtually eat one's supper. So, one could easily understand my dire strait during these times. I could not sleep at nights. The more these bills became a thorn in my side, equally, or even doubly, was my wife's assaults and taunts.

I started to get rather withdrawn. I locked away in my small apartment embedded in a largely immigrant inhabited area of Toronto. An area that lacks the kind of yearning that I so earnestly groped and thought would have been mine when I emigrated there. I spoke to no-one. I hated the ring of the phone. To me, it signified torture. It always meant that there was some lady or some man at the other end, bothering me for money. I thought I was going to die and thought about taking my life. However, I just could not have given in to such selfish way. I thought that would have been a very selfish act to commit suicide. Think about it. I have three children and loved ones, to have done the worse, would to have depicted utter scant regard and feelings to my few, but existent loved ones. I could not have developed the selfish gut to do it. How could I kill myself and leave my lovely daughters and son, Michael, without a father? That was the question I asked my troubled heart. I knew what it was like not having a father to hug me, to guide me. I missed that male role model in my life. I could not deliberately do the same to my son. That is to destroy his father who should provide love, support, guidance, and joy. I had to remain positive and I had, even to this day.

I had to find solitude somewhere though. I had to find some form of respite for my tortured, painful soul. So, I turned to what I knew I do best. I started to read a lot and join online groups on the Internet. I started to resume writing in newspapers on just about everything. This provided much therapy for me and helped to heal the pain, if even temporarily. I started to get letters from all over the world congratulating me for my excellent commentaries and solutions that I was offering for Jamaica, for example. I wondered how comes I was so skilful at coming up with these solutions for a country of 2.7 million people and others of even greater magnitude and power, but could not come up with not even a tiny, tiny half of a solution for my existence in my small apartment pitched in the heart of my immigrant, crime infested, Toronto area. I found it extremely strange. I wondered whether it was easier to solve others' problems than it was to solve one's own. Then next, I turned to writing poetry, a hobby I had developed when I lost my father to murderers. I wrote them and then I read them. I recited them aloud by myself for hours, sometimes staying up all night. I started to feel closer to my online friends than I did to my wife and people I saw around me. At least, they did not curse me or let me feel as if I was a failure, a no-good. They expressed how talented I was, and I enjoyed the flattery. I found myself being contacted to attend meetings of one sort or the other. I always gave then my word, but I knew I would never go. I couldn't even smile properly, I thought. How could I go to meet these great ones? I thought to myself. I could not take them to my place of abode, then how would I meet these people who saw me as this intelligent wizard? I found it ironic that if I should run into an online friend in my elevator, he or she might not have even had a nod of my head, but I was quite vocal online.

The reality is that most individuals are attracted to successful people only. In my poetry, and in my writings in the newspapers, in my online dispositions, only successful people can have the ideas that I had, or so I felt they felt. So, I hid away in my small apartment, oh so lonely. Very lonely indeed.

This was the period 1995 to 2000, when my greatest pain began. I lost most of the few friends I had. They started to feel that I did not want to share and be friends with them anymore. Little did they know that I just got so overwhelmed and exhausted of my lot that I just did not have that fervour to live or speak or interrelate with people on a one and one basis. The Internet provided, ironically, this safety shield. It protected me from them and from me. I started to enjoy my own company. When I had to talk with anyone, I would just act my way through the whole process. However, I was really dying for the conversation to die, even me.

The poem that follows below summed up my hurt and longings, for the approximate period alluded to in the foregoing.

Time Passes in a Flash

Its happy yesterdays and yesteryears flashed by

With lightning speed right before its eyes

Its toddlerhood spanned so narrowly, so brief

At times it has got to struggle with itself to stave off the grief

A bright, wide eyed, masculine seedling

Ejected from its safe fertile soil

Into trampled, unfertilized, and overused domain

Comedian and centre of attention

A garden's jubilee.

So free, so happy, so strong

With the glee radiated from a garden

Common to itself and its sibling's seedlings

Blossomed quickly into a blooming flower

But without the sun's rays to graze

It is dazed.

Its garden, its sun's rays, and fertilizers

Are quickly snatched away

Its chlorophyll becomes almost non-existent

There is a feeling that nothing lasts forever

And that's right.

Time passes in a flash

Like a hundred metre dash

Within seconds, it's at the end of its race

Facing what was to be for decades

A truly rapid pace.

A race of time

A pace of struggles

A memory that is merely reflective and fatigued

By the wicked elements of nature

The challenges ahead before its dead

As time passes in a flash.

Time passes in a flash

It recoils and time's pace has left it far behind

Struggling to find momentum and thrust

To make force times distance equal work Work

in seconds— not in Joules, in times.

It faces its fortieth year with trepidation

Long life for a plant!

Penetrating and elongating its roots, radicles,
and root hairs

But recoiling too often to feed from its past
source

Looking back at the past

Wanting to turn around

To defy tropism—phototropism

To evade the outer external glare

To change direction

But that's it!

It must face reality, the glare

The past is the past

It no longer exists and will never return

The facts of life must be faced

Time passes in a flash!

CHAPTER NINE

The Fire Hire Scenarios

Insurance sales got progressively worse as the time passed with me being employed with the life insurance department of this bank. I would make up to two hundred telephone calls during the day, in the evenings and nights everyday but if I were lucky, would get only about two interviews. That was way below what established science research had proven to have been the case in soliciting interviews and sales through this medium. For every ten persons contacted, the research found that one person would respond in the affirmative. In other words, ten percent of my calls should have ended in some business. That science, however, did not work with me. I started to wonder what I was doing wrong on the phone. Both the Branch Manager and the Associate Branch Manager of the organization stopped in after hours to listen to me interacting with prospective and current clients on the phone. This was done for a few days during my sales drought. They discovered and advised that on the phone, I was the most fluent, knowledgeable, and smooth talker they had met. My colleagues were also in the habit of offering me the same accolades. They could not find the reasons for my poor sales. They suggested that I changed my target market. Prior to their comments, I tended to target a Caribbean based market only. That is to say, I would specifically target the black communities comprising individuals who were either born in the Caribbean or had roots there. To their suggestions, I started to target, in addition, a mixture of local, upper middle-class individuals, and small and medium sized businesses, but the sales were augmented by a big, fat zero. I remained poor at my sales, like it had always been in recent months. When I spoke to businessmen and women in business partnership, I would point out that it was important for them to insure each other's life to the tune of their businesses' values. This was necessary in case one of the partners should die. When one dies, the partnership would have to be dissolved. However, with the partners insured, in the event one should die, the other partner would have the option, and the insurance money, to buy out the business and operate as a sole proprietor.

The concept was new to most small business partnerships that I approached. They even expressed interest. Some had me visiting even three to four times to offer more details, but always when there was time to sign off these life insurance policies, not one would reach realization. I was always in for great disappointments in these regards.

I also used the transfer tax approach to attempt to write life insurance policies with businesspeople. I outlined that if say, a businessman or woman had a big, medium, or small business, and should, unfortunately, die, for this business to be transferred to his or her son, daughter, or any next of kin or anyone for that matter, a massive transfer tax (a certain percent of the business's value) must be paid to government. To avoid his or her son or loved one having to find this money to pay the tax due to government, or worse, having to take it from the business which decreases its profit and productivity, a life insurance policy on his life
should be taken out. The insurance policy's face value should be an amount equal to the transfer tax amount that would be needed to legally transfer the business to the heir. This sale presentation also got the ears and eyes of a few businesspeople, but I had not a single sale from providing this professional advice to any of my several prospects. As in the case described prior, I had meetings and discussions but no written business as a consequence of my efforts. Instead, it seemed some of these upper end business people used this knowledge to actually contact

established insurance agents and their buddies, with a means to purchase life insurance from these big-wig insurance representatives. In the process, showing off to their agents how prudent they were business-wise. I also utilized the idea that one could take out a million dollars of insurance and then could pass on in a couple of days, even immediately after its purchase. The idea that the money would be able to take care of his funeral expenses and his family, did not work much either. Some even got angry with me when I used that sales tactic. They thought that I was being negative and that I was calling down death on them. I knew the chance of that happening was quite low myself. However, I was trained to put forth that argument, so I did so reluctantly. I guess many of my clients and prospective clients sensed that I was not very convinced myself from the lack of vigour with which I usually presented that argument.

Some of my prospective clients would argue that they would rather invest their money in stocks and mutual funds, etc. That the interests and dividends would be enough to take care of themselves and families in the remote eventuality that my death wish and trap should come to pass. I always countered with the argument that it took both money and time to achieve those millions of dollars. A few dollars paid for a month's premium of a policy of ten million dollars, say, become payable immediately and available for his or her children's education, funeral expenses, even to purchase a luxury home, and so on. There was no need for several years to pass, to accrue that vast sum of money. It was an immediate sum accrued just like magic, the very moment the client was approved for the insurance policy and signed the document. I further added to the discussion that this was guaranteed, and it was not like playing lottery where the probability of winning was stocked against the purchaser. However, I was just hitting rock bottom in the insurance sales business irrespective of my vast sales strategies and industry knowledge. I felt like I was banging my head against the wall every single time I went on the road to procure life insurance business. It was just too much a rugged task to sell the intangible.

I recall even during my first year in the insurance business that I would become so frustrated at times. Some days I would just drive in the parking lot of a mall and rolled down my car's windows and then went to sleep, if it was a warm day. At other times, I would just stay home to save gas and to avoid wasting my time and energy. I started to feel, even then, that probably sales, especially the sale of an intangible product, like life insurance, was not my thing. I would go to the occasional function or run into someone and would never hand them my business card or mention my line of work. I was always well-dressed in my suit and I thought I looked great. That was the only part of the work I really enjoyed. I thought some people were convinced in their minds that I was a topnotch lawyer, the way they would examine me when I walked confidently in the malls or across the roads. Little did they know that everything was a mere show, including the walk and the clothes. I had actually bought some of those suits at a used clothes store for five dollars, even less. I said to myself that the whole thing was indeed a farce, a big farce.

Every now and again I felt like a big loser on the inside but I resisted the thoughts every, single time with all my being, every single time, that it entered my cognitive structures, my intellectual realm, I would push it aside to the recess of my cerebrum and cerebellum. I could not afford to be defeated or stay defeated. I could not make those who wish me to fail celebrate. I could not allow all the money spent on my education in my local country, Jamaica and now my new home, Canada, go in vain. I had to be strong. I had to keep going as long as my heart was beating and I was able to inhale and exhale, to breathe. I breathed hard sometimes, extremely hard to relieve my stress and suicidal thoughts, but I never one day shared the latter thoughts with anyone. Not even my close, yet distanced, online friends in the virtual world. I simply shared them with me, and me alone in disguise and through my poetic prose, disguised, concealed, hidden.

My first year in insurance sales, I had actually done above average in the insurance business. However, my downfall was the lapses that occurred after the sales. When I sold a policy and I incurred lapses within two years of the policy's sale, the commission, or part thereof, was withdrawn. If it was just a few months on the books, I would virtually have to give back all my commission. As a result, many months passed that I did not get a paycheque. While all this was going on, the bills continued to pile up like Mount Everest in my small, roach-infested apartment. It was quite frustrating. I enjoyed the work to the extent that I dressed nicely in suits and drove around meeting people, pretending to be successful. The reality was that I had absolutely nothing, excepting a Mount Everest of unpaid bills, interspersed with a few roaches, here and there.

The branch manager had called me into his office to design a plan that would ensure that I would begin to improve my sales within three weeks of that meeting, to reduce the amount of money that I had started to owe the company. I worked out a plan and gave it to the manager. The plan had included me spending more time on the field, driving to business places outside of Toronto, meeting each day at least two businessmen or women, endeavouring to get at least three leads from every woman, man, girl, boy, chick, or child with whom I made contact.

It happened that the lease for my 1998 Toyota Camry had come to an end. It was now 2002 March. I was so elated that even though I had struggled with my monthly payments for my Toyota Camry, I had finally managed to pay off for the car. At least that was my conclusion. Upon my arrival at the car dealership to sign off my car, the salesperson and I began to have a discussion.

"Mr. Spencer, are you going to return the car or do you want to own it?" he asked.

"I now own it, I missed only one payment and I paid it it up a few weeks after," I said, confidently.

"There must be a misunderstanding, Mr. Spencer. You have to pay twelve thousand dollars to own the car today," he said.

I could not believe my ears. I pointed out that I was told at the time that I leased the car, that it was a lease-to-own arrangement and that at the end of the four years, I would own the vehicle. I pointed out that I had asked him if I would own the car, after the four years and he had responded in the affirmative to my questions, four years ago. The car salesman said he did not say anything of the sort. He flipped the pages of my contract and stopped at one page which had in fact stated that I would have to pay the twelve thousand dollars to own it, at the end of the four-year lease. I was in utter shock. The reality was that I did not read the fine print, way at the back. I had already paid over seventeen thousand, nine hundred dollars over the four-year period. Now I would have to pluck out twelve thousand dollars more cash to own this car. The second reality was that if I needed twelve hundred cents to buy the car that day, I would not have been able to own it. A compromise was worked out. I was allowed to lease another Toyota Camry, a new 2002 Toyota Camry. Unlike the first lease, I was not required to pay down a two thousand dollar deposit. I signed the documents and drove the car home, thinking deeply from where the first payment would have been derived.

My cousin in Boston, my Aunt Evelyn's son, had invited me to his wedding. Originally, I had no plan to attend. However, now that I had the new car, I decided to drive over. However, upon my return to Toronto, I realized that I could not keep the car. The insurance business was too slow. I was not making any money. I had to return the car. My insurance sales job was dependent on a car, now I had nothing, no car or money. However, there was no other option left to me. The bills continued to mount high in my apartment, all unpaid.

I drove the car into the dealer's premises and advised that I had to return it. They advised that I had to drive it to some place about half an hour from the dealership. There they would check the vehicle and it would be determined whether it could be returned or if there were any damages of which I would have to pay. I was also told that there might have been some penalty to terminate my contract before the expiry date. They might even have to report the transaction to the credit bureau which would further cripple my credit rating. I thought I would have died. The vehicle was subsequently checked, and everything was fine. They were a bit upset that I had run up the mileage on the car. However, they did not make a big deal out of it. Congratulations to Toyota!

I had to take about four different buses home on the return of the car that day. Like spite, it had suddenly started to rain. I got really wet to get on the main road, where I could get a bus from the area I had brought the car. In a way, I was happy that it was raining. It helped to mask my tears. I got the first TTC bus and there were no available seats on which I could rest my tired soul. I stood tightly against the others like a tin of sardines in the good old, Jamaica days. The rain continued to pour outside, imitating the tears pouring down inside, flowing down and washing my face. The second bus to which I transferred was also full but at least, I did not feel like I was a sardine in a full tin. Perhaps more-so like a tin of sardines of the current times. I felt somewhat uncomfortable, but I could move somewhat. The situation reminded me very much of the situation in my native land. However, to me, here it was even worse. Jamaica is labelled third world but Canada, first world. I just I could not see the difference that day I had to resume taking the bus.

The three weeks had long passed since I had given my sales plan to the branch manager. Every time subsequently that I went in the office, if he was present, I would move quickly outside. However, I ran out of luck this day. As I walked up the steps, I heard footsteps behind me. I turned around to see him. He said I should meet him in his office.

"Mr. Spencer, I think I am a reasonable man. However, business cannot be run by just being reasonable," he said.

I said nothing. I knew that I was in big trouble.

"It is now six weeks and three days, that we had our discussions. Nothing has changed," he screamed.

I told him that one of the reasons I was unable to effect my agreed plan was that I had to return my leased car. I argued that if he gave me some time, I would try to work with one of my colleagues and then get myself some business to write.

"Mr. Spencer, I hate to do this. You are a fine individual. I admire your attitude and hard work, but I have to let you go," he said calmly.

I wondered if I was hearing correctly.

"I understand your position, sir, but I am asking you please, sir, to give me a second chance," I begged.

"I have given you enough chances. You now owe the company thirty-eight thousand dollars! It's either you go or me go. It's obvious that I am performing my duties well, so it has to be you," he said firmly, with a cunning smile hitched to his face.

"You know I am a hard worker, sir. You have also acknowledged that yourself. Please give me three more weeks, sir," I pleaded.

"Mr. Spencer, you're fired! I'll help you to clear your desk and take away any of the company's belongings you have with you," he said.

He got up from his desk, opened the door of his office and led the way to my desk. He asked me to clear the drawers, hand over all documents, the security pass to the building, etc., and escorted me to the door of the building and downstairs, as my colleagues watched on in bewilderment.

I walked aimlessly out of the building, my eyes bulged with tears. I used the palm of my hands to dry and clean my tearful face. I walked across a mall and sat there for awhile, watching people walk and interact with themselves or each other. I wondered what the following day would be like for me and even for some of the people I was watching, looking no less dejected than I was. I wondered what would happen next. I wondered what my wife would say now that I was unemployed. I started to cry once again. This time I was really bawling. I used my cellphone to call my old friend Glendon to let him know I was just fired. He gave me a dose of encouragement. I then called my 'brother', Oliver Nelson in Jamaica.

"Oliver, I just got fired, man. I just don't know what to do or why I came to Canada," I cried, again tears flowing down my soaked face.

"Keep heart, my brother. Better days must come," he reassured me.

Before he could say another word, I told him I was going to hang up the phone, and I did. I felt like hanging up my life with it, or better my neck on a tree as well, but I resisted the temptation once again. I remembered my friend had just said better days would come, and my three children, whom I knew loved me very much, and whom I love world without end. I could not do that to them. I walked out the mall with my briefcase and walked out onto the street to get a ride home.

There was no severance pay or anything to get, from being fired in lieu of notice in this company. That was how the insurance business operated. The company was described as a mere sponsor of my life insurance and disability and accident licence but that was as far as the relationship went. They would give me back a tiny, very tiny portion of the money I make when I sell their goods. Beyond that, they owe me nothing. I thought about how unfair Capitalism was, and how they constantly exploit workers and were heartless. Profit at all cost, I thought.

A few days later, I got a letter from the company having the company name and its logo on the envelope. I was wondering if they had a change of heart and wanted me to come back. I also thought they must have worked out some sort of transportation for me, so I could get back on the job to help in meeting their really steeped weekly, monthly, and quarterly targets. I must have been dreaming. When I opened the letter, its content was to remind me that I owed them thirty-eight thousand Canadian dollars (C$38,000.00) and that I had ninety days in which to settle the account. I thought these people were not merely unreasonable but insane. How could they expect me to pay thirty-eight thousand Canadian dollars in ninety days when I could not find three hundred and seventy three dollars monthly so I could keep my leased Toyota Camry and accordingly, my job? I screamed in my thoughts. What stupidity I uttered in my head! I called the office and advised that it was virtually impossible to come up with the money in ninety days. One person told me to borrow it from my family. I told them I had no family. They laughed and said they had to go.

The ninety days had passed, and I was incapable of paying them the money, so they handed over the debt to collections. The latter harassed me night in, and day out, for the payments. I just could not pay it. I had to tell them that I was not Jesus. That I could not turn water into wine or my unemployment or paper, into money.

I started to focus on employment, specifically in the banking sector. I recalled that while I worked with the insurance company, I had done a number of financial related courses that probably could get me a job in the banking system as a personal banker or assistant financial adviser or any such related position. I no longer had to work in the bank simply to sell life insurance, I thought. I updated my résumé and started to focus specifically on the banking system. I did my job searches at the banks' websites, making sure to educate myself about each and everyone of them, in the event I was called for an interview. Also, in 2003, I had applied to the Ontario College of Teachers (O.C.T.) to be licensed to teach in Ontario and was successful. In that same year, I had also applied for, and acquired, my Canadian citizenship. I had not applied prior for these, as I was aware that the dropped charges might have appeared on any background check done on me and likely would cause some delay. Hence the reason that I did not apply for my teaching licence immediately after graduating from York University in 1998. Since I had been licensed with no problem with the O.C.T. and acquired my citizenship, and background checks were done in both cases, I was appalled later on in 2005 to have found that the dropped charges were still being referenced on certain of my police records. I was quite appalled to have found out that these dropped charges had appeared when I applied to a school board for a teaching position in 2005. It seemed it depended on the extent of the police report. I remember, however, obtaining a police record sometime earlier (2004) from the York Region Police, to do some voluntary work and that too was fine. There was no mention of the dropped charges. I guess then, that if one does not have a criminal record, as is the case with me, but had charges dropped, unless the dropped charges were expunged from the police data base, they could appear or don't appear, depending on the level of search done. I am happy today that these dropped charges had been expunged and I have a clean police record. There is no way that I will let any kind of provocation put me through all that pain ever in my life. It was one of the toughest ordeals I had to endure, to having been regarded as a criminal. I remember one day I was rushing to take my son, Michael, who is asthmatic, to the doctor as he was having an asthma attack. I had failed to come to a complete stop at the stop sign near to my home. The police placed on his flashing amber lights plus siren to which I pulled over.

"May I have your driver's licence and ownership, please?" he requested.

I handed him the documents. I asked him the reason I was being pulled over to which he responded that I did not come to a complete stop at the stop sign. I wanted to say, cool it officer. That it was a quiet, minor road, just by my gate but instead I told him the reason I was in a hurry. He also said that was the more reason that I should have been driving more carefully as I had my baby son in the car. I begged him for a chance and pointed out that I was a great person and had no criminal or other infractions with traffic or the law. I had totally forgotten about the dropped charges nor did I think he would have had access to that information. He went to his police vehicle, wrote me the ticket for one hundred sixty dollars and commented that how comes I was pretending to be this 'goody goody' person when in fact I had dropped assault and assault with a weapon charges against me. I took the tickets and thanked him as the tears once again, rolled down my cheeks. I wanted to ask, why should I still be paying for something of which I clearly was not found guilty? I was also shocked that the police officers were actually driving around in their cars, having access to personal information like that, even though I was not found guilty of anything by the courts. I found that very unfair. However, I was helpless in the situation.

In late 2002, I got called for an interview with another major Canadian banking institution. I was successful in its first interview. I was subsequently called for a second interview and was also successful. However, I was advised by the panel of interviewers that my official appointment to the post would have been contingent on my successfully passing the company's background check and upon the positive and successful information they gathered from my references.

Needless to say, how worried I was. For one thing, I was fired from my last job as you know. This company specifically stated that they wanted a reference from my last manager. I was worried that the latter would not recommend me for the job because of my poor sales record. I was also worried that the dropped charges might appear on my police record. Even though my police record itself is clean, the fact that I was charged for something, even though it had been forgiven or dropped, some companies still used it against the individual. I was deeply distressed.

I was told by the team of interviewers that all background checks and references would take about one week to be completed. I continued to job hunt on the Internet and to send out résumés to other financial institutions. I also tried some non-profit organizations. I am usually not a great sleeper, but it got even worse during the time I had to wait for a response. Within four days, my phone rang. Normally, I was not quick to answer the phone, however, I grabbed it at the first ring when I saw the company's name on the phone display. It was the human resources department of the company.

"May I speak to Mr. Spencer, please?" she asked.

"Speaking," I said.

"Mr. Spencer, congratulations!" she said.

I felt like I had won a million dollars.

In my native country to work in a bank was a big deal. Teachers earn much less than bankers in my native land. I thought the same was true in my new home, Canada. However, I soon found out that that was not the case.

"Thank you," I said, trying to hide how elated I was.

"Could you come in today to sign the papers?" she asked.

"Certainly," I said.

"Could you be here in thirty minutes?" she asked.

"Sure," I said.

After saying that I could be there in thirty minutes, I remember that I did not yet have a bath and that I no longer had a car.

I decided to forfeit the bath, telling myself that it was okay, just once, not to bathe. I really did not want to be late for the signing, which probably could have resulted in them changing their minds before I got to sign the documents. I wanted to ensure that my acquiring of the job was official and final. So, I rather to be dirty than to have been unemployed, I thought.

I arrived just within thirty minutes. She beckoned me in the room to read and sign a whole bunch of papers. I was so relieved after having signed them all.

The documents stated that I was on three months probation. I felt a little nervous when I read that section, but I said that that was fine. I did not have to drive or walk around bothering people to buy life insurance. My salary was set for twenty-nine thousand dollars yearly. I thought that was great. I figured I could start paying down on some of the many outstanding bills. The job title was Personal Online Banker. I would be servicing the banks' clients online. I would be trained for six weeks. During the training period, I would be paid my full salary and attend training Mondays through Fridays, 9:00 A.M. to 5:00 P. M. However, after the six-week period, my working hours would be 5:00 P.M. to 1:00 A.M. I thought about the late time I would be reaching home in the mornings, but I was happy I had a job.

I successfully completed the six-week training and started to work live, online with my clients. A few weeks after I started working, a gentleman by the name of Taiwo Osuntoyinbo joined us. We worked the same shift. Before he joined us, I was sometimes at the bus stop standing at the last intersection to my home at 3:00 A.M. The bus would take forever to arrive those hours of the morning. I was usually well dressed, having my briefcase and worried if I would have been attacked one of those mornings. When Taiwo found out that I did not have a car, he would drop me home every night and then would drive home quite a distance after doing so. The journey to my home was actually out of his way, but he just wanted to help me. He was and still is my very good friend. One day in 2003, he decided to visit me at my home. Since we became good friends, I started to show him some of my family's pictures with brothers and sisters, etc. Among the pictures, were a few for one of my sisters who was, at the time, in prison in England for having been found with drugs on entry into the country. She was also pregnant at the time she was caught. My relatively young sister was actually just doing a favour for someone, a close relative, who also does not use drugs. This was the first time ever that she had ever done anything of that sort. As I showed Taiwo the pictures, I became overwhelmed. I told him the whole story subsequently. To date, my then wife still does not know that I had a sister who had gone through this ordeal. However, I was greatly overwhelmed and had to share it with someone I knew I could trust. I was hurting for months upon months when I finally found out from a stranger that my sister had been arrested in England for using herself as a mule. I thought I was going to go crazy. When Taiwo left, I was forced to pen this poem.

Oh Sister!

Oh sister, I feel your pain

When I look at your pictures

And show them to friends too

Oh sister, I really, really do feel your pain.

When I remember the sparks

The sparks in your eyes

The natural vitality of youth in your being

Your creativity, your passion for life and glee

Oh sister, I feel your pain.

When I know there is nothing

Big brother can do to set you free

When I imagine how much you're missing

Missing your jubilee

Dear sister, oh sister

I share your pain!

Oh sister, dear sister!

It's hard to imagine

And admit that this is your bit

What regret you must hone

In your new European home.

Sister, this piece is for you

Even though I dear not send it to your palace

For fear of disturbing your solace

Oh sister, I really do feel your pain.

Oh sister, you have learned

A hard lesson

Too bad your teacher, is our sister

Oh sisters, I feel your pains!

I continued to work in the online banking system for a few months. Around April 1, 2004, I got a telephone call from Oliver. He stated to me that he was coming to Canada on a short visit and he would arrive on April 8, 2004. I was glad that I was going to see my brother. I had not seen him since my first visit to Jamaica in 1998. He had gone out of his way for me during that trip. He had gone to pick me up at the airport where he actually worked. He had arranged an elaborate welcome home party for me. He had managed to get all our close friends since the Sam Sharpe Teachers' College days to attend that welcome home party. There were the butchering of goats and the best of the local meals and soups that one could find. He had also arranged the different places we would travel and provided free transportation for me to move around, to travel with myself and my daughters back home. My wife and baby son, Michael Spencer, did not accompany me on this trip.

It was therefore a bitter-sweet news to have learnt that my 'brother', Oliver Nelson was coming to Canada. It was sweet because he was and still is my best friend and I wanted to see him, but bitter because I was not going to be able to extend the kind of courtesy he was able to, when I went on my vacation to Jamaica. At the time, I was still without a vehicle, so I would not be able even to take him out to a club or anywhere. I was devastated. I also knew that it was going to be impossible to get a loan with my bad credit, even though I worked with a bank.

I went to bed that night and I sat up virtually all night, thinking. I said to myself that I had been without a car for a long time. If there was a time that I was ever going to own a car once again, it would have to be then and there, and before Oliver got in town. I told my wife that I had to get a car before my 'brother' got in town and her remark was that I was just trying to show off. Worse, she knew that with my bad credit, I would not have been able to secure a car loan from anyone or anywhere.

I developed a plan. The plan was to go online or check magazines that advertised cars for sale that offered so-called bad credit loans. I wondered if I would be lucky enough to get one. I ran into a few online and called but they all required me to make a deposit of say, four thousand dollars toward the loan for any vehicle I would choose. Even though I worked with the bank, I still could not afford the deposit, as I was working on paying a few of my debts down. I had no savings. As a matter of fact, the money was still not enough to scratch my numerous bills.

It was about April 6, 2004 and I was really frustrated. My 'brother' was due in the country in two days' time. So, I took a walk around, looking for any signs that could get me in a vehicle by April 8, 2004. I walked into a pharmacy and as I did so, I saw one of those magazines that advertised used cars that were available for sale. I picked up the booklet and began to leaf through its pages. Suddenly, I came upon the name of an individual whose advertisement read something to the effect that whether one had good, bad or no credit at all, this person could get you a car loan and in an immaculate and superb, used car, in less than twenty four hours. I said to myself that was too good to be true. The office of this salesperson/loans officer was located at Team Chrysler Jeep Dodge Inc., 5500-D Dixie Road, Mississauga, Ontario L4W 4N3 and its telephone number was also listed. Despite my feeling somewhat suspicious about the advertisement, I called the number.

"Hello, I just read an ad that said irrespective of one's credit, you could get him or her a loan and in a used vehicle in twenty-four hours," I said.

"What kind of work do you do?" he asked.

"I am a banker," I said, somewhat ashamed.

Here was a banker, working with one of the top banks in Canada who was seeking a loan in the category for individuals with bad credit. I thought that my life was full of intrigue.

"Come on over and I will get you in a car in twenty-four hours," he boasted.

It was my day off. I called my neighbour, Renato Puno also known as René.

"René, can you do me a big favour?" I asked.

"It depends," he laughed.

"I need to get to the Team Chrysler at 5500 Dixie Road in Mississauga. Is it possible to drop me there?" I asked.

Rene was a close family friend and hailed from the Philippines as does my then wife. He was more than willing to help. We got there and I inquired for the gentleman whose name evaded me at the time of writing. He sat me down in his office. I asked my friend to stay outside. He surprisingly, despite his ad in the magazine, requested and pulled a credit check on me.

"Mr. Spencer, you have excellent credit," he remarked.

I wanted to laugh. This man must have been out of his mind or he was a great conman, I thought.

However, when he showed me my credit report, I realized that it was not that bad at all. The only problem was that I had missed a few payments once in a while and there was the Insurance money reported. But overall, he had seen much worse credit. He outlined that because of the vast numbers of credit, the loan was going to be extremely expensive over the five-year period. I told him it did not matter to me. I really wanted to be in a car by April 8, so I could entertain Oliver when he arrived, and also be at the Pearson Airport, along with his sister who lived in Brampton, to receive him on that date.

The car salesman took me outside to choose the car I wanted. I saw a 2000 Chrysler Neon and said I would take that one. He asked me to test drive the car which I did, and we went back inside his office. He told me that the following day, he would contact the credit company known as Carfinco situated in Vancouver, Canada, as it was too late to do so that night. It happened that the loan was not finalized until late evening, April 7, 2004. I decided to go in early the day of April 8, the day Oliver would arrive in Canada. I signed off the papers. The vehicle's purchase price was Canadian nine thousand, four hundred fifteen dollars and twenty-six cents (C$9, 415.26). There was also a warranty fee of six hundred twenty dollars ($620.00), documentation fees of two hundred, ninety nine dollars ($299.00), taxes—P.S.T./G.S.T. of one thousand five hundred, fifty dollars and fourteen cents ($1550.14), registration and administration fee was four hundred ninety nine dollars ($499.00). The cost of borrowing was ten thousand, two hundred ninety-one dollars and forty cents ($10, 291.40). The term for payment was sixty months or five years. The total repayment amount at the end of this sixty-month period would be a whopping twenty-one thousand, two hundred seventy-four dollars and eighty cents

($21, 274.80). The last payment on this car was on July 16, 2009.

I went over to the car dealer's premises quite early. However, by the time the car was licensed and registered and so on, it was very late. By then, my 'brother', Oliver had already landed, and his sister took him home to Brampton. I was so disappointed. I tried to drive over that night, but I got lost and had to wait until the following day after work, that late night to visit him. I recalled him saying how new the car appeared and why I had not put the car mats on the floor. I responded that I took them out to clean it. I also told him that I had recently bought the car about three weeks ago. I was too ashamed to explain what had happened. To date, I had not told Oliver of this unique occurrence, I guess he will read it in this book.

Some time later during my stint with this Canadian financial organisation, I applied to the branch system. I was getting tired of the night work as well as the inconvenient times I had to work which included Sundays, Saturdays and public holidays. I usually got my days off during the weekdays. My application was successful. I was still categorized at the same level in the branch, but my titles now included, in addition to being a Personal Banker, Mutual Funds Representative, and Manager's Backup. The latter being synonymous with the term assistant manager in some parts of the world. This was a medium-sized branch. There were, the manager, two personal bankers, an assistant personal banker plus a financial adviser. I was actually working for a colleague who had taken off some indefinite leave as I was to learn later.

An interesting thing happened one day. It turned out that the person whose job I had occupied came in to apply for one of the company's products. Upon doing the transaction with this individual, I discovered that this person had not only been working for a shorter period of time with the company than I had, but was far less qualified and had acquired a mere high school diploma. This individual had not successfully passed the securities course as I had. All this information was volunteered to me during the interview for the product, some as part of writing the business, others volunteered freely and unnecessarily. The salary I worked then, would not have qualified me for that product even had I gotten an excellent credit. Subsequent to the meeting with my client and colleague, I contacted the powers-that-be with respect to my discovery. Needles to say, they were all upset that I was trying to get more pay. These are capitalist institutions and if they can get away with underpaying their staff while improving profits, they will do so without a blink. I was told the matter would have been looked into with a view to remedy the situation. Another issue here was that the workers were not allowed to be unionized. I had actually started to see if I could get a few people to go that route, but nearly got in trouble with that too. Within two months, or so, the person for whom I was working, returned. I was transferred to another branch.

This branch to which I was transferred was much smaller. It was in fact classified as a sub-branch. That is to say, my manager had to be supervised by the manager of a branch with full status. My new manager was also less qualified than I was and had also failed the securities course on several occasions. Accordingly, in that branch, I was the only person who could conduct business in mutual funds. At first, the manager and I were very close. As this individual did not own a car, I used to take this person to the subway after work each business day. I found it strange that there was a bank manager who did not own a car. That would have been unheard of in my native country. The manager would be driving a Mercedes Benz or a BMW. The branch had four tellers and one assistant personal banker. I was enjoying my job at first, doing reasonably well. However, I noticed that there started to develop some kind of animosity between myself and the manager. Soon, e-mails were started to being sent to the powers-that-be that I was too aggressive, etc. The head of our district came to speak to me to find out what the problem was between us. We dealt with all the problems and thought everything was settled. I was to be disappointed.

It was now time for a salary review. I got my notice which advised that my salary was to move from its current level to thirty-one thousand dollars annually. Under normal conditions, that would have been great. However, I had previously discovered that at least one other personal banker with less qualification was earning 7.25 percent more than I was with less experience and academic and financial qualifications as I have already pointed out. Consequently, I responded to the letter that I would not accept that increase in light of the knowledge I had gleaned earlier and of which I was promised by the powers-that-be that the matter would have been addressed with a view to correct same. Again, the big boss came to see me. He tried to talk me out of it and instead suggested that I would get a better bonus at the end of the year, that would take care of my shortage in pay. However, I could not be fooled. He, ultimately, agreed to raise my salary to thirty-five thousand dollars annually. Even though this amount was less than the other person's salary that I described earlier, I decided to take this offer.

All hell let loose. My manager upon learning of my increase, along with the assistant banker all got jealous. The manager thought it was unfair that both of us were literally getting the same salary. I advised the manager to talk to the-powers-that-be about that, not me. To make it brief, everything went down hill from this point. Phone calls were continuously made behind my back, e-mails sent, and so on.

I had been doing extremely well. I met all my targets: daily, weekly, monthly, and quarterly. I was even given rewards of five hundred dollars and more for my work. The last five hundred dollars I received was the money I used to purchase the digital camera I still own today.

I was in my office when the big boss came in without even knocking, advising that when I was finished with the client, he wanted to speak to me. So, after I had completed the interview with my client, I invited the big boss inside my office.

"Joshua, I am tired of all the comments and arguments I am receiving about you. It must stop. If it does not stop, I will let you go," he said.

"What comments and arguments? Am I being tried behind my back now?" I asked.

The big boss just got up and left without saying a word. I could not make any sense of what he had said or the reason that my manager was badmouthing me. All I was doing was my job. The customers liked me as I was very explicit and detailed in making my presentations to them. The teacher was still in me, so I used my training to help my clients make the right choices. However, the atmosphere had started to get quite cloudy. I thought mostly because my manager and banking assistant were afraid that my sun was shining too brightly. They had to collude or extinguish that powerful glow, that beautiful flame.

The evening after the big boss left and the tellers balanced their money, I asked the manager for a meeting. I questioned why I was being undermined. An argument pursued. I advised that I respected, but I was not afraid of the branch's authority. The branch manager walked away before we could even have a sensible and decent discussion re the issues.

The following day after the meeting with myself and the manager, was a very busy one in the morning into the early afternoon. As I was the only one who could legally do the Mutual Fund transactions, I was busy, quite busy. Out of the blue, it seemed everyone needed Mutual Funds that day. I left late for lunch. Normally, when I was leaving, and vice versa, I would tell the manager that I would be gone for awhile. However, that day when I left, I did not see the manager.

I took my hour's lunch and returned to see the big boss sitting in my office with a number of clients waiting at my office's door.

"Joshua, please close the door," he commanded.

I complied. My heart skipped a beat. What was his problem today? I questioned myself. Why was he in my office again, now asking me to close my door and giving me that wicked look? I continued to question myself, nervously, what in heavens is he up to today? I felt a strange feeling deep down in my stomach.

"Joshua, yesterday I came in this very office and talked to you, right?" he asked.

"Right," I echoed.

"So why did I have to come back here today, once again, about the same thing?" he asked.

"I don't understand," I said.

"You will understand in a few minutes," he said, barely making eye contact with me.

From that moment, I could tell that the big boss was up to no good. I knew he too was upset that I had learnt that there were staff members in his very banking district, doing the same work, being paid varying salaries. I thought he was concerned that individuals like me were threats to the status quo. He could not afford everyone to learn of what was going on. Also, if my manager and I could not get along, it was in his best interest to get rid of me, not the manager. First, the manager was well underpaid and was a chicken and would not speak up. He had a business decision to make and I could sense there and then that he felt it was urgent. He was going to exploit the opportunity to get things back on track. To have things as they were before this alien came aboard with his smart self.

"Okay," I submitted to the worse.

"Yesterday after I left the office, why did you attack the manager?" he queried.

"Sir, I did not attack the manager. I simply asked, why was I being undermined? Why was I not contacted if there was a problem? That was all," I said.

The big boss disregarded my response.

"Look what you did just now, and I came here and witnessed it for myself. You left the branch all afternoon with the clients all stranded at your office's door," he said.

"That's not exactly correct, sir. I went for lunch late and took a mere one hour. When I left the manager was no where insight," I said.

So, you are saying that I am a liar, right? he asked.

"Right, I mean I understand, but I did not leave the clients. There was no one when I left," I insisted.

"Joshua, I am fed up with this tug of war," he said.

He went on to say that I was fired. He had me sign a pile of papers for payment in lieu of, and so on. I opened the door of my office and walked to the back and close to the tellers. I told them I was just fired for no reason. I started to file the mutual fund documents that I had left in a tray at the back, when the big boss shouted to me to leave immediately and that the manager would take care of them.

"The manager has no authority to touch these documents," I shouted back at him.

He allowed me to file them away. I collected the letters and all the documents I signed related to severance pay in lieu of, and so on. I handed over my security pass and combination information I had, grabbed my briefcase, held my head high went into my car and drove away. I stopped at the York Gate Mall, pulled out my cellphone and once again, advised Oliver that I had just been fired. I hung up the phone without listening what he had to say. I called Glendon and a female friend to inform them of my end as well. They gave me the usual encouragement. I hung up feeling satisfied that my friends had known my new status in Canada.

I told my wife that I had been fired. Surprisingly, she was quite supportive. I was glad she was. Had she been any less, I would have probably just done something erratic or outright stupid.

CHAPTER TEN

A New Life

I recalled that Oliver's sister was a teacher in Ontario. I told him to ask his sister if she could serve as a reference for me. I also asked him to find out if she knew of any opening at the school she taught, or at any other school. Oliver contacted his sister and she, in turn, contacted me. The first challenge was to get an interview with the school board with which she taught. This was a requirement to be placed on the Occasional Teaching Roster as well as the Eligible-to-Hire List. One had to be on the latter, this still is the case as I write, to be hired permanently by the board in question. The former is necessary to teach as an occasional teacher. I eventually got an interview with the board and was at first placed on the Occasional Teaching Roster. It happened that in September 2005, there was a position available for two weeks of teaching. Oliver's sister, Mrs. Morant, advised me that there was an opening for an occasional teacher whose services would have been needed for about two weeks. Mrs. Nancy Spencer (We are not related. We even share different races) granted me an interview. When

I arrived at the school for the interview, I was quite surprised to learn of the number of other individuals who were also interested in this two-week teaching assignment. Fortunately, I acquired the teaching position. It turned out that I ended up spending two full years at the school as what is known as a Long Term Occasional (L.T.O.) teacher. At the school in question, I got some great help and support from its administration and staff.

Teaching in Canada is completely different from teaching in Jamaica. Had it not been for the support of the principal, Mrs. Nancy Spencer, Mrs. Massia Morant who later served as my mentor, the vice principal, Mrs. Andrea Douglas et al, I didn't know how I would have managed. In 2004 or sometime earlier in 2005, the then vice principal at The Elms Junior Middle School, Mrs. Allman, had also given me an opportunity to volunteer at her school. Mrs. Allman, at the time of writing, is now a principal. She had also served as one of my references when I applied for the several teaching posts, temporary or permanent, that I had applied to, prior to starting at Mrs. Nancy Spencer's school. While I served at the school, I also met a retired principal, Mrs. Sitwell, who acted as a VP at the school, briefly. She also said I could use her as one of my referrals in my search for permanent teaching in the system. I am extremely grateful to these individuals who had helped me to begin on a pathway to the new life. I had no idea that it would have been as difficult as it was for me, to acquire and resume serving in my career as a teacher in Canada.

At this school, I got involved in a number of extracurricular activities, among which were a boys' book club, ran jointly by myself and one, Ms. Russell, the Spelling Bee club, Mathematics Enrichment classes, literacy and numeracy clubs. It later became obvious that not only had students benefitted from these programs, but apparently my colleagues and the school's administration were also taking notice of my efforts. These efforts, on my part, were later to help to launch me closer to acquiring a permanent teaching position. It was for my efforts too that I worked for a full two years at this school.

During the summer of 2006, my daughter, Kaliese Spencer who is an athlete, was involved in the World's Junior Championship in Beijing, China. On August 17 that year, she won the 400M hurdles, becoming the World's Junior Champion for female in the event. I was so elated for this feat. I remember this happened at a time when I was going through much emotional turmoil due to financial constraints and domestic challenges. Her

438

success could not have had a better timing. I called her in Beijing to congratulate her and we were both quite elated. The media also contacted me for interviews. I got a big write up, picture included, in the Jamaica Observer, dated August 18, 2006. Later in 2009, Kaliese was to go on to acquire fourth place, as mentioned earlier, in the 400M hurdles in the World's Championship Games held in Berlin, Germany. Her compatriot and friend, Melaine Walker won the race with a record-breaking time of 52.42 seconds. Kaliese had also done a personal best of 53.56. A few days later, Monday, August 31, 2009, Kaliese Spencer, created an upset in the 400M hurdles winning the race over her friend, Melaine Walker, who came in a close second.

The year 2007 was quite a bitter-sweet year for me. On February 17, 2007, while I awaited my son, Michael Spencer, who was at his piano class, I suddenly fell ill. Just prior to my sudden feeling of illness, I felt a little thirsty. As I had a box of orange juice in my car, I went for it and imbibed it all. Shortly thereafter, I started to feel an excruciating pain in my stomach. I thought that probably it was simply caused by the juice which was probably spoilt. However, it got progressively worse by the passing minutes. I thought of going to let

Michael know that I was not feeling well. However, I resisted that urge.

Firstly, there was about fifteen minutes of the class to go. The second reason was that I did not want to let my son know that I was not feeling well. I did not want to worry my son with what I thought originally was just a simple pain, probably caused by a spoiled box of orange juice. I decided to wait through the fifteen minutes for my son's class to end. It was the longest, most painful fifteen minutes I would have ever had to wait and endure in my life. At the end of the class, I quickly went to get him from his class.

I didn't know whether Michael had noticed that I was not talking to him. I usually asked him as routine, how the class was, what new he had done but that day I said nothing. I didn't know whether Michael had noticed that I was not feeling well either because surprisingly, he did not talk to me at all.

We went to the car and I sat in front of the steering wheel. I thought I was going to die then and there. I did not want Michael to panic. I decided I would not tell him what was going on inside my body. I truly cannot explain here how I managed to drive home safely. Michael must have noticed that I was not driving well or probably to him, that was the way I always drove.

Luckily, I reached home. I parked the car, and my son and I took the elevator. During all that time, I was writhing in pain. As I disembarked from the elevator and approached the door to my suite, I fell to the floor.

"Daddy, daddy, I don't want you to die!" I heard Michael scream.

Upon hearing Michael's words, I became a little stronger. I quickly remembered how I grew up without a dad, first through separation from my mother, then finally through being murdered. I wanted to live to see him through university and I tried to remain strong. My then wife, Reflor was inside the apartment and heard the commotion at the door. She ran out inquisitively to see me on the verge of dying at the front of the door. She called 911. It was taking too long for an ambulance to arrive so Reflor called our neighbour, Renato Puno, who grabbed me and rushed me to the hospital.

At the hospital, a battery of tests was done on me. It was discovered that there was a huge hole in my duodenum, the first part of my small intestine. They gave me some medication to ease the pain and conducted other medical acts as a temporary measure until surgery. I was told by the doctors that I had to do surgery and there was not much time. It had to be done quickly, I was told.

I had never done surgery before. As a matter of fact, if I was the only patient on which doctors rely to make a livelihood, they would certainly die for hungry. I just do not enjoy visiting doctors' offices too much. As a matter of fact, I am one of those persons, who believes that if it is not broken, one should not try to fix it. I thought, and probably, still do, that most doctors, would prescribe some kind of medication even when it was not necessary. This was as a means to confirm that they had in fact seen the patients. In this way, they avoid any suspicion that they might just make claim on the public coffers without treating patients. I also believe that taking medicines unnecessarily is not good for the body. One can just imagine how shocked and afraid I was then, at the suggestion of surgery. I told the doctors that I was not going to do the surgery. They asked me if I wanted to die. That would have been the end result if I did not do surgery and quickly, they thought.

My then wife was all for surgery. However, I knew she would go to the doctor if her nose itches, she was a doctor lover. I felt I needed some other opinions. I asked Renato, and he too, said that as far as the doctors believed, surgery was not optional. It was mandatory and I should do it for the sake of my children. I just had to get it done. I, however, was still not certain that I should let these doctors put me to sleep and then be staring inside of me as if I was a car engine. The whole idea even got me more nervous and terrified. Luckily, they had me connected and being fed and breathing, intravenously.

I wanted to speak with one final individual before I allowed the mechanics to go to work. That was how I started to see the doctors, as mechanics going to fix me, the car. I contacted Mrs. Massia Morant and her husband, Mr. Garrett Morant. The former was my mentor at the school I taught, as you may recall, and also my 'brother', Oliver's sister. They called them in their Brampton home. Within minutes, they were in the hospital. I had a feeling that the doctors and others had conferred with her prior to her and her husband coming into my hospital room.

"Joshua, you must do the surgery. You will come out of this fine," she said.

I wanted to believe her. I always regarded her highly as a great thinker. However, I was questioning myself whether she was just saying this because the doctors urged her that it was important. I wondered whether

her gut feelings were contrary from the words that emitted from her mouth. However, I decided to go along with the suggestion. Surgery, it would be, I thought, nervously. They all wished me well and the doctors took me away.

On my way to the operating theatre, I recalled saying to the doctors that the following day would have been my son, Michael's birthday and I really did not want to die. I told them that I had lost my dad at a tender age and that I would not want that to repeat itself with my little Michael Spencer. When I said that, I noticed the older looking doctor face changed to pale.

"Joshua, I am a dad too. I understand. You will be fine," he said.

From that point I knew nothing else. It seemed they had already given me the anaesthesia or the smooth talk of the senior-looking and caring doctor had knocked me out or a combination of the two had.

Approximately four hours later I heard,

"Mr. Spencer, the surgery has been successful."

I was so happy. They wheeled me to a semiprivate room upstairs. The Sunday morning Michael had come to visit me on his way to the Canadian Music League (C.M.L.) competition. Since Michael had started at four years old, it was the first time that I was not going to be present when he would be performing at either a concert or a competition. I felt very sad inside, but I tried to show my best face. I was actually feeling better. It was also his birthday and that too, we were in the habit of celebrating each year. There was going to be none that evening.

"Michael, happy birthday, my son," I forced myself to say without showing my emotions.

"Thanks daddy," he said.

Our family friend and my then wife's cousin, Cely, then said they had to leave for the music competition. I felt so sad inside that I was going to miss Michael perform.

For a couple of days, I was getting better. However, there was a lot of fluid inside me that they had to suck out of my system. Then later I started to develop complications. I was told that as a result of the surgery, I had developed a blood clot in one of my lungs. I now had a tube that was pushed down my nostril. I also had on the intravenous connections. I started to pass fluids and you know what, freely. I was getting really worse. They rushed me to a lower floor of the hospital a few times to do CAT SCANS and a whole number of medical examinations. I had to get injections throughout the nights and was being monitored constantly. I truly believed that this was it. My children would call from Jamaica, but it was so painful to speak to them being connected to all the wirings and the tube in my nose. I started to have diarrhoea and had to wear diaper constantly. I could not believe that this was happening to me. Here was a man who had never been ill. I was told that as a child I was really sickly, but since I had been an adolescent, I had never been ill or hospitalized other than the time I was stabbed by a girl in the face. I very seldom had the common cold. However, here I was being reduced to being a baby once again. At this point of my illness, I advised my then wife not to allow Michael to visit me. I did not want him to see my condition. I would talk to him every day and tried to sound the best I could. I would also say I was getting better but that was far from being the truth at the time.

I spent approximately two weeks in the hospital after the surgery. I gradually started to improve. My then wife came everyday to give me a shower or at least to wipe my body clean. I started to think that despite our challenges, she was a great woman. I still think she is, even though we still have a lot of things to straighten out in our relationship. She had never left my side while I was sick. She would come in early in the mornings and leave late in the evenings.

Michael was being taken care of by Renato's family. They have children too, so Michael was not bored. He played computer games and had fun, the best he could, under the circumstances.

While I was in the hospital, I would have a lot of thoughts going through my head, constantly. Below is one of the poems I wrote when I was hospitalized. I had no paper on which to write my thoughts at the time, so I had to write it on toilet tissue. I later transferred it to my other pieces of work.

Reflecting

Reflecting on my life

Reflecting on my doctor's knife

Pondering whether my children from this point

I will have to disappoint

Muscling courage to have these views go out of sight.

Reflecting on my abdominal pains

Encouraging restraints

Singing, hoping, and dancing

To the musical blues

Radiating straight from my perforated, digestive tubes.

Reflecting on my life, my wife

Our struggles, our frustrations, and conflicts

But now for her dedication, she now in my eyes, is a champion

Regretting my numerous screams and steams of tantrums.

Reflecting on my dreams

Staring at their solid, weakening masses

Through my stained eyeglasses

Silently doubting but hoping

Hoping to sleep to maintain these dreams

Blurred images in my brain

I endeavour to remain sane.

Reflecting on my thoughts

Reflecting on my inbuilt wraths

Evaporating the juiciness of my tearful, weepy eyes

Ultimately leaving them scaly and dry questioning if it is now time for my bye bye.

Reflecting on me in the surgeon's operating room

Endeavouring to eliminate the thoughts of doom and gloom

Reflecting on the above

And all whom I've loved

And even hated

Praying silently for forgiveness

Struggling to bind my happiness.

This surgery has caused great pain

But I had much to gain

It purified my body and soul

To make me glow.

From the solace, peace, and tranquillity

I have been made merry

Appreciate life and those in it, just that more

Reflections on my life.

I eventually got better and was finally dismissed from the hospital. I had to spend an additional two weeks at home before returning to work, at school. I also had to visit one of the surgeons a few days after the surgery. When I turned up in his office he was elated.

"Joshua, look at you," he said.

I was not sure what he meant until he continued to speak.

"We thought you were going to die. You had a slim chance of living," I heard the surgeon say.

I just could not believe my ears. I had such a slim chance of surviving and no one told me that until now. I started to think that probably it was better that I did not know. I probably would have died. I truly believe that one's thoughts are as powerful as anything in the world. The way one thinks can most definitely lead to success or on the other hand, failure.

"Joshua, in April, we must go back inside of you to see how it is healing," he said.

I agreed to his comments, but I knew I was not going to let them get back inside of me. I had decided then and there that if I was going to have anyone else looking inside my engine, it would have to be for another surgical requirement. It was not going to be the one that had a mere slim chance of success. I did not go back. Instead, I went to my family doctor. He examined me and said that I seemed fine. He, however, advised that I should still go to the surgeon. I agreed, but I knew that was not going to happen. To this day, I feel, and am fine. I did not return and have no intention to do so, any time soon.

I was always active at my son's school. I had been elected as the school's Parent Council Chair. I had served in this role for approximately three years. In the summer of 2007, just months after my illness, the principal of the school of which my son, Michael was a student, Mrs. Norma Baichoo, discovered that I was not permanently employed as a teacher. All along she thought I was a permanently employed teacher. I had not asked her to serve as one of my references at the time I was job hunting. She was shocked that I did not ask her to serve in that role before. She thought that I was a great person. She encouraged me to use her name as one of my referrals as well. So, I did. The first time that I used her name I hit the jackpot, so to speak. I had an interview, just days before school reopened in September that year. I had actually been offered another L.T.O position by Mrs. Nancy Spencer at my then school, but I was fortunate in acquiring a full time, contract at the school, I currently teach. I thank Mrs. Carmen Wynter-Ellis, the principal of the school, for having given me the opportunity to serve in a permanent teaching role. The interview was quite intense, but I had been well prepared. The moment the interview was over, I knew that that was it. The new life was about to start.

I have been there since I was officially hired September 1, 2007. I actually started working the first Tuesday in September which I think was September 7, 2007. I had worked extremely hard to resume a career that I truly enjoy. I do not take my work for granted. I know there are several other teachers who are, on a daily basis, endeavouring to obtain what I currently enjoy. I also know that I have a huge responsibility every time I step onto this school's compound, and even more so, when I walk into my classrooms to attend to these minds put to my charge. I do not take this work lightly for an iota of a second. I know this has been a learning process, but I endeavour to do all it takes to be the best teacher I can be to mould these minds and to contribute, even in a small way, to those who are constantly being placed to my charge, to mould and create their future. I know many of the students I teach, like myself, were not born with gold spoons in their mouths. I therefore have to make sure that I do not short-change them. I also have an eleven-year old in school. Every teaching experience I have with my pupils, I constantly and regularly ask myself if Michael, my son, were my student, if I would have been satisfied that I did everything to enhance his learning. Put another way, I have to ensure that my teaching is what I would be happy with my son receiving from another teacher. This is my constant safeguard. I endeavour to apply this litmus every single time I interact with my pupils educationally.

Teaching is quite a challenge, notwithstanding the above points. One has to be really committed to do well. It can be very frustrating as well. However, if my colleagues approach this field with professionalism and with the knowledge that it takes an entire community to educate our children, we, and our students, will succeed. We must, at all times, put our students at the centre of everything we do in the classroom. We must work as a team and share best practices and experiences. We cannot sit quietly in a corner and criticize what our colleagues do. We need to approach our colleagues and guide them in those areas that may be wanting of some boost. That's the approach we as teachers must take. I must say that the experience that I have had at my current school is significantly one of cooperation and teamwork. I am glad I got the opportunity to work with such a wonderful team, a team that had no idea that they have been making salient contributions in my acquiring the so well desired and deserved, new life, even in Canada.

Those who criticize teachers in a wholesale manner, simply do not understand clearly the nature of this work. Recently, someone, a parent, said teachers were so lucky. She argued that in summer we are away from work with full pay for two months. I corrected her that that was not exactly true. That it was outright false. I pointed out that teachers' pay in summer was actually money that we actually worked during the school year, part of which is being banked and then given to us during the summer holidays. This parent was shocked. I pointed out that teaching or preparation for it, is done twenty-four hours a day, seven days a week. For example, I advised this individual that many evenings teachers are at my school, Elia Middle School until 6:00 P.M. when they were, in fact, merely required to be there only to 3:30 P.M. We also work weekends, including Sundays, to support students in extracurricular activities such as sports, Spelling Bee competitions, Science fairs, and so on.

My being permanently employed has been helping in taking care of my outstanding accounts. However, the struggle, though being abated, is not fully eliminated. For example, since my visit to Jamaica in 1998, five years after arriving in Canada, I had not revisited the country until 2008. It must be noted here, that this is the country where my two daughters still reside as well as my five siblings, Georgia, Polly, Raffick, Anzil and Oliver. (Sadly, my youngest sibling, Oliver, died a few years ago.) It must also be remembered that when I emigrated to Canada in 1993, Kadisha and Kaliese were a mere nine and six years old, respectively.

In 2008, a friend of mine, Carlton Grant, who resides in the United States, upon realizing that I had not travelled to Jamaica in ten years, bought my son, Michael and I two tickets. It was one of the best gifts I could receive. Just around the same time, I had received some retroactive pay. Money that was due to me from the start of my teaching career in Canada. When I started to teach, I was underpaid as the school board needed evidence of my teaching experience to establish my correct salary. I did not have the written, acceptable evidence at the time, I gained employment. It took some time to obtain the required document from the Jamaica Ministry of Education. However, the time it arrived was quite timely. I had some money that I used to have a good time in Jamaica. It was Michael's first visit, and the first time to meet his sister, Kadisha. At the time of writing, Michael was yet to meet Kaliese, my other daughter of the same marriage. The last time I saw Kaliese myself, she was Michael's age, eleven years old. Even though we communicate often via e-mails, text messaging, phone calls, I long to hold my daughter and to talk to her face to face. I hope that opportunity will present itself in the very near future.

Kaliese was due to attend the 2008 Olympic Games. However, she had some injuries and was not in full, physical form. She, unfortunately, did not make the team. Notwithstanding this fact, Kaliese and her M.V.P. Team, as is the case each summer, was at their summer camp in Italy.

My visit in Jamaica was a quite enjoyable one. We had a full and exciting five weeks on the island, my original home where my journey to the new life started. Who knows where and when it will end!

I have taken you through a very long journey. It was a journey that began in 1959. It, at this point, culminates in 2009, my fiftieth year of existence. Sometimes the road along this journey was extremely rugged for you as well as me. At points in writing this journey, to share with you, I had severe migraine. I also had laughter. It involved an unearthing of a past that was somewhat traumatic in many instances. However, as I said in the introduction to my autobiography, I just felt that I had to do it. Does this mean that I may be nearing a new spiritual transcending? That you or I may not know. That I cannot ascertain at this time. Only time will tell. In the meantime, I endeavour to use my skills to the best of my ability.

In everyone, with no exception, there is an inborn ability to be great. There may be environmental, economic, political factors or a combination of them that frustrate one's full actualization. However, I humbly believe that it is in every single man and woman, this innate ability to excel at, at least, one thing.

Had you ever met someone with whom you had interacted and whom, is in general terms, and by his or her current experiences, regarded as lowly? However, when you interacted with this individual on a personal basis, you sensed something more than that which came to the surface, than that which came to your eyes.

In my mind, one is in a sense, in such a situation, feeling the potential of that being. Had it not been stunted by geographical location, economic factors, politics, or a combination of these constraints, that individual would awe the world and herself or himself. It is for these reasons, that I am compelled to regard every single individual that I meet, with the utmost respect. It is just by mere good fortune that I enjoy the opportunities I do today in Canada. Notice the complicated way it was initiated and came to fruition.

The above point brings me to the view that I sometime harbour, that everyone has a kind of timetable that was shoved upon him or her from the time the sperm fused with the ovum. This timetable will be realized in most cases, irrespective of the circumstances in which one was born. I remember my close shave with death, three times. The first two events were drowning related, and the last, was related to a problem with my duodenum and one of my lungs. My views are that my timetable had those events as parts of my journey in life. However, it was not mentioned as the vehicle of my extinction.

The new life is still in progress and I have a great sense that toward the end of 2009 to early 2010, there will be much material gain on my part. There will be more than enough in which to share and enjoy. Whatever the future brings, I believe in hard work and I am pregnant with optimism, always. I also believe that each person on the face of this earth has a true talent, a talent, one or more, if properly honed, that will bring the individual great happiness. I know that my true talent lies in my ability to write well. It is for this reason that I envision climbing the social and economic ladder utilizing this skill. I am ready for this onward journey in Canada or any other jurisdiction that it takes me, are you? If you are, please share my story with the world.

Joshua Spencer

Reference – Historical Source

Augier, F.R., Augier, Roy., Gordon, S.C., Hall, D.G., *The Making of The West* Indies (5th Edition). Longman Caribbean, 1960.

Made in the USA
Middletown, DE
05 September 2022

72279386R00272